Chinese Thought

Chinese Thought

from

Confucius to Mao Tsê-tung

BY HERRLEE G. CREEL

THE UNIVERSITY OF CHICAGO PRESS

ISBN: 0-226-12029-5 (clothbound); 0-226-12030-9 (paperbound)
Library of Congress Catalog Card Number: 53-10054

THE UNIVERSITY OF CHICAGO PRESS, CHICAGO 60637
The University of Chicago Press, Ltd., London

Preface

THIS book is a nontechnical account of the main outlines of the history of Chinese thought, from the earliest times that are known to the present day. It does not pretend to be an exhaustive history of Chinese philosophy. It has been written in the belief that it is important, for a number of reasons, that we in the West should know Chinese thought far better than we do, and that many of us would find it extremely interesting if we once got into it. It is hoped that it may serve as an introduction to the subject, which will facilitate the enjoyment of more complete and technical works.

A disproportionately large amount of space has been given to the history of Chinese thought before the beginning of the Christian Era. This is not because later developments are considered either unimportant or uninteresting; they are neither, and deserve more careful study than they have received. This volume is especially concerned, however, with the thought of the Chinese themselves, and Chinese thought prior to the Christian Era appears to have been essentially indigenous, while that of later times has been considerably influenced by ideas received from the outside world. Still more important, the ideas developed in the ancient period have continued to play a dominant role, even in our own day.

While this book makes no pretense of being an exhaustive treatise, it has not been written carelessly or hastily. Much of the material was originally assembled for a series of public lectures delivered at the University of Chicago three years ago. A few of those who heard them urged that the material should be published and that only a little further work on it would be necessary. The latter supposition, at least, proved to be erroneous. The preparation of a summary treatment can be more demanding than a full statement, for there is always the gnawing question of whether one has selected those elements that are representative, so that they give a true, though abridged, impression of the whole. I dare not hope that I have succeeded, but I know that I have tried.

In every case in which it was possible (and the exceptions are not more than one or two), passages translated from Chinese have been checked with the Chinese text. In some cases the translations given are wholly new; in most cases they differ to some extent from previous renderings. For the convenience of the reader, however, references have usually been given to English translations of these works where they exist. In a few cases, for special reasons, reference has been given both to a translation and to the Chinese text.

The manner in which notes and references are given is somewhat unusual. There are very few notes which add information or discussion to what is contained in the text; in every case these are given on the same page, as footnotes. References, which merely indicate sources or works cited in evidence, are indicated by numerals, and the references themselves are printed together in the back of the book. The reader may be sure that if he encounters a numeral in the text he will miss nothing by failing to look up the reference in the back of the book, unless he should wish to check on the source or the work cited in evidence.

Sinologists who read this book may be disturbed—some who have read the manuscript have been—by the absence of many Chinese names that might be expected to appear in such a work. They have not been omitted by accident. It is difficult for us, to whose eyes Chinese is familiar and to whose ears it is music, to realize that to most Western readers a page that is sprinkled with Chinese names becomes rather forbidding. It has been thought better, therefore, to include only those names of the most outstanding importance, leaving others to be encountered in further reading.

Preface

In the course of writing this book I have bothered my friends a great deal, and it owes much to their assistance. Although my wife must have become exceedingly weary of it, she has always been able to furnish, when the need arose, a fresh and inspiring suggestion to ameliorate a seemingly hopeless chapter. My colleague, T. H. Tsien, has given me invaluable aid concerning bibliography and has written the Chinese characters for the title-page. Mrs. T. H. Tsien has written the characters for the Bibliography. My special thanks are also due, for suggestions, counsel, and criticism, to George V. Bobrinskoy, John K. Fairbank, Norton S. Ginsburg, Clarence H. Hamilton, Francis L. K. Hsü, Charles O. Hucker, Edward A. Kracke, Jr., Earl H. Pritchard, Richard L. Walker, and Francis R. Walton. Miss June Work has not only prepared the manuscript for publication but has also brought to my attention valuable materials that had escaped me.

H. G. Creel

Palos Park, Illinois

vii

Contents

I. THE CHINESE VIEW 1

II. BEFORE CONFUCIUS 10

III. CONFUCIUS AND THE STRUGGLE FOR HUMAN HAPPINESS . 25

IV. MO TZŬ AND THE QUEST FOR PEACE AND ORDER . . . 46

V. MENCIUS AND THE EMPHASIS ON HUMAN NATURE . . . 68

VI. THE MYSTICAL SKEPTICISM OF THE TAOISTS 94

VII. THE AUTHORITARIANISM OF HSÜN TZŬ 115

VIII. THE TOTALITARIANISM OF THE LEGALISTS 135

IX. THE ECLECTICS OF HAN 159

X. BUDDHISM AND NEO-CONFUCIANISM 186

XI. THE REACTION AGAINST NEO-CONFUCIANISM 217

XII. THE INFLUENCE OF THE WEST 235

XIII. IN RETROSPECT 258

SUGGESTIONS FOR FURTHER READING 263

BIBLIOGRAPHY 266

REFERENCES 273

INDEX 289

Chapter I

The Chinese View

For a century two ways of life and thought have been at war for possession of the Chinese people. One is that of the West, the other that of their forefathers. A hundred years ago every Chinese vastly preferred the latter. The Chinese long believed themselves more intelligent, more cultured, and more capable than any other people. But a series of rude shocks gradually undermined their assurance. They found it impossible to protect themselves in a military sense, so that their borders were invaded. As a result, they were compelled to permit Europeans and Americans, whom they did not want, to live in China. This led to a still more disturbing invasion of the mind.

It soon seemed evident that in some ways the Chinese were not so capable as the Westerners. They did not make war so well. They were not such good mathematicians. They had little command of the sciences. They knew little of machinery and therefore could not produce goods in the fabulous volume that factories make possible.

At first these things did not greatly impress the Chinese. After all, these were for the most part material matters, in which "barbarians" (they thought of the Westerners as barbarians) might be expected to excel. We know that the barbarians of ancient Europe excelled on the field of battle at the time of the fall of the Roman Empire, but that does not convince us that the barbarians were, on the whole, better human beings than the Romans. We know that Eskimos and other people who live close to nature know far more about wild life and are far better hunters than most of us, but that gives us no sense

1

of inferiority. In the same way, it was a long time before the Chinese were overawed by the feats of Western technology. They looked on them as one does on the tricks of a magician—startling, but not really important.

Far more than these material things, the Chinese valued the things of the mind. They could see the value of skill that could combine various materials to make a machine to produce goods cheaply, but they thought more highly of the art of making it possible for human beings to live together in harmony and happiness. They valued wealth—the Chinese have always valued it—but they could see little usefulness in wealth that did not bring its owner satisfaction, a fuller enjoyment of life, and a sense of security in the esteem of his fellow-men. In these respects they were by no means sure that the way of the West was better.

By a process that we shall have to consider in some detail toward the end of this book, many and perhaps most Chinese were brought, in time, to doubt the superiority of their traditional way of life and thought. Many of them were converted to the Western philosophy known as Communism—enough of them to give the political control of China to the Chinese Communists.

Some of us may be reluctant to think of Communism as a Western doctrine. To be sure, Russian Communism has its own peculiarities, and Russian culture has undergone a certain amount of Asiatic influence. But the philosophy of Marx and Lenin is one of the end-products of a line of thinking that can be traced far back in Western philosophy. In its tendency to control people by organizing them into large groups, its emphasis on material things, and the importance it gives to economics, it is far more similar to the philosophy of the West in general than to the traditional thought it has displaced in China.

It might have been expected that when the Chinese adopted one variety of Western doctrine, this would have brought them into greater sympathy with the West as a whole. As everyone knows, it did not. On the contrary, the Chinese Communists bitterly denounced the Western democracies, and Chinese soldiers engaged in open warfare against the forces of the United Nations in Korea.

These actions profoundly shocked a great many people in the West. They felt that the Western democracies had demonstrated, time after time, that they were the truest friends of China. They had sent missionaries, teachers, doctors, and vast sums of money to China. They helped her in her struggle against Japan. Yet the Chinese turned upon them. Many are ready to conclude that the mysterious East is mysterious indeed and that it is impossible to understand the Chinese.

However natural this feeling may be, it solves no problems. And for us the Chinese are a very pressing problem. By this time it is perfectly clear that five hundred million Chinese cannot be ignored. We shall have to deal with them, in one way or another. We cannot deal with them successfully unless we understand them.

Why did the Chinese turn against the Western democracies? Why did they become Communist?

According to Communist dogma, all social changes and political revolutions are to be explained primarily in economic terms. Thus Communists, as well as many who are not Communists, interpret the success of Chinese Communism as due almost entirely to the revolt of China's oppressed and poverty-stricken masses.

This is partly true. But what it omits is perhaps the most important part of the picture. All students of Chinese Communism seem to agree that it has been organized and led, not by peasants or factory workers, but by students, professors, and the intellectuals in general.

When we ask why China's intellectuals were attracted to Communism, we get a curious answer. There is no one explanation, but more important than any other single reason is their burning desire to achieve, for their nation, a position of independence and a place of equality, respect, and esteem in the eyes of the world. They felt, not without justification, that the world regarded them as incapable, disorganized, and backward. They saw in Communism a method of national vindication. They found in Soviet Russia a nation that undertook to treat them as equals.

This leads us to a rather strange conclusion. The Chinese abandoned their traditional ways of life and thought (in so far as they did abandon them) in protest against the attitude and actions of the West, which branded their traditional ways as backward. In rejecting the claim to superiority of Western thought in general, they accepted as superior a particular variety of Western philosophy, Communism.

This had another paradoxical result. During the first half of this century the Chinese had a tendency to feel apologetic about their culture; undoubtedly this was linked with the decline in power and prestige of the Chinese state. Soon after the Chinese Communists came to power, their soldiers could claim to have won victories over the troops of some of the world's most powerful nations, and Communist China became a force to be reckoned with. Thus, while it may seem surprising, it is not unnatural that in their new-found self-confidence the Chinese Communists, whose official philosophy is of European origin, should point with pride to the glories of Chinese history and claim the great Chinese thinkers of the past as belonging to the intellectual heritage of the Chinese Communist party.

If some of the things the Chinese think and do seem hard to understand, it accomplishes little to shrug our shoulders and say that they are a quaint, mysterious, or unreasonable people. If we take the trouble to try to learn why they think and act as they do, we may find that they are quite as reasonable as we are. Much of the difference arises from the fact that they have not always valued the things that we prize most, but have cared more for things to which we give little thought. This is illustrated in the following story that is told by one of their early philosophers.

A student, traveling one day in the country, came upon a farmer who was watering a large vegetable garden in a very curious manner. He had laid out ditches as if for a regular irrigation project. Then he took an earthen pot, climbed down into his well, filled it, and walked back, puffing with exertion and clutching the pot in his arms, to empty it into one of the ditches.

The student watched him do this several times, with great labor but very little effect. Then he spoke to the farmer kindly.

"You know," he said, "there is a sort of mechanism you could use, that would water a hundred gardens like yours in a single day. It requires very little effort to accomplish a great deal. Wouldn't you like to use it?"

The farmer looked up at him and asked, "How does it work?"

"You cut a wooden beam so that it is heavy behind and light in front. Using it as a lever you can lift water as easily as if you were scooping it up in your hand, and as rapidly as boiling water flows over the sides of a kettle."

The farmer laughed scornfully and said, "I have been taught that in order to produce mechanical devices there must be elaborate contriving, and that elaborate contriving requires an artful mind. When the mind is artful, one's natural character can no longer maintain its integrity, and peace of mind is impossible. . . . I know well enough the sort of device you are talking about, but I would be ashamed to use it."[1]

This condemnation of the machine age was written in China well over two thousand years ago. It is interesting to compare it with some remarks that the British novelist E. M. Forster published in 1951. He wrote: "We cannot reach social and political stability for the reason that we continue to make scientific discoveries and apply them, and thus to destroy the arrangements that were based on more elementary discoveries.

. . . Science . . . gave us the internal combustion engine, and before we had digested and assimilated it with terrible pains into our social system, she harnessed the atom, and destroyed any new order that seemed to be evolving. How can man get into any harmony with his surroundings when he is constantly altering them? The failure of our race is, in this direction, more unpleasant than we care to admit, and it has sometimes seemed to me that its best chance lies through apathy, uninventiveness, and inertia."[2]

This is not identical with the Chinese statement of the problem, but when we consider that these two criticisms of machinery were written by authors who were separated by more than two thousand years and ten thousand miles, they are remarkably similar. Of course, Mr. Forster's conclusion is one that very few people living in the Western world would accept. No matter how much we may deplore the existence of the atomic bomb, most of us wish that there will be, not fewer inventions, but more and better ones—including, we devoutly hope, some means to keep us and our children from being blown off the planet.

The Chinese have seldom been as devoted to machinery as we are, but few of them have ever been willing to accept, as a practical matter, the complete abstinence from all use of mechanical devices and all "ingenious contriving" that was advocated by the farmer in the story. Although they have not developed a great deal of theoretical science, the Chinese have usually been eager to adopt devices that would obviously contribute to their well-being.

The story of the farmer who wanted to remain in his condition of simple naturalness in order to preserve his peace of mind is not, therefore, wholly representative of all of Chinese thinking. It is characteristic of the Chinese view, however, in that it lays the emphasis not upon some divine injunction or philosophical principle but upon the human individual—and not upon his state of grace or material well-being but upon his state of mind.

And it is typical of most of the thinking of most of China's famous philosophers, in that it deals with a persistent human problem, a problem that faces us today as much as (or perhaps even more than) it faced the Chinese of the time at which it was written.

Even in the Western world it is not merely in our own day that thoughtful persons have looked upon a tranquil mind as the most precious of all possessions. In A.D. 305 Diocletian, one of the greatest and most successful of Roman emperors, voluntarily abdicated at the age of fifty-nine and at the height of his power. He retired to a country villa, where he laid out a garden and tended it with his own hands. When his former associate urged him to become emperor again, Diocletian assured Maximian that if he could only see his beautiful cabbages, there would be no question of expecting him to give up happiness for mere power.[3]

More recently Jean-Jacques Rousseau and Henry David Thoreau, to name only two of many, have praised the simple life. In the nineteenth century there were a great many practical attempts to realize it by communities of men and women who sought to find tranquility by withdrawing from the world and creating a less complicated society of their own. "Brook Farm," near Boston, where Nathaniel Hawthorne lived for a time, was the most famous of these experiments. Most of them ended in disillusionment; but it is an interesting fact that even today those who have been outstandingly successful in our industrialized cities commonly try, as soon as they have enough money, to buy homes outside them. Very often they spend their weekends working like farm laborers.

As our world increases in complexity, the mounting pressure that it exerts upon the human spirit becomes a more and more difficult problem. One clear evidence of this is the number of books that are bought by men and women seeking peace of mind and relief from nervous tension. Psychiatrists are among the most overworked members of our society, as they try vain-ly to keep pace with the increase in the number of those for whom the world has become more than they can bear.

To escape from the world becomes more and more difficult. Most of the Chinese have never tried to. Instead, they have looked for ways in which it is possible to dwell with other people without being irritated by them, and to live in the world without being oppressed by it. On the whole, they have been quite successful in this. It would be a mistake, of course, to expect that these Chinese solutions could be applied to our own situation without any modification; yet there is no question at all that we can learn a great deal from them. At the very least, they set our own problems in a new light and let us look at them more objectively.

This is perhaps the greatest use that a knowledge of China can have for us. We are too close to ourselves; we cannot get outside our own skins and our own civilization. Do we do the things we do because they are the only sensible, the only "human" things to do? Or do we do them because centuries of social habit and the pressure of the circumstances under which we live compel us to act as we do? How can we tell?

One way to get some light on this question is to see how other peoples, who have different social habits and live under different circumstances, have solved the same problems. That is one reason why the reports of anthropologists concerning so-called "primitive" societies make such fascinating reading. Yet for this purpose relatively simple societies have one great drawback. They are too different from our own; we feel, rightly or not, that our culture is on an entirely different level and cannot really be compared with them. Chinese civilization, on the other hand, while it is very different from our own, is in many ways quite comparable with it. Certainly ours is superior to it in some ways, but there is no doubt that in some other respects the advantage has rested with the Chinese for centuries, and possibly still does.

Most important of all, China's civilization has grown up independently of our own. Among the several greatest cultures that humanity has produced, there is no other that has had, in its formative period, so few relationships of mutual influence with our own Western culture.* Thus we can view China as a great social laboratory, in which for three thousand years of recorded history men and women have been doing things with ideas and institutions that are often quite different from the things we do. This book proposes to take the reader on a brief visit to this laboratory, to see something of what has been going on and something of what it means. We shall consider in particular detail the thought of those periods in which Chinese civilization was most purely and simply Chinese. And, finally, we shall look at the ways in which Chinese thought has reacted to influences from India, from western Europe and America, and from Russia.

* An exception to this statement that might be urged is the culture of India; but, ever since Alexander the Great pushed his conquests into India in 326 B.C., India and Europe have undergone mutual influences, which have at times been considerable.

Chapter II

Before Confucius

A GREAT deal is known about Stone Age men who lived in China; but, since we have nothing that they wrote, we can only guess about what they may have thought. Our earliest Chinese writing comes from a city that was the capital of the Shang kings around 1400 B.C. It was the center of a civilization that was already remarkably advanced, as is proved by its large buildings, beautiful bronze vessels, elaborately woven silks, and many other things. Although these people had books they have long since rotted away, so that the only writings we have from them are short inscriptions on bone and stone. These brief records give us a tantalizing peep at their elaborate religious ceremonials and considerable political organization, but they are not sufficient to tell us much about their philosophy.

These highly cultured Shang people were conquered (in 1122 B.C., according to the traditional dating) by rude tribesmen from western China. The conquerors were led by a group known as the Chou, who established the famous Chou dynasty. At the beginning, these hardy warriors had a difficult time; for, while they knew well enough how to take territory by fighting, it was another matter to hold it by means of a well-ordered government.

A few years after the conquest the Chou king died. His son was crowned as his successor, but he was too young to rule with the firmness that the situation required. The Chou empire began to fall apart. It was saved from ruin by an uncle of the young king, who is known as the Duke of Chou. He stepped in and proclaimed himself regent, took over the armies, punished all those who tried to rebel, and ruled with a firm hand. His nephew, the young king, probably expected to be murdered, but the duke proved to be a man of high principle. Once the danger was past, he substituted conciliatory mildness for force and displayed great genius in organizing the empire on a sound basis. After seven years he turned back the power to the king.

Although the Duke of Chou lived many centuries before Confucius, he has been honored in China as the founder of the "Confucian" tradition. Some Chinese have regarded him even more highly than Confucius. This is not only because of his character but also because there were forged, in the heat of the stirring events in which he took part, certain ideas that have been important in Chinese thinking ever since. To understand them, we must look at the way in which Chinese society was organized at this time.

Almost every aspect of life was dominated by the hereditary aristocracy, in Chou times and probably in Shang times as well. The reputed founders of aristocratic families were, in many cases at least, mythological heroes or even deities.

The family of the Chou kings was believed to be descended from an ancestor called Hou Chi. Literally this means "Millet Ruler," and it seems clear that he was originally an agricultural deity. We read in the ancient classic called the *Book of Poetry* that he was miraculously conceived when his mother stepped in a footprint made by the principal deity. Like a number of other famous infants he was abandoned, but miraculously escaped all harm. The poem says:

> He was laid in a narrow lane,
> But sheep and oxen protected him tenderly.
> He was placed in a large forest,
> But woodcutters found him there.
> He was laid on the cold ice,
> But birds covered him with their wings.[1]

When he grew up, this remarkable ancestor taught the people how to cultivate grain.

It was not only the remote founder of an aristocratic family but all its ancestors who gave it its power. After death the great aristocrats were conceived as living in the heavens, where they supervised the destiny of their posterity. Normally, unless they were extremely displeased with their descendants, they gave them victory in war and prosperity in peace. In return for these favors it was expected that the descendants would provide for them the usual sacrifices and accord with their wishes in so far as these might be learned by divination or other means. The dependence of rulers great and small upon their ancestors is made clear in a great many documents. In an inscription on a bronze vessel we find one noble boasting that his illustrious ancestors above "grandly open up a path for their descendants below."[2] One of the verses in the *Book of Poetry* ascribed the power of the Chou house, at a particular time, to the fact that it had "three [former] rulers in heaven" in addition to the one who reigned on earth.[3]

In such a situation no plebeian could hope to become a ruler, either small or great. He lacked the essential qualification, powerful ancestors. Almost all the plebeians, except for a few who were artisans, were peasants, probably serfs. It is doubtful that they had any definite rights as against the nobility, who apparently treated them as they pleased. An early proclamation classes runaway male and female servants in the same category with strayed cattle.[4] One of the verses in the *Book of Poetry* says: "The common people are contented, For every day they have enough to eat and to drink."[5] Yet the same classic makes it clear that, in fact, they did not always have even enough to eat. One poem says:

> Merciful Heaven has become awe-inspiring in its anger;
> It is showering us with ruin,
> Afflicting us with famine.
> All the people are scattered in flight,
> The settled regions and the open countryside are alike
>   in their desolation.[6]

Another tells us:

> Good fortune has forsaken the people
> For Heaven is striking them down.
> The rich may get along,
> But alas for the lone and solitary.[7]

Were the common people content, if only they had enough to eat and drink? For the early period, it is hard to tell. Few, if any, plebeians could write, so that little of what they had to say has come down to us. Nevertheless, we find some evidence of protest, particularly against forced military service that tore sons from their parents and husbands from their wives, with no guaranty and sometimes little probability that they would ever see them again.

The aristocrats seem to have been able to treat their plebeian underlings just as they pleased, taxing, exacting forced labor, and punishing as suited their whims. Nevertheless, it would have been very poor policy for the aristocrats to make life too difficult for the people as a whole. This was particularly the case just after the Chou conquest.

At that time the Chou rulers and their feudal vassals were newcomers in most of north China (the Chou conquests do not seem to have extended into south China). They lived in walled cities, surrounded by a population that was either hostile or apathetic. Like most successful conquerors, they quickly recognized that, while it had been possible to conquer their territory by force, they could not hold it by force alone. For that, they were wise enough to realize, they needed popular good will.

The Duke of Chou knew this well. He was a warrior, and he knew how to threaten and punish. Despite the sacred nature of family ties, he exiled one of his own brothers and put another to death because they had dared to assist the Shang people in an unsuccessful attempt to revolt. But after the revolt was quelled and its leaders punished, he tried to conciliate the Shang people. He told them that they would be punished without mercy if they were recalcitrant but that if they would co-operate with the Chou, their future was bright. In a proclamation that is preserved to us the duke told the Shang aristocrats: "Heaven will show compassion toward you, and we of Chou will greatly assist and reward you, choosing you to stand in our royal court. If you perform your duties well you may rank among our great officers."[8]

We have a number of documents preserved from early Chou times. A considerable proportion of them have traditionally been attributed to the authorship of the Duke of Chou. Some scholars think that, while he actually wrote some of them, others were written by other Chou leaders but have wrongly been credited to the Duke of Chou because of the prestige that his name has acquired. We need not go into these controversies. For us it is enough to note that the Duke of Chou, and perhaps some of the other early Chou aristocrats as well, showed a definitely conciliatory tendency not only toward the aristocrats they had conquered but even toward the common people.

Instructions issued by a Chou ruler to one of his vassals said: "I will explain to you how virtue should control the use of punishments. At this time the people are not quiet; their hearts are not yet tranquil; though repeatedly urged to accord with us, they have not yet done so. . . . Be earnest! Do not do what will create resentment; do not follow false counsels and uncommon ways. Make your judgments justly and sincerely . . . look to your virtue, be farseeing in all your planning, in order to bring the people to tranquillity. Do these things and I shall not have to remove you from your place, or cut you off."[9] Elsewhere the writer says that one should deal with the people as if one were "protecting infants."[10]

A similar document says: "When the kings set up officials to govern the people they said to them, 'Do not be violent or oppressive, but extend [your protection] even to widowers and widows.' "[11] Statements of this sort are rather abundant. We find them not only in the literature that has been handed down, where we might suspect that they had been added later, but even in inscriptions on bronzes that have been preserved from that time to this. They remind us of the rather similar pious declarations made by European rulers, who have sometimes proclaimed themselves to be the protectors and defenders not only of the church but also of "widows and orphans and strangers." Clearly enough, such statements are made for a variety of reasons and may or may not be evidence of genuinely humane feeling on the part of those who make them. But this does not alter the fact that the mere uttering of such views may have important effects upon history. A particularly important role was played by one such conception that was developed in the aftermath of the Chou conquest.

The Shang kings had sacrificed lavishly to their ancestors and believed that their assistance in various undertakings was of decisive importance. Undoubtedly the Shang rulers, like the Chou kings who succeeded them, believed that they ruled by divine right. The Chou had conquered by force of arms, but this could not be said, without further elaboration, to have transferred the divine *right* to rule. The justification of conquest has always been an embarrassing business. It usually calls for a certain amount of mythology, washed down the throats of the people by means of propaganda. Recently this mythology has often taken the form of a doctrine of "manifest destiny"; the Chou rulers called their doctrine that of "the decree of Heaven." "Heaven" was the name of the most important deity.

The Chou said that it had not been their desire to conquer the Shang territories. On the contrary, the burden of this conquest had been laid upon them by Heaven. Why? Because the last Shang king was a drunken scoundrel who oppressed his subjects and flouted the gods, cheating them of their sacrificial victims. For this reason Heaven had come to despair of his line and had withdrawn its "decree" to rule China from him. This decree had then been handed over to the leader of the Chou people, who had been commanded by Heaven to conquer Shang and take over the throne.

Although it is difficult to check on a story that concerns the conduct of the gods, and our knowledge of this period is meager, we nevertheless know enough to discredit this account. Archeological evidence indicates that the last Shang king was not, in fact, a wastrel. On the contrary, he seems to have been particularly energetic. Far from having been guilty of the neglect of religious ritual with which he is charged, he took an unusual personal interest in such practices and seems to have been very careful in performing them. But this, of course, would have made no difference to the Chou leaders, if only they could get people to believe their version of history. Eventually they did. Some documents which have come down to us appear to be literary forgeries, produced at that time to help the Chou propaganda. There is also some reason to believe that there was in existence a body of Shang literature that would have embarrassed that propaganda. It has disappeared, and it is logical to suppose that the Chou may have destroyed it, although there is no actual evidence that they did so.

The Chou justified their conquest of the Shang people by alleging that history had merely repeated itself. Many centuries earlier, they said, the Shang ruler known as T'ang the Successful had been appointed by Heaven, in exactly the same way, to replace the wicked last king of the previous dynasty, known as the Hsia (although there is a great deal of tradition concerning a Hsia dynasty, as yet we have no archeological evidence that can definitely be linked with it). This version of history provided the Chou conquest with a precedent and made it merely an incident in a recurring cycle. A Shang version of Shang history, still preserved to us in the *Book of Poetry*, records the matter quite differently.[12] Thus it is possible that the Chou leaders, to justify their conquest, changed the whole pattern of Chinese history.

In the writings that have come down to us the Duke of Chou

appears as a leading advocate of the doctrine of the decree of Heaven. He set it forth at great length in a proclamation that he made to the conquered Shang people. It will be noted that he sometimes refers to the chief deity as Ti, sometimes as Heaven; these names were used alternatively, at this time. The duke, speaking in the name of the king, said:

Ti sent down correction on Hsia, but the Hsia sovereign merely increased his luxurious ease, and was not willing to speak consolingly to the people. He was licentious and benighted, and could not for a single day yield himself to the guidance of Ti—these things you have heard. He was contemptuous of the commands of Ti. . . . His inflictions of heavy punishments only heightened the disorders within the domain of Hsia. He did not treat the multitude well . . . and their grief and vexation became greater every day. . . .

At this point Heaven sought a true lord for the people, and sent down its bright favoring decree to T'ang the Successful, who punished and destroyed the sovereign of Hsia. . . . From him down to Ti I [the last Shang king but one] the sovereigns all, with illustrious virtue, were careful in the use of punishments, and thus were able to exercise a stimulating influence over the people. . . . But when it came to your late ruler [the last Shang king] he was not able with your many states to continue to enjoy the Decree of Heaven.

Oh! the king speaks to the following effect: I announce and declare to you . . . it was not that Heaven desired to do away with the sovereign of Hsia, or with the sovereign of Shang.* But your ruler . . . was extremely dissolute, and despised the commands of Heaven . . . he was lazy and slothful, slighted the labors of government, and did not make pure sacrifices, so that Heaven sent down this ruin on him. . . .

Heaven then sought among your many regions . . . for one who might be attentive to its commands, but there was none able to do so. There was, however, our Chou king, who treated the multitudes well and was virtuous, and presided carefully over the sacrifices to the spirits and to Heaven. Heaven therefore instructed us to avail ourselves of its favor; it chose us and gave us the decree of Shang, to rule over your many regions.[13]

It would be impossible to exaggerate the importance of this idea for the history of Chinese politics and Chinese thought.

---

* The text, at this point and one other in this translated passage, reads "Yin," which is another name for "Shang." I have changed these to the latter, for simplicity's sake.

From this time on, it was the normal pattern for rebels to claim possession of the "decree of Heaven." As late as our own century the revolutionary party of Dr. Sun Yat-sen was at one time called "The Association for Changing the Decree."

Even more important were the reasons for which it was alleged that Heaven had transferred its favor. In the document just quoted and in many others it was stated that Heaven rejected rulers because, among other crimes, they did not treat the people well. The result was to establish, in theory, the principle that the rulers existed for the sake of the people, rather than the reverse, and that they held their powers only in trust, as a kind of stewardship, subject to revocation if they did not use them well. At the beginning this was little more than a theory, and a theory born of the necessities of propaganda, but no matter. The theory existed, and in time it would come to be very important.

In this very early period that we are now considering, there were already in existence certain other ideas that have continued to be very important in Chinese thought. One was the emphasis on the family. As early as we have any clear knowledge of Chinese civilization, the paramount importance of the family is unmistakable. In the *Book of Poetry* we read:

> Of all the men in the world
> None are equal to brothers. . . .
> Brothers quarrel inside the walls,
> But they stand united against insult from without
> While even the best of friends,
> However numerous, will not fight for you.[14]

Western writers sometimes give the impression that Confucius almost invented filial piety, or at least that he emphasized it as it had never been emphasized before. But in a passage written long before the time of Confucius the *Book of Poetry* says: "No one is to be looked up to like a father, No one is to be depended on like a mother."[15] Even at the beginning of the Chou period we find it said that filial piety is not merely a moral but even a legal obligation. A charge to a Chou vassal states that certain criminals are even worse than murderers, to wit: "the son who does not serve his father respectfully, but greatly wounds his father's heart; and the father who cannot cherish his son, but hates him; and the younger brother who does not bear in mind the evident intention of Heaven, and will not respect his elder brother; and the elder brother who forgets the tender regard in which he should hold his younger brother, and is unfriendly to him." All such criminals, it is declared, must be punished without mercy.[16]

The task that confronted the Chou rulers after their conquest was not an easy one. Their problem was not lack of territory to rule but lack of means to rule it. The only means of communication was by road, and the roads were poor. Although there were certain media of exchange, convenient money in our sense did not exist. Without good communications and money, direct rule over a large territory is almost impossible. The Chou rulers did what was almost the only thing they could do; they parceled out their territories to vassals, who were for the most part their relatives or the chiefs of other tribes that had assisted them in the conquest. These feudal lords were left free to govern their local territories very much as they wished, so long as they kept the peace, paid the required tribute to the king, and led their soldiers to help him when they were needed.

At the beginning this feudal system worked very well. The Chou feudatories were little more than the commanders of walled garrison towns, who kept watch over a newly conquered and hostile populace. They needed the support of the Chou king and of one another. When individual vassals became unruly, the king punished them. In extreme cases he took their lands away and gave them to others.

After a few generations, however, the situation changed. The descendants of the original feudal lords were no longer strangers in their territories, and the former hostility of their people had in large measure vanished. Time had sanctified their authority, and local pride and self-interest rendered most of their subjects loyal. The stronger feudal lords annexed the territories of their weaker neighbors, and, when the king tried to interfere with this practice, they resisted him. The nobles formed parties and alliances, which quarreled among themselves and with the king. Finally in 771 B.C. an attack by such a coalition, in league with certain "barbarian" tribes, ended in the death of the reigning Chou king. His heir was established in a capital farther to the east, but from this time forward the Chou kings were little more than puppets in the hands of their most powerful vassals.

China was thus left without any effective central government. The wars between groups of feudal lords became more and more frequent and furious. The barbarian tribes on the borders not only invaded China but sometimes were called in by Chinese as allies against other Chinese. Even the powerless Chou king sometimes invited barbarian tribes to help him win back his patrimony, with unfortunate results. If the barbarians could have co-operated effectively, there is little doubt that they would have overrun China then, as coalitions of barbarian tribes sometimes did later.

The danger was recognized, and it was generally agreed that China should have a strong king, in place of the Chou puppets. The great feudal lords were in harmony on this point; they disagreed only on the question of which one of them should establish a new dynasty. Each one had a candidate: himself. To settle the point cost many centuries of war and uncounted hundreds of thousands of Chinese lives.

In the meantime the process of decentralization went on. Not only did the feudal lords disregard the orders of the king, usurp his powers, and do as they pleased. In a number of states the chief officials of the rulers treated their overlords in the same manner. Thus, for instance, in Lu, the native state of Confucius, the duke still nominally reigned, but all power was held by three of his relatives, who were the principal officers of the state. They not only ruled as they wished but sometimes murdered heirs to the ducal throne in order to place others, whom they favored, on it. In 517 B.C. (when Confucius was thirty-four) the reigning Duke of Lu attempted to revolt against these usurping officers. He was unsuccessful and had to flee the state and live out the rest of his life in exile.

Not only the feudal lords were subject to such treatment. Their usurping officials were, in turn, preyed upon by their underlings. Thus, when Confucius was forty-seven, the principal usurper of power among the officers of the Duke of Lu was attacked by his own chief retainer, imprisoned, and forced to swear to obey the commands of his nominal subordinate. This swashbuckling retainer ruled the state with a high hand for several years. He finally decided to kill off all the nominally principal officers of the state and take the titular as well as the actual power. A last-minute hitch frustrated the plot, however, and the bravo had to flee.

Lu was not alone in being the victim of such disorders. Some states were in much worse condition. In general, it may be said that at this time "law and order" scarcely existed, for there was no strong central authority to enforce them. Since the king was powerless, states fought among themselves constantly. By the sixth century B.C., in which Confucius was born, there were four large states of pre-eminent power on the periphery of the Chinese world and a number of smaller states in the center. The large states customarily met to fight their battles in the territory of the central states; sometimes they did this annually, for as much as ten years without intermission.

Within states, since many of the rulers were weak, the most powerful of the noble clans fought among themselves in the same way; some states were divided into armed camps, in a more or less constant state of siege. Finally, even within families, individuals quarreled and led their personal retainers in what may best be described as "private wars."

Considering the fact that China was, even at this time, one of the most civilized of nations, her situation was wretched indeed. Scarcely any individual, whether of the highest rank or the meanest condition, could be said to enjoy security. The plight of the common people was pitiful. They were the principal victims of war. One result of the decentralization was that even minor aristocrats tried to ape the luxury of the greatest nobles; to do this they taxed the people so severely and exploited them so much at forced labor that in years when the harvests were poor a great many literally starved to death.

In some respects conditions had probably been better in the early years of the dynasty, immediately after the Chou conquest. In those days the aristocrats had been not only under the necessity of conciliating the people but also under the discipline of the tribal morality that had been developed in a simpler situation. The common people had had to work hard and enjoyed few luxuries, but the *Book of Poetry* gives the impression that the lords of great estates took a direct personal interest in those who tilled the soil, while the peasants felt a definite loyalty toward the lord. Increased sophistication did not bring ethical advance, but retrogression. The aristocrats became absorbed in vying with one another in luxury and fighting one another in constant wars. Treaties were made under the threat of force and broken as soon as it became expedient, but the breakers did not suffer the awful penalties that the spirits were supposed to inflict. This inevitably undermined the belief in religion. The conditions of the time in general fostered the idea that only a fool would keep his word or act in any manner except that which his own selfish interest dictated.

The feudal system had, in the beginning, made for good government. It permitted the king to appoint capable men to rule the various parts of the kingdom and to dismiss them if they ruled badly. It appears that in China, as later in Europe, fiefs were not at first hereditary; if a son was believed fit to carry on his father's office, he had to be appointed to it anew by the king. But as noble families became more powerful and the king weaker, he was compelled by circumstances to confirm the heirs of vassals automatically; finally, this was dispensed with altogether. As this condition spread and applied even to lower functionaries, China came to be ruled by officials who simply inherited their places. Quite commonly they had neither aptitude for nor interest in their functions. Many of them considered their offices to be little more than the symbols of their right to power, privilege, and luxury. The inevitable result was misgovernment.

Many men realized this; even some of the aristocrats themselves recognized that many members of their class had come to be mere parasites upon society. This was particularly easy for the rulers of states to see, for they were victimized by the nobles almost as much as the people were. The principal officers of the ruler of a state were nominally his subordinates, charged with the various functions of the government. But commonly they not only neglected these duties but even used their private armies to flout, if not to usurp, the authority of the ruler.

In 535 B.C., when Confucius was sixteen years old, the duke of one small state tried to rectify this condition. Instead of giving the principal offices in his government to his noble relatives, who had undoubtedly been in the habit of bequeathing them to their sons as hereditary possessions of their families, this duke discharged his relatives from office. In their places he installed men from other states to perform their functions. This so enraged his relatives that they banded together, assassinated the duke, and put a stop to this invasion of custom and privilege.[17]

Who were these men from other states, whom the luckless duke tried to use as his officers? History does not tell us, but it is easy to guess. They can hardly have been plebeians; few plebeians would have known how to read and write, to say nothing of how to govern. These men probably belonged to the growing class of impoverished descendants of the nobility. The aristocrats practiced polygamy on a large scale; as a result, there soon came to be so many younger sons that it was quite impossible to provide fiefs and posts for all of them. Thus a large number of men, descended from the aristocrats, were cast adrift to fend for themselves. Some of them became mercenary soldiers. Others became minor functionaries at the courts, and some of these went from state to state seeking better jobs. It was probably such men that the duke in question tried to use as his officers. From his point of view they would have had two advantages. Since he had appointed them to office and could remove them, they were more likely to be loyal to him than were nobles of independent power. Furthermore, it is reasonable to suppose that, as the result of competition, they were better able to govern well and almost certainly were more interested in doing so than most of the aristocrats who merely inherited their positions.

These depressed descendants of the nobility played an important role in history. They formed a mediating class, in touch with the common people and aware of their grievances, but educated and able to protest effectively, as the people were not. Beginning around the time of Confucius, some of these men were able to attain to increasingly higher office and to wield considerable influence upon the events of their day. We know their names, but little more about them.

One of them, however, was almost a complete failure in so far as realizing his ambitions in his own lifetime was concerned. He was a man of outstanding intellect and lofty ideals. Because he refused to compromise, none of the rulers of the day would give him any effective post in their governments. For this reason he was thrown back on teaching and forced to spend his time in elaborating his ideas to his students. As a result, although he personally failed, his ideas succeeded after his death in effecting drastic alterations in the theory and practice of government in China. It is for this reason that, even after twenty-five hundred years, we know the name of Confucius better than that of any other Chinese.

Chapter III

Confucius and the Struggle for
Human Happiness

CONFUCIUS was one of the handful of men who have deeply influenced human history by the force of their personal and intellectual gifts and achievements. The fact that such men appear upon the scene can never be completely explained; but, by examining the circumstances of their lives, we can at least increase our ability to understand them.

Our attempt to understand Confucius is made difficult by the large mass of legend and tradition that has accumulated about his name so thickly, over the centuries, that it becomes very hard to see the truth. These elaborations, not to say distortions, spring from two quite different motives. On the one hand, the faithful have wished to exalt him and have therefore performed such pious acts as building up an elaborate genealogy that traces his ancestry back to emperors. On the other, those whose interests were menaced by this revolutionary thinker have sought, and with partial success, to nullify his attacks upon intrenched privilege by distorting and misrepresenting what he had to say. Our only safe course, therefore, is completely to disregard the elaborate traditional story of his life and thought and trust only the more meager testimony that can be gleaned from documents that can be proved to be early and reliable.[1]

Confucius was born in 551 B.C. in the small state of Lu, which was located in what is now Shantung Province. What his ancestry was we cannot be certain, but it is probable that there were aristocrats among his forebears. As a young man he was, however, by his own testimony, "without rank and in humble circumstances."[2] He had to make his own living, at tasks that

25

were more or less menial. He was able to study, but seems to have been largely self-taught.

These experiences undoubtedly gave him a close view of the sufferings of the common people, about which he became deeply concerned. He felt that the world was sadly out of joint and that it was vital that drastic changes be made. He had opportunity not only to know the people but also to become familiar with the aristocrats, who were the hereditary lords of creation. Of most of the aristocrats he had a very poor opinion. He was undoubtedly speaking of the parasitic nobles of his time when he said: "It is difficult to expect anything from men who stuff themselves with food the whole day, while never using their minds in any way at all. Even gamblers do *something*, and to that degree are better than these idlers."[3]

Unfortunately, however, the aristocrats were not always idle. They used considerable ingenuity in devising ever more expensive adjuncts to luxurious living, for which the people paid with taxes and forced labor. Above all, the nobles practiced the art of war. In China, as perhaps in most other nations, the nobility was military in origin. In an earlier day these military officers had performed a useful function in protecting society, but as a class they had largely outlived their usefulness, and now they preyed on the people and on one another. Most of them felt that the arts of war were the only occupations worthy of the serious attention of a gentleman, and they made fun of those, even among their own numbers, who concerned themselves with the need for good government and orderly administration.

Confucius was not a pacifist. He believed that, regrettably, there are times when force must be used by moral men, in order to prevent themselves and the world from being enslaved by those for whom force is the only argument and the only sanction. But he considered force a last resort and one that must always be subordinate, not only ideally but as a matter of hard fact, to the power of justice. On the ideal and personal level he said: "If I feel in my heart that I am wrong, I must stand in fear even though my opponent is the least formidable of men. But if my own heart tells me that I am right, I shall go forward even against thousands and tens of thousands."[4] On the more practical level, he believed that an army could not fight effectively unless even its common soldiers knew why they were fighting and were convinced of the justice of their cause. He believed that morale is dependent on moral conviction. He said: "To lead a people who have not been educated to war, is to throw them away."[5]

Confucius was aware that such ideas were completely at variance with those of the nobility. He not only realized it but tried to do something about it. Up to his time the term *chün tzŭ*, "gentleman," had almost universally had a significance somewhat like the original meaning of our word "gentleman." It denoted, that is, a man of good birth, whose ancestors had belonged to a stratum above that of the common herd. Such a person was a gentleman by birth; no one not born so could become a gentleman, and no gentleman could ever become less than one, no matter how vile his conduct might be. Confucius changed this usage completely. He asserted that any man might be a gentleman, if his conduct were noble, unselfish, just, and kind. On the other hand, he asserted that no man could be considered a gentleman on the ground of birth; this was solely a question of conduct and character.

Confucius was always markedly contemptuous of eloquence and of ornate language, and there is no record that he ever delivered a public lecture. Nevertheless, he must have been an unusually persuasive speaker to one person or to small groups. Even today, as we read the things he said, we can feel the magnetism of his personality. He talked about his ideas for reforming the world, which were many and bold, to those with whom he came in contact, and gradually there were attracted to him a number of men who became his students, or, as we commonly call them, his disciples. At the beginning some of them were only a little younger than himself.

In so far as we know, this group, composed of Confucius and those who studied with him, formed the first private school devoted to higher education in Chinese history. The sons of rulers and aristocrats had long had tutors; and men who were destined to be minor officials in the courts had studied, as apprentices of officials, with their superiors. That kind of teaching seems to have consisted chiefly of training in techniques, to enable men to carry on certain traditional functions. Confucius, however, was not concerned merely to train his charges, but to *educate* them, in the sense of, as one dictionary definition explains the word, "to develop and cultivate mentally or morally, to expand, strengthen, and discipline."

There was a definite reason why Confucius diverged from the traditional pattern in his conception of the function of schooling. The two programs were similar, in that both were designed to equip the student to be a governmental official. But, whereas in the usual view such an official was expected to be simply an instrument of his ruler, putting into practice what the ruler wished to be done and administering the government in the customary manner, Confucius expected his students to play the dynamic role of revolutionizing any government in which they might take part and making it serve the needs of the people. If they were to do so, they would obviously have to be prepared for this strenuous function by having their initiative, their character, and their intelligence developed to the utmost. No mere training in routine techniques would suffice.

With Confucius the belief that any man might become a gentleman, regardless of his birth, did not remain a matter of theory. He undertook to make his students into gentlemen, and he accepted them from the lowest as well as the highest social strata. "In education," he said, "there should be no class distinctions."[6] Of his own catholicity in receiving students he said: "I have never refused to teach anyone, even though he came to me on foot, with nothing more to offer as tuition than a package of dried meat."[7]

Among his students there were, in fact, members of the nobility along with others who were very poor. Confucius seems to have been impartial; but if he had any preference, it was probably for those who had little. He praised one of his disciples for being able, "though wearing a tattered hemp-quilted gown, to stand beside those wearing costly furs without the slightest embarrassment."[8]

Interestingly enough this same disciple, who here wears a tattered gown, was later on a very high official, occupying what was perhaps the most influential office in the state that could be held by one who did not inherit his place. This illustrates the fact that Confucius was not engaged in education merely for the sake of education, but was preparing his students to go out into the world to work and struggle for his principles. For this reason, although he accepted men of all classes as his students, he was very strict in his requirements as to their intellectual abilities. He said: "I point out the way only to the student who has first looked for it himself, and make him find his own illustrations before I give him one. If, when I give the student one corner of the subject, he cannot find the other three for himself, I do not repeat my lesson."[9]

Since he was undertaking to make men of humble background into "gentlemen," able to hold their own in the halls of state with the most polished courtiers, he had to teach them court etiquette. He did so; but here again he profoundly altered the character of an ancient institution, in a manner that was to have the most important consequences. The Chinese term by which such etiquette is known is *li;* it is commonly translated, even as Confucius uses it, as "ritual" or "the rules of propriety." These translations will do well enough, no doubt, for this institution as Confucius found it, but they are hopelessly inadequate to express what he made of it.

The original meaning of *li* was "to sacrifice"; it still has this sense in modern Chinese. It was extended to denote the ritual used in sacrifice and then to cover every sort of ceremony and the "courtesy" that characterized the conduct of those who made up a ruler's court.

Confucius started from there. If rulers were gravely serious in sacrificing to their ancestors, why should they not be equally so in attending to the government of the realm? If ministers treated one another with courtesy, in the daily intercourse of the court, why should they not be equally considerate toward the common people, who were the backbone of the state? Thus he said to one of his disciples that, wherever he went in the world, he should treat all those with whom he came in contact as if he were "receiving an important guest"; and if he became an official of the government, he should deal with the people as if he were "officiating at a great sacrifice."[10] Such conduct would, of course, contrast sharply with the careless conduct of most of the aristocrats.

Court etiquette was then, as it has been in most times and places, conceived as a more or less well-defined body of fixed rules. Even in some of the so-called Confucian "classics" we find the most minute directions for behavior, which tell one exactly where each finger should be placed in picking up a ritual object. But Confucius himself conceived of *li* quite differently. It was the spirit that counted, and he was contemptuous of those who believed that, by mere ostentatious display of costly trappings and sedulous aping of the behavior of others, they could excel in *li*.

One of his disciples asked what was the essence of *li*. The master replied: "An important question! In matters of ceremony, if one must err on one side or the other it is better to be too economical rather than vulgarly ostentatious. In funerals and ceremonies of mourning, it is better that the mourners feel true grief, than that they be meticulously correct in every ceremonial detail."[11]

Confucius himself said that he had no hesitation in departing from the conventionally accepted etiquette when he felt such departure to be dictated by reasons of common sense and good taste. On the other hand, he did not for a moment underestimate the importance of convention.

His whole system of ethics and, indeed, most of his philosophy seem to have been based upon a consideration of what is the nature of the human being. He did not make either of two mistakes that have sometimes been made in this connection. On the one hand, he did not think of the individual as existing quite separately from society. On the other, he did not think of society as a kind of metaphysical entity that is so completely prior to the individual that the individual can hardly be said to exist, except as he is wholly absorbed in it.

Confucius believed that men are essentially social beings. They are to a very considerable extent (though by no means totally) made what they are by society. On the other hand, since society is nothing more than the interaction of men, society is made what it is by the individuals who compose it. Confucius believed that the conscience of the individual must equally forbid him either to withdraw from society or to surrender his moral judgment to it. It is equally wrong, then, either to become a recluse or to "follow the crowd." The moral man must not be a cipher in, but a co-operating member of, society. Wherever the conventional practices seem to him immoral or harmful, he not only will refrain from conforming with them but will try to persuade others to change the convention. Necessarily, however, the areas in which he does this will be limited. As a sensible and social man, he will accord with convention wherever the common practice seems reasonable or harmless.

It goes without saying that convention is the cement of society. If each of us ate, slept, and worked when and where

we pleased and used words that we individually invented to
mean what we individually desired them to mean, the world
would be a difficult place to live in. Confucius used the term *li*
to stand for the whole complex of conventional and social
usage, which he endowed with a *moral* connotation. Thus
combined, the sanctions of morality and courtesy reinforced
each other. We consider it courteous, but not necessarily a
moral duty, to be polite to everyone with whom we come
in contact. We consider it a moral duty, but not necessarily
an obligation of courtesy, to return property we find to the
loser, even though we may not know him. But the whole
range of the obligations imposed by the highest conceptions
of both courtesy and moral duty were included in *li*. To say
"it is *li*" was equivalent to our "it is done," which is often
far more persuasive than the most detailed argument.

This conception of *li* was extremely important in Confucius'
program of education. Psychiatrists say that our education,
although it cultivates the intellect to a high degree, often
fails signally to discipline the emotions. For this reason it is
sometimes unable to produce a well-adjusted individual, capable of taking his place as a happy and useful member of
society. Confucius considered intellectual cultivation to be of
little worth if it were not accompanied by emotional balance;
to produce such balance he depended upon education in *li*.
The learning of the gentleman, he said, must be "disciplined
by means of *li*"; one thus prepared to meet the world is
strengthened, he believed, to hold true to his principles through
any crisis and in the face of every temptation.[12]

Another concept that was of basic importance in his
philosophy and his education was that of the *tao*, usually
translated as "the way." The earliest meaning of *tao* was
"road" or "path." Before the time of Confucius the term was
usually employed either in this sense or as meaning a way of
conduct, which might be indifferently good or bad. After
Confucius' time it was used, especially by the Taoists (who

get their name from this term), as a mystical concept standing for the primal stuff of the universe or the totality of all things.

This later idea has very commonly been read back into Confucius' use of the term. There are a few passages in the *Analects* that seem to make this plausible, but these are also capable of a different interpretation. In my opinion it is essential, if we are to understand the philosophy of Confucius, to recognize that for him the *tao* was not something mystical. It was "the Way," with a capital *W*, that is, the way above all other ways that men should follow. Its goal was happiness, in this life, here and now, for all mankind. Just as *li* comprehended both courtesy and morality, so the Way included, on the one hand, the ethical code of the individual and, on the other, the pattern of government that should bring about the fullest possible measure of well-being and self-realization for every human being.

When one says that the Way was not mystical, this does not mean that it was not regarded with enthusiasm. Confucius said: "If a man in the morning hear the Way, he may die the same evening without regret."[13] This is not, of course, because he will then go to heaven; Confucius refused to discuss the question of life after death. It is rather because of Confucius' steadfast emphasis on the qualitative rather than the quantitative. The measure of a man's life is not "how long?" but "how good?" If one has heard the Way (and we have to assume that this means that he has also understood it), he has achieved the highest possible degree of moral enlightenment and has entered into a way of life and thought that is in the highest degree satisfying. It is not desirable that he should die the same evening; but if he must, it can be borne.

Yet this *tao*, this Way, was not a *thing* in the mystical sense in which the Taoists later regarded it as such. Confucius made this clear when he said, "Men can enlarge the Way, but the Way does not [by itself] enlarge the man."[14] When

Confucius had been dead for thirteen centuries, the T'ang dynasty scholar Han Yü, one of the greatest figures in the history of Chinese literature, wrote his famous essay "On the Way," in which he deplored the fact that the Confucian conception had become confused with that of the Taoists. The Confucian Way, Han Yü said, was a way of action; action animated by the ideal of justice (which in the Chinese sense means "appropriateness") and motivated by love for all men. This ideal of the Way was handed down, Han Yü wrote, by the sage rulers of the past to the Duke of Chou and thus to Confucius and Mencius. But it was not, he insisted, a fixed and immutable thing, but one that varied with the individual and the circumstances.[15]

Yet if Confucius did not regard the Way as a cosmic absolute, he was none the less exacting in his demand that his disciples adhere to it unswervingly. He rejected the standard of feudal loyalty due to an overlord and in its place demanded loyalty to principle, to the Way.[16] Despite the fact that he did not base his philosophy on religious beliefs or on any particular dogma as to the ultimate nature of the universe, he was able to inspire a remarkable number of men with the most complete devotion to his ideals.

Confucius demanded the utmost zeal of his followers. He expected them, as a matter of course, to be prepared at all times to lay down their lives for their principles.[17] And they did so. Over the centuries, the Confucians have produced a goodly company of martyrs, who have given their lives in defense of the Way. Some of them have died as revolutionaries, who had taken up arms against tyranny; this was the fate of Confucius' own heir in the eighth generation. Others have died at the hand of the executioner, for daring to obey Confucius' injunction to criticize an erring ruler fearlessly, in behalf of the common good.[18]

Han Yü, whose essay on the Way we have considered, narrowly escaped martyrdom. He rose to high office more than once but was repeatedly punished for his outspokenly critical memorials to the throne. When his emperor became a devout Buddhist and organized an elaborate celebration in which he personally welcomed an alleged bone of the Buddha that was transported with great honors as a relic, Han Yü wrote to the emperor denouncing this action in no uncertain terms. He declared that this veneration paid to a "dry and rotten bone" would only mislead the common people into superstition, and urged that the relic be destroyed. The emperor was, of course, furious. Han's life was saved by the intercession of friends, but he was banished to the wilds of the southern coast. There he devoted himself to improving the life of the people and bore his exile with fortitude, secure in the knowledge that he had fought the good fight and joined the company of those who, in many times and places, had remained true to the Way. He would have faced death in the same manner. The function of the Way, for Confucians, has been much like that of "the faith" for Christians.

The problem of Confucius' relationship to religion is a difficult one. Certainly he was not primarily, as has sometimes been supposed, a religious prophet or teacher. In fact, it is easy to cite passages from the *Analects* that show that he was reluctant to discuss religious questions. Although he talked a great deal about the way that men should follow, one of his disciples said that he did not discuss "the way [that is, the *tao*] of Heaven."[19] Another disciple asked how one should serve spirits; Confucius told him: "You are not yet able to serve men; how can you serve spirits?" The disciple asked about death; the Master told him: "You do not yet understand life; how can you understand death?"[20]

From these and certain other passages it has sometimes been concluded that Confucius was insincere. Some have thought that he was, in fact, skeptical or even atheistic but that, for lack of courage or for some other reason, he refrained from telling his disciples the truth. This seems to resolve a difficult problem too simply.

There are several passages in which Confucius speaks of Heaven, the principal deity of the Chinese. He seems, in fact, to have felt that he had been intrusted by Heaven with a mission to cure the ills of the Chinese world, and he hoped that Heaven would not permit him to fail.[21] Once when he cried out in despair that there was no one who understood him, he added, "But Heaven understands me!"[22]

What did Confucius understand by the term "Heaven"? Not an anthropomorphic being. Heaven was seldom so conceived in his time, and there is explicit reason for rejecting this idea in connection with Confucius. If we examine the ways in which Confucius refers to Heaven, it appears that this term stood, in his thinking, for a vaguely conceived moral force in the universe. He placed the utmost emphasis on striving by the individual, but he seems to have hoped that Heaven would, as we say, "help those who help themselves." Yet even this could not be counted on, for, as he sadly observed, the wicked often prosper and the efforts of the good sometimes come to nought. Nevertheless, the idea of Heaven gave him the feeling that somehow, somewhere, there was a power that stood on the side of the lonely man who struggles for the right.

The religion of the day said little about life after death and made little or no use of it as a deterrent to wickedness or a stimulus to virtue. Confucius, as we have seen, would not discuss this topic. In numerous respects he broke sharply with the traditional religion. In accord with his usual practice, however, he did not call attention to these departures from precedent, so that they are sometimes overlooked. In general, sacrifice was considered a barter transaction, in which so much goods was sacrified to the ancestors and other spirits in the expectation of receiving so many blessings. Confucius condemned this attitude. He believed that the traditional sacrifices should be made, but in the same spirit in which one is courteous to one's friends: not because of what one expects to get from them, but because it is the right thing to do. Did he believe that the spirits conferred blessings? We simply do not know; it is possible that he did not.

Human sacrifice had been very prevalent in an earlier day, and still continued to some extent in his time and for centuries after. Confucius condemned it,[23] and there seems to be little doubt that it is the Confucians who were principally responsible for its eventual decline.

We noticed earlier that the office of the ruler had definite religious connotations. The king was called the Son of Heaven, and feudal lords were believed to rule by virtue of the assistance of their powerful noble ancestors, who lived in the heavens and supervised the destiny of their descendants. This idea protected the intrenched privilege of the aristocracy, for no plebeian, however wise and capable, could bring to the throne such supernatural backing. Confucius did not attack this traditional view. He simply said nothing about it whatever. Instead, he made the title to rule wholly dependent upon character, ability, and education, without regard to birth. And he asserted that one of his disciples, who was not the heir of a ruling house, might properly occupy a throne.[24]

Although Confucius had certain religious convictions, he does not seem to have used them as the basis of his philosophy. Here his attitude seems to have had some resemblance to that of the modern scientist. Probably no scientist would say that the existence of God can be proved by scientific technique; even theologians have asserted that this cannot be done. On the other hand, it is doubtful that any careful scientist would say that God can be scientifically proved *not* to exist. For science is not concerned with the ultimate nature of the universe but with making certain observations from experience and formulating these into principles that represent preponderant probabilities. By foregoing the right to speak of ultimate truth, science gains the ability to help us act practically and fruitfully.

Confucius operated in much the same way. He made no claim to the possession of the ultimate truth. He was groping toward the truth, by the method of observation and analysis. He said that one should "hear much, leave to one side that which is doubtful, and speak with due caution concerning the remainder. . . . See much, but leave to one side that of which the meaning is not clear, and act carefully with regard to the rest."[25] He said nothing about attaining the truth through a sudden flash of mystical enlightenment; on the contrary, he stated flatly that meditation alone does not lead to wisdom.[26] He also said: "To hear much, select what is good, and follow it; to see much and remember it; these are the steps by which understanding is attained."[27]

Thus it is clear enough that, however religious Confucius may have been, he was far from feeling assured of his own omniscience or infallibility concerning the ultimate nature of the universe. He was trying to set up a structure of ideas that would last, and be strong enough to serve as a foundation upon which to build the freedom and happiness of the human race. For this he had to build with materials which he not merely hoped, but which as nearly as possible he knew, to be sound. He took as his basis, therefore, neither theological dogma nor religious hope but the nature of man and society as he observed them.

It is perhaps more true of Confucius than of any equally famous thinker that he divorced ethics from metaphysics. Max Weber has written: "In the sense of the absence of all metaphysics and almost all residues of religious anchorage, Confucianism is rationalist to such a far-going extent that it stands at the extreme boundary of what one might possibly call a 'religious' ethic. At the same time, Confucianism is more rationalist and sober, in the sense of the absence and the rejection of all non-utilitarian yardsticks, than any other ethical system, with the possible exception of J. Bentham's."[28]

Confucius based his ethics, we have said, upon the nature of man and society. But what is the nature of man and society? Obviously this is the crucial question, and if Confucius had tried to answer it hastily or dogmatically his empirical approach would have been little more than pretense. He did not. Unlike Mencius, the great Confucian philosopher of the fourth century B.C., Confucius did not say that human nature is "good." Nor did he, like another slightly later Confucian, Hsün Tzŭ, say that human nature is "bad." We shall see that for both these later thinkers their conclusions, while opposite, had in common the fact that they were generalizations that led to some consequences which their own authors would have deplored.

Confucius stayed closer to the concrete. Perhaps his most important observation about men was that they are essentially equal. Probably the fact that he had himself been born into depressed circumstances, from which he wished to rise, had much to do with this. He saw, too, that men who were born with every hereditary claim to exalted rank and noble character often behaved like beasts or clods, while others without these advantages often conducted themselves in a manner far more worthy of respect.

He also made the simple observation that all men, however differently they may define it, desire happiness. Since there was not in his background any religious or philosophical dogma that branded happiness, or the desire for it, as bad, he believed that in so far as possible men should have what they wanted. All about him, however, he saw that people in general were anything but happy. The masses were in want, sometimes starving, oppressed by war and by the aristocrats; and even the aristocrats did not always derive much pleasure from their irregular and often precarious way of life. Here, then, was an obvious goal: to make men happy. Thus we find him defining a good government as one that makes its people happy.[29]

Since happiness is the good and man is normally a social being, it was only a short step to Confucius' principle of reciprocity. Obviously, if everyone worked for the happiness of all, we should have a situation more likely to bring about general happiness than any other. Confucius once defined reciprocity as "not doing to others what one does not wish them to do to one's self."[30] He stated the same idea more positively as follows: "The truly virtuous man, desiring to be established himself, seeks to establish others; desiring success for himself, he strives to help others succeed. To find in the wishes of one's own heart the principle for his conduct toward others is the method of true virtue."[31]

Yet Confucius was not so naïve as to suppose that the mere recognition of these principles would solve men's problems. All men want happiness, and most of us like to see those about us happy. But most of us will act unwisely, choosing a lesser immediate pleasure instead of a greater, deferred one. And we commonly act unsocially, preferring to secure our own happiness even at the expense of that of others. To correct these tendencies and to enlighten men and socialize them, Confucius clearly recognized and constantly insisted upon the necessity of some degree of universal education. He considered an enlightened citizenry the necessary foundation for the state. Punishment may temporarily compel men to do what they should, but it is at best a poor and unreliable substitute for education. He said: "If one tries to guide the people by means of rules, and keep order by means of punishments, the people will merely seek to avoid the penalties without having any sense of moral obligation. But if one leads them with virtue [both by precept and by example], and depends upon *li* to maintain order, the people will then feel their moral obligation to correct themselves."[32]

If one pursued this ideal far enough, it might even lead to

the dream of the philosophic anarchists, who think that all government will some day be unnecessary. But Confucius did not go to extremes. He recognized the need for good government and traced the most glaring abuses of his own day to the lack of it. Why was government bad? Because, he believed, those who governed were not disposed by their character to desire good government, or qualified by their abilities or education to bring it about. Why? Because they inherited their positions.

No concise statement of the political philosophy of Confucius has come down to us, but it is possible to reconstruct its main outlines. Clearly, he believed that government should be aimed at bringing about the welfare and happiness of the whole people. This, he thought, could be done only when the government was administered by the most capable men in the country. Such capability has nothing to do with birth, or wealth, or position, but is solely a matter of character and knowledge. These are produced by proper education. Education should therefore be widely diffused, so that the most talented men in the whole population might be prepared for the business of government. And the administration of the government should be handed over to such men, without regard to their origin.

Confucius did not, however, demand that the hereditary rulers vacate their thrones. If he had, it is doubtful that he would have accomplished anything by it, and his teaching would probably have been suppressed. Instead, he tried to persuade the hereditary rulers that they should "reign but not rule," handing over all administrative authority to ministers chosen for their qualifications.

Confucius attributed to the minister the highest degree of moral responsibility. Thus, while a minister ought to be loyal to his ruler, "can there be loyalty," Confucius asked, "which does not lead to the instruction of its object?"[33] When one of his disciples asked Confucius how a minister ought to be-

41

have toward his ruler, he replied: "He should not deceive him, but when necessary he should take issue with him openly."[34] Confucius once told the Duke of Lu that if a ruler's policies are bad, and yet none of those about him oppose them, such spinelessness is enough to ruin a state.[35]

There was a very obvious weak point in this political program that Confucius proposed. The rulers would still have the power to choose their ministers, and thus to control the government. But there was scarcely any alternative open to Confucius. Voting was unheard of in ancient China, and the common people of his day were, in any case, both uneducated and without political experience. Almost the only thing he could do, therefore, was to try, through education, to influence young men who were to be ministers, and, when possible, those who were to be rulers, and to develop a pressure of public opinion in favor of putting the most qualified men in the most responsible posts.

What did the rulers think of this plan? We have little information on this point, but certainly some of them thought Confucius was eccentric, if not dangerous. He seems to have owed his success, to the extent that he did succeed, chiefly to one aristocrat, by name Chi K'ang Tzŭ. Chi was the head of the most powerful family in the state of Lu and, as such, was the actual ruler, dominating the duke, who was no more than a puppet. Chi may have had a rival assassinated, though this is uncertain; but he certainly did tax excessively to maintain his luxurious way of life, wage aggressive war, and in various ways exemplify all the evils against which Confucius held forth. When this powerful noble deigned to notice him, Confucius did not abate his condemnation in any way. Almost every statement which has come down to us, that he made to Chi, is outspokenly critical. Thus, when Chi asked how he might deal effectively with thieves, Confucius replied: "If you, sir, did not covet things that don't belong to you, they wouldn't steal if you paid them to!"[36]

42

Instead of becoming angry, Chi K'ang Tzǔ admired Confucius' courage. He did not carry this admiration to the extreme of giving Confucius what he wanted—a position of authority in the government—but he did give official posts to several of his disciples. He did this primarily because he believed that they would make good officials. He believed this for two reasons. In the first place, while the nobles themselves acted with a great deal of license, it was obviously to their interest that their subordinates should be, in most respects at least, moral men. It is true that Confucius specifically repudiated the idea of feudal loyalty to individuals, insisting that his disciples must instead remain true to moral principle. But they nevertheless could be depended upon by their superiors much more completely than could most of the hereditary aristocrats, whose first thought was for the interests of themselves and the clans to which they belonged. In the second place, Confucius taught his students how to think, how to conduct themselves in the various situations in which an official might find himself, and something about the principles of government. His disciples proved, in actual practice, that these things made them effective officers. We know that at least half of the disciples who are mentioned in the *Analects* ultimately held government posts; some of these were quite important.

Yet Confucius was far from content. He had never intended to make a career of teaching. His plan was to reform the world, and he was teaching only until his opportunity came along. He wanted nothing less than to direct the government of the state. It was hardly reasonable to expect, however, that a man of his radical views would be given such power. If he had been willing to compromise, perhaps. But his unquestionable sincerity must have given the men who ran the government chills, when they thought about it.

Finally, after several of his disciples were in office, a place was found for Confucius. He was given an office probably equivalent to "Member of the Council of State." He accepted because he hoped that he could accomplish something, but, in fact, he had been given a sinecure to keep him quiet. When he realized this, he resigned in disgust.

Although Confucius was now in his fifties, he left his native state and spent about ten years in traveling from state to state in north China, seeking a ruler who would use his philosophy in his government. He never found one. In some places he was treated with scant courtesy; at least once an attempt was made on his life. In only one case did a noble who wielded the chief power in a state treat Confucius with great deference and constantly ask his advice. But this man was so corrupt that, when an invitation came to return to his native state, Confucius did so gladly.

At this time the policies of the Chi family, headed by Chi K'ang Tzŭ, which still held the principal power in Lu, were guided by one of Confucius' disciples. But as the price of his success this disciple had, in effect, renounced the principles of his teacher. When, to fill the bursting treasuries of the Chi to overflowing, this disciple raised the taxes, the Master publicly disowned him.[37]

Confucius spent the last years of his life in teaching in Lu. He was deeply disappointed, but not embittered; if he ever whined, we have no record of it. Once, when he was seriously ill, one of his disciples wished to offer prayers that he might recover. But Confucius smiled and told him: "My kind of praying was done long ago."[38] When he was so ill that he was unconscious, some of his disciples dressed themselves up in court robes and stood about his bed in the attitude of the ministers he would have had if he had realized his ambition to be a high official. Regaining consciousness and seeing this pantomime, Confucius said to them: "By making this pretence of having ministers when in fact I have none, whom do you think I am going to deceive? Heaven? And is it not better that I should die in the hands of you, my friends, than in the hands of ministers?"[39]

When he died, in 479 B.C., there were probably very few who did not think that this rather pathetic old man had died a failure. Certainly he himself thought so. Yet few human lives have influenced history more profoundly than that of Confucius. The appeal of his thought has been perennial. In China, generation after generation has made him its own; today, even some of the Chinese Communists claim him for their own revolutionary tradition. In the West his influence has been greater than we sometimes realize. This was particularly the case during the seventeenth and eighteenth centuries, so that Reichwein says that "Confucius became the patron saint of eighteenth-century Enlightenment."[40]

If we look for the secret of his appeal, it seems probable that it lies in his insistence upon the supremacy of human values. Wisdom, he said, is to know men; virtue is to love men.[41]

Perhaps even more important than this, because it is still more rare, is what might be called his "intellectual democracy." A great many men have been willing that the people should govern themselves, but relatively few philosophers have been willing to trust men in general to think for themselves—unless, that is, they are willing to think for themselves along the line which the philosopher graciously points out for their own good. Confucius was not only willing that men should think for themselves; he insisted upon it. He was willing to help them and to teach them *how* to think, but the answers they must find for themselves. He frankly admitted that he himself did not know the truth, but only a way to look for it.

He believed that humanity could find happiness only as a co-operative community of free men. But men cannot be free while forever following a star pointed out by another. And he believed that to give them, under the guise of the immutable truth, a dogma that represented only the imperfect insight of one individual would be to betray their trust. He never did so. He said: "If a man does not constantly ask himself, 'What is the right thing to do?' I really don't know what is to be done about him."[42]

Chapter IV

Mo Tzŭ and the Quest for Peace and Order

Although Confucius had emphasized *li*, one aspect of which is ritual, he considered the forms of ritual wholly secondary to the feelings it expressed, and believed its value to lie in its ability to socialize the individual. There was a change of emphasis in regard to *li*, however, even among some of Confucius' immediate disciples. Some of the most influential of them gave almost exclusive attention to ritual forms, laying the basis for the tradition in the Confucian school that placed the utmost stress on meticulous attention to ceremonial detail. Some of the disciples are said even to have insisted that a proper Confucian must wear a certain peculiar kind of clothing.

We have seen that filial piety was important in China long before Confucius. Confucius enjoined its practice and approved of long mourning for parents. Some of the Confucians emphasized filial piety and mourning out of all proportion. They also advocated lavish funerals—which we know Confucius considered in bad taste. Apparently some of the lesser Confucians came to specialize in conducting funerals with elaborate ceremony, and it is said that some of them made their livings in this way.

Confucius was what might be called "a teacher in spite of himself." He was a good teacher, and he liked to teach, but his real ambition was to transform the world, as a practical statesman. Even though he never had this opportunity, the nature of his goal and his interest colored everything he did. Some of his earlier disciples actually did hold government posts of considerable importance, but most of his later disciples seem to have considered themselves to be teachers primarily. Since it was their teaching that transmitted the tradition, their interests also colored the Confucian movement, which came to consist of teaching scholars to a degree that would have surprised and displeased Confucius.

The most successful of these teachers were the tutors of rulers. In this position they had excellent opportunities to influence the government, as consultants on political questions; but some of them hesitated to step out of this privileged position into the competitive arena of practical politics. They never ceased to work, as Confucius had done, to better the lot of the common people. But it seems that this was something they had learned they should do, not something that an intense personal conviction compelled them to do, as it had Confucius. By comparison, they seem rather more concerned with the success of their personal careers than with the welfare of mankind. At least one man, in the generation that immediately followed the death of Confucius, found them contemptible, and attacked them violently. We know him as Mo Tzŭ.

Our knowledge of Mo Tzŭ is derived chiefly from the book that bears his name. Although it has sometimes been supposed that he personally wrote this book, it is clear that he could not have written some parts of it. It appears that some of its chapters were written by his disciples, while others may be by himself. Hu Shih has stated that chapters 1–7 are late interpolations into the text,[1] and this seems probable. There seems to be no doubt whatever that chapter 39 is false, and a late addition; it is betrayed, among other things, by historical anachronisms. Chapters 40–45 are believed to be productions of the Moist school, but to have been written at a date considerably later than that of Mo Tzŭ. Finally, of the seventy-one chapters that the work is supposed once to have included, eighteen are now lost.

Nevertheless, what remains after all these subtractions is a great deal. This is the earliest piece of Chinese literature we have that includes lengthy dialogues and numerous complete essays. And it gives us a reasonably adequate picture of Mo Tzŭ, the man.

The dates of his life are not certainly known, but it appears that he was born not earlier than 480 B.C. (the year before the death of Confucius) and died not later than 390. Some scholars think he was born in Confucius' native state of Lu, while others make him a native of Sung. It is said that he held office in Sung.

Mo Tzŭ was evidently a man of relatively humble origin, as was Confucius.[2] He is said to have studied at first with those who transmitted the doctrines of Confucius. He felt, however, that Confucianism as it was practiced in his day did not get at the root of the troubles that made the people miserable. On the contrary, he asserted that in some ways it aggravated them.

He therefore broke away from the Confucians and founded his own school. Yet it is perfectly clear that, although he attacked the Confucians violently, he shared many of their points of view. He spoke of the Way, the *tao*, much as Confucius did, saying for instance that "those who know the Way will untiringly instruct others."[3] He said that government should correspond to the desires of the common people. His basic formula for bringing about good government was very similar to that of Confucius. In his book we read:

Mo Tzŭ said: Nowadays all rulers wish their domains to be wealthy, their people to be numerous, and their administration to produce order. But in fact they obtain not wealth but poverty, not populousness but paucity of population, not order but chaos—thus they lose what they want and get what they abhor. What is the reason?

Mo Tzŭ said: It is because the rulers are unable to exalt the virtuous and to cause the capable to administer their governments. When virtuous officers are numerous in a state, it is well governed; when they are few, it is governed badly. Therefore it is the business of the rulers merely to cause the virtuous to be numerous. By what method can this be done?

Mo Tzŭ said: Suppose, for example, that one wishes to cause good archers and charioteers to be numerous. In this case one will certainly enrich them, give them rank, respect them, and laud them. Once these things are done, good archers and charioteers will become numerous. How much more should this be done in the case of the virtuous and excellent who are rich in virtuous conduct, versed in argumentation, and experienced in the arts of the Way. These are certainly the treasures of the nation and the supports of the state. They too must be enriched, given rank, respected, and lauded; once this is done, they too will be numerous.[4]

Clearly, Mo Tzŭ agreed with Confucius that the hereditary rulers should turn over the administration of their governments to men of virtue and capacity. But, if so, why should they not turn over their thrones as well? Why should rulers not be selected for their merit rather than for their pedigrees? The old answer would have been that a ruler of plebeian origin could not command the support of powerful spirits, but in Confucius' thinking this idea had been swept into the discard. Confucius did go so far as to say that one of his disciples might properly occupy a throne, but he did not directly assail the title of the hereditary rulers to their places. It is probable, however, that he refrained because of a very reasonable prudence. He did not preach rebellion, which would have made trouble both for himself and for others, but instead proclaimed a doctrine that would more certainly, if more slowly, bear eventual fruit.

Traditional Chinese history records a long line of early emperors who are supposed to have reigned before the establishment of the first dynasty, during the third millennium B.C. This is a period concerning which we have no scientifically established historical data. Furthermore, critical Chinese scholars have long since pointed out that these early emperors are not mentioned in any document that was written at a time earlier than that of Confucius. The name of one of them, Yü, does appear in early works, but only as that of a culture hero who performed marvelous deeds in draining the marshes to reclaim land for cultivation, dredging out rivers, and so forth. In the Confucian *Analects*, however, we find Yü mentioned as an early emperor, along with two others, Yao and Shun. It should be noted that Yao and Shun are assigned to an earlier date than is Yü. This accords with a principle that Chinese scholars have discovered in connection with these mythical emperors. The *later* an emperor appears in the literature, the *earlier*, as a rule, is the date assigned to him. This is because, as this mythology was expanded, new figures had to be assigned to vacant periods, and only the earlier periods remained vacant.

Although Confucius mentions Yao, Shun, and Yü in the *Analects* as worthy emperors of old, no genuinely early passage in the *Analects* states that they did not acquire their thrones in the usual hereditary manner. In the book of *Mo Tzŭ*, however, we find a new note, as follows:

> Suppose a ruler wants . . . a garment made from cloth that is difficult to cut properly; he will certainly look for a skillful tailor. . . . To cure a sick horse, he will seek a skillful physician. For all such tasks the ruler will not employ his relatives, nor those who are rich and noble but lack merit, nor those who are merely good-looking, for he understands that they are not capable of performing them. . . . But when it is a question of governing the state, it is not so. For this task, the ruler selects those who are his relatives, the rich and noble without merit, and those who are merely good-looking. . . . Does he care less for the state than for a sick horse or a suit of clothes? . . .
>
> When the sage-kings of old governed the world, those whom they enriched and ennobled were not necessarily their relatives, or the rich and noble, or the good-looking. Thus Shun had been a farmer . . . a potter . . . a fisherman . . . and a peddler. But Yao discovered him . . . , made him emperor, and turned over to him the control of the empire and the government of the people.[5]

As the legends developed, it was said that Shun in his turn had not left the throne to his son but instead had selected Yü, because of his virtue and capacities, to be his heir. Mo Tzŭ may have known this tradition.[6]

Because our earliest record of these traditions is found in the book of *Mo Tzŭ*, it has been argued that Mo Tzŭ invented them. This is unlikely. We have seen that they represent a logical next step from the doctrines of Confucius, and, as a matter of fact, the *Mo Tzŭ* shows clearly that the Confucians of Mo Tzŭ's day had the same idea. A Confucian is recorded in the *Mo Tzŭ* as saying: "Anciently the sage-kings, in assigning rank, set up the most sage man as Son of Heaven [that is, king]. . . . If Confucius had lived under a sage-king, why then would he not have been made Son of Heaven?"[7]

The reason that lay back of this theory is very easy to see. It carried the fight against the hereditary aristocracy directly to the enemy. Did the rulers demur when told that they ought to hand over the principal offices to virtuous and talented men of obscure birth? Now the rulers could be told that, by rights, they ought to hand over their very thrones, on which they were little better than usurpers. In antiquity, when rulers were great, they had all, it was now said, followed this practice.

As we follow the development of Chinese philosophy, we shall see more and more of the argument from antiquity. The emphasis on precedent was by no means new. As far back as the beginning of the Chou dynasty we find the Chou conquerors stressing the importance of following the ways of "the former wise kings" of the dynasty they had conquered,[8] and ascribing its fall to a neglect of "the old ways."[9] Confucius made some reference to antiquity, but as compared with the men of his world he was a bold innovator. He almost never justified a course merely on the basis of precedent.

But the Confucians of Mo Tzŭ's day, and Mo Tzŭ himself, argued from precedent a great deal. One of Mo Tzŭ's chief arguments for his doctrines was that they accorded with those of the sage-kings. He said: "'I have decided that the best thing to do is to familiarize myself with the Way of the former kings and seek to understand it, and to examine into the pronouncements of the sages, and with these to persuade the rulers and the common people."[10] Again he said: "All precepts and all actions that accord with those of the sage-kings [of former times] . . . should be practiced. All precepts and all actions that accord with those of the wicked kings [of former times] . . . should be eschewed."[11]

Such precedent was not Mo Tzŭ's only criterion, by any

means. He even blamed the Confucians of his day for being too wedded to precedent, and said that if an action is good that is sufficient justification for it. Nevertheless, it is certainly true that both Mo Tzŭ and the Confucians of his time were much less concerned with teaching men to think for themselves than Confucius was, and were much more interested in setting up fixed rules for them to follow. This is natural. It is easy to train a man to use a machine but far harder to teach him how to make one. Really to educate him, so that he may invent a still better machine for himself, is superlatively difficult. It is no wonder that most teachers, and most philosophers, choose the easier way.

By referring their fixed rules to antiquity, Chinese philosophers conferred upon their doctrines the greatest prestige possible in the Chinese world. Antiquity also had the advantage of being (beyond a thousand years or so in the past) almost totally unknown, so that it provided a blank space that the philosophers could fill as fancy might dictate. Of course, this space remained blank only so long as it had not been used. In general, there was much less jumping of claims than might be expected. For the most part, instead of arguing about what happened in antiquity, rival schools said in effect: "What you say is no doubt quite true, but when we go still farther back we find. . . ." Thus Mo Tzŭ said to a Confucian: "What you call antiquity is not really antique." "You merely pattern yourself after Chou, and not after Hsia."[12] Here Mo Tzŭ went back two dynasties, to repose on the solid antiquity of real age.

Some differences with the Confucians that Mo Tzŭ stressed do not seem clearly grounded in philosophical differences. For instance, Mo Tzŭ devotes much time to an attack on the doctrine that "poverty and wealth, long life and premature death, all depend on Heaven and are unalterable."[13] He seems to have attributed this doctrine to the Confucians, or at least to some of them. It is clear, however, that neither Confucius himself nor Mencius, who lived after Mo Tzŭ, preached that man has no power in the face of destiny. But it is possible that some Confucians held this view, perhaps to excuse themselves for not making more strenuous efforts to right the ills of the world.

Some of Mo Tzŭ's most violent criticism was directed against the practice of expensive funerals and long mourning. He describes the elaborate funeral practices which were advocated by some, in a manner that may caricature them a little, but probably not very much. He concludes: "Thus the funeral of even a common man would exhaust the resources of his family. At the death of a feudal lord the treasury of the state would be emptied to surround his body with gold, jade, and pearls, and fill his grave with bundles of silk and carts and horses."[14] Mourning for the closest relatives, as prescribed by such regulations, would require that the individual spend three years in complete abstinence from his usual mode of life, doing no work, living in a mourning hut, eating sparingly, and so forth. Taken together, Mo Tzŭ says, these practices of burial and mourning impoverish the state, interfere with the orderly processes of economic production and government, and (because of the chastity that must be observed during the mourning period) reduce the population. Therefore, they are to be condemned.

We know that Confucius personally deplored unsuitably lavish funerals,[15] but he did advocate mourning for three years. There is no doubt that, from a Western point of view, Mo Tzŭ has the right of this argument.

In deploring war, Mo Tzŭ was at one with the Confucians. He considered the predatory warfare that the great states were constantly making on the small ones to be the greatest of evils. The reason is clear. Mo Tzŭ was associated with, and perhaps a native of, Sung. This small central state was a favorite battleground of its larger neighbors and suffered all the horrors of war. It is related that on one occasion the capital of Sung was besieged until the people were reduced to cannibalism to remain alive.[16]

Mo Tzŭ attacked the problem of war in two ways. The first

was to try to persuade the rulers of states that war was unprofitable. When his adversaries point out to him that four states have won large territories and great power by waging war, Mo Tzŭ replies that there were originally more than ten thousand Chinese states, while now all but four have been swallowed up (this figure was not strictly accurate, but accurate enough, since the other small states that remained were almost powerless). Mo Tzŭ concludes that to say that war has been beneficial is like arguing from the case of "a physician who treats more than ten thousand patients, and cures only four. He can hardly be called a good physician."[17]

From the point of view of the world in general, it is clear enough that war is not beneficial. But from the point of view of the state that conquers, this argument of Mo Tzŭ's would carry little conviction; here he does not deny that, in fact, the great states have gained in territory and in power. Elsewhere, however, Mo Tzŭ says that "the attack of a large state upon a small state injures both, and the large state always suffers for the wrong it has committed."[18] He tries to prove this by arguments from history, but his demonstrations are rather forced and tend to misinterpret and even misrepresent the facts.[19]

He is more persuasive when he asserts that war is not a productive but a destructive process, for the victor as well as for the vanquished. Territories that are conquered, he points out, are often laid waste in the process. Furthermore, those who conquer for the love of conquest usually have far more territory to begin with than they actually make use of. Conquerors are, in fact, great thieves, who steal not because they need more territory but because they are kleptomaniacs.[20] [It is interesting to note that the ancient Chinese seem to have been quite familiar with kleptomania, since we find it mentioned in more than one work.] Mo Tzŭ concludes that the world cannot be truly conquered by the sword, but only by virtue, justice, and good faith, which cause men truly and willingly to submit, and to co-operate with the ruler and with one another for the common good of all.

There is some question, however, whether even this argument would suffice to stop a powerful ruler avid for conquest. Evidently, Mo Tzŭ himself had some doubt about this, for he gave a great deal of attention to the practical techniques of defensive warfare, which might be used to oppose a ruler undeterred by persuasion. Thus in his book we find chapters with such titles as "The Fortification of a City Gate," "Defence against Scaling-Ladders," "Defence against Inundation," "Defence against Tunneling," and so forth. Mo Tzŭ was an unusual philosopher, in that he was not content merely to talk and write about his ideas on defensive warfare, but put them into actual practice. He trained his students in his methods, and it is recorded that at least one of them died in battle.

Chapter 40 of the *Mo Tzŭ* relates that the philosopher heard that a certain strategist, named Kung Shu Pan, had built "Cloud-Ladders" for the great southern state of Ch'u and was going to attack Sung with them. Mo Tzŭ at once hurried to Ch'u and tried to dissuade its ruler, but without success. Thereupon:

Mo Tzŭ took off his belt and laid it down to represent a fortified city. As a weapon he used a small stick. Kung Shu Pan employed nine different stratagems of attack; Mo Tzŭ repulsed him nine times. Kung Shu Pan had exhausted his devices for attack; Mo Tzŭ still had methods of defence in reserve.

Kung Shu Pan was embarrassed and said, "I know how you could be defeated, but I won't tell." Mo Tzŭ said, "I know what you have in mind, but I won't tell." The ruler of Ch'u asked what it was. Mo Tzŭ replied, "Kung Shu Pan thinks that if I were murdered, then there would be no one to defend Sung.... But in fact three hundred of my disciples ... supplied with all my implements of defence, are at this moment waiting on the walls of Sung for bandits from Ch'u. You may murder me, but you can't get rid of them." The ruler of Ch'u said, "Very well, let's give up this idea of attacking Sung."[21]

This manner of dealing with war, while effective, was negative. Mo Tzŭ had a more positive program. As a fundamental remedy for war and for a great many other evils he proposed what he called "universal love." Here again he was differing with the Confucians. They emphasized love of one's parents and relatives and said that, by analogy with this, one should love all men, though in lesser degree. This putting of the family first has always, from the most ancient times we know until the present, been characteristic of Chinese culture. It is responsible for some of its greatest strengths and for some of its chief weaknesses, such as nepotism. Mo Tzŭ saw only the weaknesses of family loyalty and condemned it utterly. Everyone, he believed, ought to love everyone else in the world, without distinction. Thus he says:

> Suppose that everyone in the world practiced universal love, so that everyone loved every other person as much as he loves himself. Would anyone then be lacking in filial devotion? If everyone regarded his father, his elder brother, and his ruler just as he does himself, toward whom could he be lacking in devotion? Would there then be anyone who was not affectionate? . . . Could there be any thieves and robbers? If everyone looked upon other men's houses as if they were his own, who would steal? . . . Would noble clans contend among themselves? Would states attack each other? . . . If everyone in the world would practice universal love . . . then the whole world would enjoy peace and good order.[22]

This sounds very easy, but, in fact, of course, it would be very difficult to make all men love one another. We should note, however, what Mo Tzŭ means by "love." The Chinese term he uses is *ai* 愛, for which "love" is the only possible translation. It must be noted, however, that while many Christians have hailed Mo Tzŭ as a kindred spirit, his "love" is not the emotional love of Christianity or, for that matter, of Confucianism. For, unlike the Confucians, Mo Tzŭ disapproves of emotion and at one point says that all emotions must be abolished, including "love."[23] Here he uses the same character, *ai*, but he is not really inconsistent. For the "love" in "universal love" is not emotional but (as Mo Tzŭ conceives it) purely a thing of the mind.

How can people be caused to exercise such a mental love?

Mo Tzŭ mentions two chief ways. On the one hand, they must be encouraged and exhorted by the ruler to practice universal love; of this more later. On the other, they must be made to understand that it is useful, and in their own interest, to do so. This is, then, a doctrine of "enlightened self-interest." Mo Tzŭ gives a great many arguments to show that his "universal love" is good policy. He is on strong ground when he points out that a ruler who practices universal love will be liked and trusted by his people, while one who is selfish and partial will not.[24] He is somewhat less convincing when he postulates the case of a man who is going on a long journey from which he may not return, and who has to intrust the care of his family to a friend. In such circumstances, he says, everyone, even though he himself may oppose the doctrine of universal love, will select as the guardian of his family one who believes in it. No one, Mo Tzŭ asserts, will be such a fool as to select a "partial" friend for this service.[25] Actually this is not certain, since the "universally loving" friend would, for instance, divide up whatever food there was not only with his friend's family but with everyone. Yet it is true that one would not select for this service a totally selfish person.

Someone said to Mo Tzŭ: "Your doctrine of universal love may be good, but of what use is it?" Mo Tzŭ replied: "If it were not useful I myself would disapprove of it. But how can there be anything that is good and yet not useful?"[26] Here we have Mo Tzŭ's famous doctrine of utilitarianism. But utility by itself is not a standard; everyone does what he finds useful in attaining some purpose, if it be no more than the purpose of loafing. What, then, we must ask, are the ends for Mo Tzŭ's utility? He seems to believe five goods to be especially desirable, to wit: enriching the country, increasing the population, bringing about good order, preventing aggressive war, and obtaining blessings from the spirits.[27] All these are self-explanatory except the desire to increase the population. Today we think of China as overpopulated, but her population has grown hugely in recent centuries. It has been estimated that, as recently as three hundred years ago, there were only one-seventh as many Chinese as today. In Mo Tzŭ's time it was underpopulation that was the problem.

To attain the end of a rich, numerous, orderly, peaceful, and literally "blessed" population, Mo Tzŭ was willing to sacrifice very nearly everything else. Clothing should keep out the cold in winter and the heat in summer but should not be attractive. Food should be nourishing but not well-seasoned. Houses should keep out the cold and heat, the rain and thieves, but should have no useless decoration. All must marry, whether they wish to or not, in order to augment the population.

Nothing not useful in Mo Tzŭ's terms was to be tolerated. He was particularly opposed to music, which used men's time and wealth in the making and playing of instruments, yet created nothing tangible. Thus we read: "What is it that causes rulers to neglect government and common men to neglect their work? Music. Therefore, Mo Tzŭ says, 'It is wrong to play music.' "28

This is quite different from the Confucian view, which is stated in one of the classics thus: "Music produces pleasure, without which man's nature cannot do."29 Mo Tzŭ would have disputed this. He realized that his whole system stood in danger of being wrecked by the emotions; therefore, he simply said that they should be eliminated. Specifically, he said: "Joy and anger, pleasure and sorrow, love [and hate], are to be got rid of."30

This is more easily said than done, but Mo Tzŭ did not rely upon persuasion alone to gain his ends. He advocated a rigidly disciplined organization of the state, cemented by what he called the principle of "identification with the superior"—by which he seems to have meant an identification of will and interest. Mo Tzŭ thought that men had first lived in an anarchic condition similar to Thomas Hobbes' "state of nature," from which the chief deity, Heaven, had rescued them by establishing an emperor. The emperor had chosen subordinates; these had then chosen their subordinates; and this process went on until the whole machinery of government was created. Then the emperor issued a decree saying: "Everyone, upon hearing good or evil, shall report it to his superior. What the superior approves all must approve; what the superior condemns all must condemn. When the superior makes a mistake his subordinates shall remonstrate with him; when a subordinate has merit his superior shall discover it and recommend that he be rewarded. Those who identify themselves with their superiors, and do not form cliques with their subordinates, shall be rewarded by their superiors and praised by their subordinates." On the other hand, the emperor concluded, those who act in the opposite manner deserve blame and punishment.[31]

This system, which Mo Tzŭ declared had actually operated in antiquity, has more than one resemblance to that of the party organized by Adolf Hitler, who wrote in *Mein Kampf:* "The principle of the establishment of a whole State constitution must be the authority of every leader to those below and his responsibility upwards."[32] It is arguable that it could be a good system if it could be insured that every leader were good. Mo Tzŭ said that anciently they had been but that in some manner which he does not completely explain they had ceased to be; hence the ills of the world. One wonders, though, how subordinates can, as Mo Tzŭ says they must, remonstrate with evil superiors while at the same time thinking just as their superiors do. Mo Tzŭ has a partial answer.

It is by no means enough, Mo Tzŭ says, for the chief ministers of the emperor to identify their wills with his. To complete the process, the emperor must identify his will with that of Heaven. Only then will the system function unfailingly. If this is not done, Mo Tzŭ says,

Heaven sends down immoderate cold and heat and unseasonable snow, frost, rain and dew. The five grains do not ripen and the six domestic animals do not mature. There are diseases, epidemics, and

59

pestilence. Hurricanes and torrential downpours occur repeatedly. These are Heaven's punishments, visited on men below because they fail to identify themselves with it. Therefore the ancient sage-kings understood what Heaven and the spirits desire and avoided what they dislike. . . . With purifications and baths and clean wine and cakes they led the people in sacrificing to Heaven and the spirits. . . . They did not dare to miss the proper time for the spring and autumn sacrifices. In judging lawsuits they dared not be unjust. In dividing property they dared not be unfair. Even in informal moments they did not dare to be disrespectful.

Thus, Mo Tzŭ concludes, they were able to act so as to get the blessings of Heaven and the spirits and the approval and assistance of their people. And all this came from their use of the principle of identification with the superior.[33]

Confucius, it will be remembered, had transferred the emphasis from ritual action (such as sacrifices to the spirits) to ethical conduct, exhorting men to be kind, to govern well, and so forth. Mo Tzŭ does not go back to the old, primarily ritual, scheme; ethical action is still very important for him. But whereas religious ritual, and even religious belief, were compatible with but in no sense essential to the philosophy of Confucius, Mo Tzŭ's whole scheme of things demanded that Heaven and the spirits intervene in human affairs to punish wrongdoing. Thus we find Mo Tzŭ saying: "The Confucians consider Heaven to be without intelligence and the spirits of the dead to be without consciousness. This displeases Heaven and the spirits, and is enough to ruin the world."[34]

Mo Tzŭ gives various proofs of the activity of Heaven. He says, for instance: "How can one know that Heaven loves all the people? Because it enlightens them. How can one know it enlightens them? Because it possesses them. How can one know it possesses them? Because it accepts sacrifices from all of them." Mo Tzŭ says this is clear because people everywhere make sacrifices. He continues: "Since Heaven thus possesses the people, why should it not love them? Moreover I say that for every murder of an innocent man, there is certain to be retribution. . . . Who sends down retribution? Heaven. . . . Thus I know that Heaven loves the people."[35]

To prove the existence of spirits Mo Tzŭ cites a number of instances, from relatively recent history, in which spirits (usually those of the dead) are supposed to have avenged wrongs or rewarded virtue. These spirits, Mo Tzŭ says, were seen by large numbers of people. Yet spirits are not always visible, for he tells us: "Even in deep gorges and great forests, where there is no man, one may not act improperly. There are ghosts and spirits who will see one!"[36]

Whether the Confucians of Mo Tzŭ's day were in fact as skeptical as he indicates, we cannot be sure. But there is no question that Confucius himself was, and Confucians generally have consistently been, much less superstitious than most of the people around them. There is no reason to believe that Mo Tzŭ was making up his stories about ghosts out of whole cloth. On the contrary, it seems clear that he was bringing back into philosophical thinking an element of which Confucius had largely purged it, but which undoubtedly played a much larger part in the thinking of men in general than did the kind of ideas that Confucius had stressed. Later, as we shall see, something of this filtered back into Confucianism, though it is doubtful that Mo Tzŭ had anything directly to do with that.

In fairness to Mo Tzŭ, however, we have to remember that he did not say that men might prosper merely by offering sacrifice. On the contrary, he insisted that only the sacrifices of the virtuous would meet with favor.[37]

Since Mo Tzŭ believed that the state should be organized in a rigidly disciplined hierarchy, it is not remarkable that he organized his school in the same way. This was the more natural because of the military functions that the group sometimes performed. Military functions sometimes require, and always excuse, the exercise of arbitrary powers by those in authority.

Mo Tzŭ went to a great deal of trouble to persuade pupils to join his group. One case is recorded in which he promised a young man that if he would study with him, he would secure for him an official post. At the end of a year, when the student asked for the promised position, Mo Tzŭ blandly told him that he had made the promise only to get him to study, for his own good.[38]

When his students were neophytes, Mo Tzŭ disciplined them by feeding them only one meal a day, of vegetable soup, and making them wear the clothing of common laborers.[39] When they had graduated and gone out into the world as officials, Mo Tzŭ still considered them subject to his authority. It is recorded that one of them, whom Mo Tzŭ had dispatched to serve as an official in Ch'u, sent a large amount of money back to his master.[40] Mo Tzŭ recalled another disciple, whom he had sent to take office in Ch'i, because he took part in aggressive war waged by that state.[41] A Han dynasty work tells us: "Those who served Mo Tzŭ numbered one hundred and eighty men, whom he could cause to go into fire or walk on knife blades, and who would follow him to the death."[42]

After the time of Mo Tzŭ, his school was continued for several centuries. His great power as leader of the group was handed down to a series of individuals, who apparently held it for life. This leader could apparently enforce the death penalty against his followers.[43] It is recorded that one of these leaders was intrusted with the function of defending a small state, and that when he was unable to do so he committed suicide. At the same time, one hundred and eighty-three of his followers killed themselves with him.[44]

In the book of *Mo Tzŭ*, chapters 40–45 are given over in large part to the discussion of questions of a logical and dialectical nature. It is generally agreed that these chapters were written by later Moists rather than by Mo Tzŭ himself. Nevertheless, we can find the beginnings of interest in such subjects in Mo Tzŭ personally. Mo Tzŭ liked to argue, but very often he was not a very fair or convincing arguer. He used unconscionable tricks in discussion and sometimes seems to be seeking to bewilder his opponent into agreement. Perhaps it is just because he was not a very logical arguer that he liked to insist that he followed logical rules. In fact, neither his rules nor his fidelity to them were very impressive.

At about the same time there were other thinkers in China who were developing disputation to a high degree. The method and the subject matter of their teaching remind one sometimes of the Greek Sophists and sometimes of the Eleatics. Although these men did not all agree, they are commonly grouped together under the title of "the school of names" or "the dialecticians."

One of their most famous propositions was that "a white horse is not a horse." The philosopher Kung-Sun Lung, who developed it, wrote in support of this proposition as follows: "A white horse is not a horse. . . . The word 'horse' denotes a form, the word 'white' denotes a color. To name a color is not to name the form. Therefore I say a white horse is not a horse. . . . If you are seeking a horse, a yellow or a black one will do, but they will not answer if you want a white horse. If it be assumed that a white horse *is* a horse, then what one is seeking is one thing, namely a white horse which is not different from 'horse' in general. Yet although they are supposed not to be different, a yellow or black horse will fulfill your desire for a horse, but will not fulfill your desire for a white horse; how is this?" The philosopher goes on to develop this thesis at great length.[45]

The later Moists, in their dialectical writings, combated many of the propositions of the dialecticians. They wrote, for instance: "A white horse *is* a horse. To ride a white horse is to ride a horse. A black horse is a horse. To ride a black horse is to ride a horse. . . . Although one's younger brother may be a handsome man, to love one's younger brother is not to love a handsome man."[46] The point in this latter case seems to be that, while it may be technically true that in loving one's younger brother one is loving a handsome man, this gives a false impression, since the love is not because he is handsome but because he is one's brother. And we are presumably to extend the same principle to the term "white horse" and recognize that when we say that a white horse is a horse, we are not referring to its color but to those qualities that it possesses in common with horses in general. We are not saying that white horses are *all* horses, but that white horses are *some* horses. In the language of Western logic, the Moists seem here to be making an objection equivalent to saying that the term "horse" has not been distributed.

The Chinese written language does not normally distinguish singular and plural, or active and passive voice; in these and other ways it may be ambiguous, if it is used carelessly or with the intent to confuse. The dialecticians were pointing out these pitfalls. They also considered the problem of universals, pondered the nature of such qualities as "hardness" and "whiteness," and speculated on the acquisition of knowledge through the senses. Obviously, what they were doing was very important and very interesting. Yet it is difficult to get reliable knowledge of what they said and wrote. Only one portion of one of their works is preserved; the others are lost and survive only in quotations by their critics. The reason for this seems to be that, while some Chinese at certain periods have been intensely concerned with the techniques of logic and dialectics, the Chinese in general have been relatively little interested in such things.

Although the later Moists criticized the dialecticians, they like Mo Tzŭ were interested in disputation. They appear, too, to have esteemed it as a means of reaching the truth, for they wrote: "In dialectic, the one who wins is right," and again, "In dialectic . . . the one who is right will win."[47] This may be true—one hopes it will be true—but the Chinese in general have been much too skeptical to believe that it is necessarily true. Thus the Taoist work *Chuang Tzŭ* says that the dialecticians "could vanquish men's arguments, but could not convince their minds."[48] A Han dynasty essayist said: "They paid exhaustive attention to terminology, but neglected the feelings of men."[49] Hsün Tzǔ, perhaps the most critical of all the Confucians, said of one of the dialecticians that he was "blinded by words, and did not know reality."[50] This is a very Chinese verdict.

Since dialectic is so important in Western philosophy, it is not easy for us to realize how little some Chinese have esteemed it. One writer early in the Christian Era commented that dialectical theorizing contributes nothing to the practice of government and is really a form of useless discussion. Nevertheless, he said, as a form of recreation for gilded youths, the exercise of arguing about terms and analyzing principles has distinct advantages. It at least keeps them out of mischief.[51]

In its early centuries the Moist school flourished and seems to have been a principal rival of Confucianism. In the uprisings against Ch'in totalitarianism in 209 B.C., both Confucians and Moists flocked to the standard of revolt as soon as it was raised.[52] We find the Moists mentioned as a numerous group as late as the first century B.C.[53] Shortly thereafter they disappear from sight, and interest in Mo Tzǔ seems to have become virtually extinct until it was revived in relatively recent times.

It is not difficult to account for the fact that Mo Tzǔ's doctrines had little lasting appeal for the Chinese people. His authoritarian system of "identification with the superior" and the dogmatic tone of his statements are the antithesis of the reasonableness that has usually been considered a cardinal virtue in China. Mo Tzǔ said: "My teachings are sufficient for every purpose. To reject my teachings and think for one's self is like rejecting the harvest and picking up individual grains. To try to refute my words with one's own words is like throwing eggs at a rock. One may use up all the eggs in the world, but the rock remains the same, for it is invulnerable."[54]

Mo Tzŭ's condemnation of all pleasure, and even of all emotion, runs counter to the normal Chinese attitude, which is to maintain balance in all things and to regard pleasure in reasonable moderation as good, not evil. Thus the Taoist work *Chuang Tzŭ* said of Mo Tzŭ's precepts: "His doctrine is too limited. It would make men miserable. . . . It is contrary to men's nature; they will not tolerate it."[55]

Yet Mo Tzŭ meant exceedingly well. Even Mencius, who attacked his philosophy, attested to his altruism.[56] Mo Tzŭ was as deeply concerned as Confucius had been over the suffering caused by poverty, disorder, and war. But, unlike Confucius, Mo Tzŭ did not see very far beyond the immediate goal of removing these conditions. Confucius had advocated a program that he believed would make men happy. Mo Tzŭ advocated a program designed to remedy specific evils, and in order to do this he was ready to sacrifice everything, including human happiness. This was not because he wanted men to be unhappy but because he was unable to see beyond a condition in which the present evils might be removed. He conceived of a world at peace, in which a large and orderly population was adequately clothed and fed, as enjoying the best possible state of affairs.

Those who are coldly calculating sometimes try to make others think that their actions are dictated by emotion. Those who are ruled by their hearts sometimes like to believe that they are exceptionally rational persons. Mo Tzŭ was of the latter sort. He seems to have devoted his life to a sincere effort to help his fellow-men, without any hope of selfish reward. Yet he tried to justify all his actions and all his philosophy by reason alone. Even his "universal love" was supposed to be founded not on emotion but on intellectual considerations.

Mo Tzŭ's intellect, however, was inferior to his heart. Although he contributed importantly to the development of interest in logic, his own argument was often singularly illogical. In attacking fatalism, for instance, he said that fate did not exist because "no one has ever seen fate or heard fate."[57] Exactly the same argument could be used to discredit his doctrines of "universal love" and "identification with the superior."

Cynics would have us believe that altruism is rare. It seems possible, however, that the best of intentions are not nearly so rare as the wisdom that is necessary to implement them.

Chapter V

Mencius and the Emphasis on Human Nature

THE Han dynasty work called the *Historical Records* tells us that "after the death of Confucius his seventy disciples scattered and traveled about among the feudal lords. The greater among them became teachers [of rulers], or ministers; the lesser were friends and teachers of officials, or went into retirement and were no longer seen." It states that four students of the disciple Tzŭ-hsia "became the tutors of kings," while Tzŭ-hsia himself was tutor to the ruler of the state of Wei.[1] The book of *Mencius* says that shortly after the time of Confucius two Confucians held ministerial posts in the government of the state of Lu. One of these was the grandson of Confucius, who was also a minister in the state of Wei.[2]

After Confucius had been dead for a century and more, there were many scholars who lived at the courts of rulers, great and small, as "guests" rather than as officials. Sometimes we find the two functions combined, in men called "guest-officials." These men were not all Confucians, by any means. Confucius was the first private teacher and scholar of whom we have any clear knowledge in Chinese history; but his example and the conditions of the times quickly produced a host of emulators, who traveled from state to state seeking to sell their abilities and their philosophies. Some of them were very successful.

The ruler of the state of Liang, for instance, invited a number of philosophers to his capital, including the Confucian Mencius. To assure that they would condescend to honor his court, he invited them with humble language and rich presents.[3] King Hsüan of the state of Ch'i was famous as a patron of philosophers. A Han dynasty work tells us that he supported more than a thousand scholars at his capital, where men like Mencius "received the salaries of high officials and, without having to undertake the responsibilities of office, deliberated upon affairs of state."[4] The *Historical Records* adds that King Hsüan built lofty mansions for his principal guests, in order to show the world that Ch'i was able to attract the most eminent scholars to its capital.[5]

This competitive spirit was undoubtedly one reason why scholars were honored, but there were other and more obviously practical reasons, too. The Chou kings had long been puppets, and China was split into a number of autonomous warring states. Sometimes they made treaties agreeing to accept the status quo, but it was a long peace that lasted more than a few years. The ideal of a united China persisted in the background, much as the ghost of the Holy Roman Empire long hovered over Europe. Unlike the European conception, however, the Chinese spirit refused to die, and each powerful state hoped that it might be the one to gain control of the whole country. For this purpose their rulers tried to attract to themselves men of talent. Many of these "guests," it should be noted, were military men, but many also were philosophers. However different the philosophies might be, they had this in common: that their advocates claimed that each philosophy, and it alone, held the key to gaining control of the entire Chinese world. (When the Chinese have spoken of "the world," they have usually meant "the Chinese world," just as when we speak of "the world" we frequently mean "the Western world." In each case the term means "all the world that matters.") It is interesting to note that the *Historical Records* tells us that it was only after he had repeatedly been defeated in war that the king of Liang invited philosophers to his court.[6] He expected philosophy to provide not consolation but revenge.

By the fourth century B.C. a number of different philosophies were current. Mencius complained that "unemployed scholars engage in perverse discussions" and that "the words of Yang Chu and Mo Tzŭ fill the country." The principle of Yang Chu, he said, was "each one for himself," which Mencius criticized as not recognizing the authority of the ruler, while Mo Tzŭ would have the individual love all equally, which did not acknowledge the special affection due to one's father.[7] Again Mencius said, "If Yang Chu could have benefited the whole world by merely plucking out one of his hairs, he would not have done it. . . . Mo Tzŭ, on the other hand, would have rubbed his entire body smooth from head to heel if in that way he could have helped the world."[8]

Apparently, the schools of these two men and that of the Confucians were the most popular in the time of Mencius. He says: "Those who flee from the doctrines of Mo Tzŭ turn to those of Yang Chu, and those who flee from Yang Chu turn to Confucianism."[9] We have already examined the philosophy of Mo Tzŭ. In the next chapter we shall look more closely at the doctrines attributed to Yang Chu and see that there is reason to agree with those scholars who regard him as an early forerunner of the Taoist philosophy.

Mencius mentions another individual who was a virtual hermit. He was the younger brother of a rich noble, but he considered his brother's wealth ill-gotten and would therefore have none of it. Instead, he lived in the wilds, supporting himself by weaving sandals out of hemp threads that were twisted by his wife. It is related that on one occasion he nearly starved to death because of the austerity of his principles.[10]

Another group is called the "agricultural school." The *Mencius* records that at one time, while Mencius was in the state of T'êng, a philosopher of that school named Hsü Hsing came to T'êng from the south. He asked the ruler to give him a dwelling, which he did. There Hsü lived with his several tens of disciples, all of whom wore coarse clothing and wove sandals and mats for a living. Two Confucians were won over by this group; this piqued Mencius and added to the acerbity with which he refuted their doctrines.

They maintained that "a wise and virtuous ruler tills the soil together with his people in order to get his food; along with governing, he cooks his own meals morning and night." The mere fact that such a doctrine could be held and preached quite openly shows to what an extent the old idea of the almost divine status of the ruling aristocracy was under assault. Mencius criticized this philospohy, however, on a different ground. He asked whether the philosopher Hsü Hsing raised his own food, and was told that he did. Mencius then asked if he wove his own cloth and made his own plowshare and cooking pots. He was told that he did not do so, because this would interfere with his farming. Mencius pointed out that, in the same way, a ruler could hardly be expected to find the time to do his own farming and cooking while ruling the state.[11]

It is not feasible to describe here all the varieties of philosophical opinion that were prevalent in China in the fourth century B.C. They were so numerous that the book of *Chuang Tzŭ* called them "the hundred schools." Others among them will be referred to later. Our present concern is primarily with Mencius, whose fame overshadows that of all the other Chinese of his day.

Our knowledge of Mencius comes chiefly from the work that bears his name. This is undoubtedly one of the great books of the world's literature. I. A. Richards, who made a study of the *Mencius*, wrote that certain of its arguments rank with "those of Plato," "in historic and intrinsic interest."[12]

The *Mencius* is a lengthy book; it contains more than thirty-five thousand Chinese characters. These would have to be multiplied several times to give the equivalent in English words. Although it has been said that Mencius himself wrote the book, it seems certain that it must have been put together by his disciples. Unlike most early Chinese books, it involves very few problems of textual authenticity. Hu Shih once wrote that "the *Mencius* is either entirely genuine or entirely false; in my opinion it is probably genuine."[13] For my own part, I suspect that one small portion of the text *may* be interpolated,[14] but, in general, with this book we are pleasantly free from the sort of troubles that beset us in most of early Chinese literature.

Mencius the man was a very interesting and a very complex character. He had both virtues and faults, and he was not petty about either of them. It is difficult to do him justice or even to understand his character. Yet we have to try, for the man is intimately reflected in his philosophy, and we cannot understand the one without the other.

Our knowledge of Mencius' life is very slight. We do not even know the dates of his birth and death. It is rather generally accepted that he lived from about 372 to about 289 B.C. He was born in a small state adjacent to the native state of Confucius, in northeastern China. It is said that his ancestors belonged to the Mêng family of the state of Lu, which had been one of the "three families" that dominated Lu in Confucius' day; but there seems to be no clear evidence of this.

Mencius studied with men who transmitted the teachings of Confucius, and lamented that he lived too late to study with the Master himself.[15] He is said to have studied with disciples of Confucius' grandson, Tzŭ-ssŭ.[16] He was always loyal to the memory of Confucius, and spoke of him in the highest terms. Mencius himself had a considerable number of disciples; but, even though the book of *Mencius* is much longer than the *Analects,* it is difficult to derive from it any clear picture of Mencius' methods as a teacher. It seems probable that he did not give as much careful thought and attention to the art of teaching as Confucius had.

Apparently he was quite as democratic as Confucius in accepting the humble as students. On one occasion when he and his students were lodged in a palace as the guests of a ruler, the custodian of the palace announced to Mencius that a single shoe was missing, and it was implied that his disciples had stolen it. When Mencius replied that this was hardly likely, he was reminded that he did not inquire into the past of those who sought to study with him, but accepted all who came with their minds set on learning.[17]

Nevertheless, he did turn away some who asked to study with him, but in some cases at least these were aristocrats who tried to presume on their status to demand special consideration. We have relatively little information about his disciples. It is recorded that one of them was once on the point of being put in charge of the government of the state of Lu.[18]

The principal aim of Mencius seems to have been to find office as the chief minister of a state and to direct its government so as to put his principles into operation. In this he resembled Confucius. Like Confucius, he never achieved such a position of great authority. He was somewhat more successful than Confucius, however, in that he held a nominally higher office, in the state of Ch'i, than Confucius ever attained in Lu. In addition, Mencius seems to have been consulted with rather more respect by the rulers of several states than Confucius had usually been. This, however, was in considerable part a symptom of the times.

It is doubtful that Mencius was ever a regular administrative official. Apparently he was a "guest minister," a sort of consultant on governmental affairs who had neither the duties nor the authority of the ordinary minister. In Ch'i he even refused to accept a salary.[19] We sometimes find him reproached, as Confucius had been, for not taking a regular office. There is no doubt, however, that he was eager to be a regular official, but he did not wish to do so unless he could have a free hand to run the government in his own way, and none of the rulers was willing to give him that.

Seeking a ruler who would embrace his way, Mencius traveled about with his disciples from state to state, remaining a longer or a shorter time according to the circumstances.

He was once asked: "Is it not extravagant of you to travel about, followed by several tens of carriages and several hundred men, living off one of the feudal lords after another?" Mencius defended his manner of living as being worth what it cost the rulers, since he was keeping alive the principles of the former kings for posterity.[20] He was supported by gifts from the princes, which were sometimes quite lavish. He cannot, however, be accused of indiscriminate avarice, for he sometimes refused gifts and seems to have limited himself to accepting what he believed he needed.

Mencius was quite correct in his belief that he was the continuator, in his day, of the Confucian tradition. He was undoubtedly sincere in his belief that his ideas and actions were in complete harmony with those of Confucius, but on this point he was mistaken. Mencius was quite another man than Confucius, and also, the times had changed.

An obvious difference lies in the fact that, whereas in the *Analects* Confucius several times says frankly that he is mistaken, Mencius seems never to have openly admitted that he was wrong. This is extremely significant. It has to do with the very foundations of their respective philosophies, as well as with the difference in their characters. It is also connected with the very different circumstances under which they lived.

Confucius seems to have been the only very important philosopher living in his world. Mencius, however, belonged to one philosophical school among many, and all these schools were competing among themselves for disciples and for the favor of the rulers, which would bring wealth, power, and position. The discussions of Confucius with his disciples were conducted in a relatively calm atmosphere and were devoted, at least in considerable part, to an attempt to arrive at and to examine the truth. The discussions of Mencius, on the other hand, are largely taken up with the enterprise of defending and propagating the true doctrine, which is of course another thing entirely.

Mencius and the Emphasis on Human Nature

We have already noted that I. A. Richards finds much that is admirable in Mencius. He is not blind, however, to his limitations. Richards characterizes certain of Mencius' arguments as follows: "(a) They are dominated by suasive purpose. (b) The purpose of eliciting the point of difference is absent. (c) The form of the opponent's argument is noticed, in the sense of *being used* in the rebuttal, but not *examined* so that the flaw, if any, may be found."[21] In other words, Mencius was usually more interested in winning the argument than in trying to find the truth. Not that he cared nothing for the truth but that he was convinced that he had it already, and needed only to persuade his opponent of that fact.

Mencius is not the only person who has argued in this way. Most of us do it more often than we would care to admit, and such argument can be found even in the works of great Western philosophers. That does not, however, make it a good practice. Mencius' attempt to maintain his infallibility led him into various pitfalls, including inconsistency. On one occasion when a disciple pointed out that he was not acting according to a principle that he had previously laid down, Mencius cut him off with the curt statement that "that was one time, this is another."[22]

In one case he seems clearly to have been guilty of dangerous casuistry in a matter of great importance. The government of the northern state of Yen was in considerable confusion, with the result that there was much suffering and disaffection among its people. At this point Mencius was asked by a minister of the state of Ch'i whether Ch'i ought to attack Yen. Accounts differ as to what Mencius said; in any case he did not oppose the invasion. Such intervention could have been justified both on political and on humanitarian grounds; but, after Ch'i's troops controlled Yen, the invaders treated those they had liberated badly, so that the people of Yen revolted. At this point Mencius was taxed with having advised Ch'i to undertake the invasion. He could probably have defended himself on perfectly valid grounds, but he sought refuge in a quibble.

Mencius said that he had only been asked, by Ch'i's minister, whether Yen might properly be attacked. Since the government of Yen was not conducting itself properly, he had answered, "It may." If Ch'i's minister had gone on to ask him *who* might properly attack it, Mencius would then, he explained, have said that only a righteous ruler appointed by Heaven for the task might attack it. But, unfortunately, the government of Ch'i had not asked him this question but had merely gone on to make the attack. Under these circumstances, Mencius asked, how could he possibly be accused of having advised Ch'i to attack Yen?[23]

It is not difficult, however, to find more admirable aspects of Mencius' character. No one has more eloquently asserted the claim of the scholar and the man of virtue to a place of honor above that which is conferred by the pomp of princes. Such a man, Mencius says, should regard worldly success and failure with indifference, secure in the knowledge that, if his character is as it should be and the world fails to acclaim him, the fault lies not with himself but with the world.[24] His success is not to be measured by the size of the sphere in which he acts but by the manner in which he conducts himself within that sphere.[25] "There is a nobility of Heaven," Mencius said, "and a nobility of men." The nobility of men consists in being a duke, a minister, or a great officer. But the nobility of Heaven consists in being "benevolent, just, high-principled, and faithful, and taking an unwearying joy in being good."[26] Rulers wear a manner peculiar to their position, Mencius observes; but how much more should an air of distinction set apart the scholar who lives in the wide house of the world.[27] He says: "Dwelling in the wide house of the world, occupying his correct place in the world, walking in the great way of the world; when his desire for office is fulfilled, practicing his principles along with others; when that desire is disappointed, practicing them alone; riches and honors cannot corrupt him, poverty and mean condition cannot change him, authority and power cannot make him bend the knee: such is the truly great man."[28]

This exalting of the scholar was not purely a matter of abstract principle. It had to do, very definitely, with the struggle for influence and power that was going on between the scholars and the aristocrats. Confucius had told the rulers that they should turn over the administration of their governments to men of virtue, ability, and education. A little later, as we have seen, the traditions concerning the legendary emperors had asserted that in antiquity even rulers had been selected on their merits rather than by heredity; this in effect demonstrated that the hereditary rulers were mere interlopers, occupying their thrones without good right. In the *Mencius* we find the great superiority of scholars to hereditary aristocrats stated unequivocally.

This was given a basis of considerable plausibility in the special position of the teacher. In China this is a position of great respect; and we find Mencius saying that a ruler's tutor stands toward him in the relation of a father or an older brother, and thus of a superior rather than a subject.[29] On the basis of this claim and their own assurance of their worth, some Confucians demanded meticulous attentions of the rulers whom they deigned to advise. Mencius says that Tzŭ-ssŭ, the grandson of Confucius, had a man always at his side to assure him constantly of the regard of the Duke of Lu; otherwise, Tzŭ-ssŭ would have left the court.[30] Mencius also tells us that this grandson of Confucius was highly displeased when his duke once suggested that they might be friends; Tzŭ-ssŭ told him that such a thing was hardly possible.[31] In fact, Mencius says that the virtuous rulers of antiquity were not even permitted to visit worthy scholars frequently, unless they showed the very utmost of respect.[32]

The subject of the presents that rulers gave to scholars was a difficult one. They were necessary to the scholars' existence, and yet such gifts put them in an embarrassingly humble position. Mencius laid down the principle that they ought to be presented with the most complete respect and in such manner that the scholar was not put to the trouble of constantly thanking the ruler for them.[33] Mencius himself was quite offended when the prime minister of Ch'i sent him a gift from the capital, without making the journey to the town where Mencius was residing to present it in person.[34]

Mencius believed that it was far beneath the dignity of a scholar like himself to be summoned to the presence of a ruler. This is demonstrated by an almost childish piece of byplay that occurred when he was in Ch'i. Mencius was on the point of going to the court, when a message came from the king. The king, wanting to summon Mencius but mindful of his sensibilities, said that he had been planning to visit Mencius but, unfortunately, was a little unwell; therefore he wondered if Mencius would come to see him. At this, Mencius dropped his plan of going to court and said he was very sorry, but he *too* was ill. The next day he went elsewhere to pay a visit, but as he was returning home he received a message from one of his disciples. The king had sent a physician to treat Mencius' illness, and the mortified disciple had said that his master was just now on his way to court. Therefore, the message urged, Mencius must not return home but immediately go to the court. Instead, Mencius went elsewhere to spend the night.[35]

In line with all this, we might expect Mencius to be even more uncompromisingly opposed to the hereditary principle in government than Confucius was. And we do find him laying great stress on the fact that the legendary emperor Yao left his throne, not to his son, but to the most able and virtuous man in the empire, a farmer named Shun.[36] Furthermore, Mencius tells the king of Ch'i that government should be turned over to those who have studied the art of government; presumably he means the Confucian scholars. And he says that for the king to interfere with the administration of such officials is as if he were to try to tell a skilled jade-carver how to carve jade.[37]

Elsewhere, however, we find Mencius emphasizing the importance of pleasing the great families that wield hereditary power.[38] He tells the same king of Ch'i that a ruler should not promote, in his government, men whose only claim is their possession of virtue and ability, unless he has no alternative. For by promoting such men the ruler will cause those who are not related to him to overpass his relatives and will place those of low condition above men of rank.[39]

These rather surprising views can be explained on two grounds. As a practical matter, it is quite true that the wrath of outraged relatives of the ruler was to be feared, if they were powerful; it might be asked, however, whether this was not a reason to try to reduce, rather than to augment, their power. The thinking of Mencius, in this connection, may have been importantly influenced by the fact that he himself is said to have been of noble ancestry[40] and that he habitually moved in aristocratic circles. We find him commenting, with a sigh, on the air of distinction that rulers wear as a result of their position,[41] and declaring that "those who counsel the great should despise them, and not look at their pomp and display." Lofty palaces, an abundance of rich food, hundreds of attendants and concubines, pleasures and wine, and the dash of hunting with a thousand chariots following after— all these, Mencius declares, "I would not have if I could. . . . What I possess is the lore of antiquity. Why should I stand in awe of kings?" This is bravely said, but one wonders whether Mencius was not human enough to be just a little envious of the rulers, if only subconsciously.[42]

Mencius was interested in the hierarchy of feudalism,[43] and we occasionally find later Confucians defending feudalism as an institution. Undoubtedly, these ideas have been read back into Confucius himself and have contributed to the idea that Confucius was a strong advocate of the feudal system, although it is very difficult to find valid evidence for that position.

None of these considerations, however, caused Mencius to stoop to currying favor with the rulers of his day, or mitigated the audacious courage with which he accused them of crimes and declared them deserving of punishment. "Is there any difference," he asked the king of Liang, "between killing a man with a club and with a blade?" "There is none," the king replied. "Is there any difference between doing it with a blade and with one's manner of governing?" "No," the king said. Then, Mencius told him, since his manner of governing was causing some of his people to starve to death, the king was in fact a murderer.[44]

Mencius told the king of Ch'i that an erring ruler might properly be disciplined by his ministers. Here, however, he made a distinction. Ministers not related to the ruler should remonstrate with him, and, if not listened to, they should quietly resign. But those ministers who are his relatives ought, if he does not mend his ways after remonstrance, to dethrone him. It is recorded that when Mencius told him this the king "changed color."[45]

The countenance of the same king must have turned a still darker shade on the occasion of another conversation with Mencius. The king said that he had heard that the last ruler of the Shang dynasty, one Chou by name, had been killed by one of his subjects, who had established a new dynasty; was this, he asked, true? "The records say so," Mencius answered. The king then asked: "May a subject then put his sovereign to death?" The king must have thought he had Mencius in a tight place, but the philosopher answered: "One who outrages the human virtues is called a brigand; one who transgresses against righteousness is called a ruffian. One who is a brigand and a ruffian is called a mere fellow. I have heard that the fellow called Chou was put to death, but I have not heard that this was killing a sovereign."[46]

Perhaps more than any other early Chinese philosopher, Mencius may be called a legislator, or at any rate one who attempted to legislate, in the sense in which Plato used that term. We find him standing back and thinking about what a state ought to be and could be, and then proposing a concrete program to make it so.

The basic postulate of Mencius' political program was simply that virtue brings success. The king of Liang told Mencius that, although his state had formerly been quite strong, during his own reign it had repeatedly been attacked and stripped of portions of its territory by neighboring states. In one of these wars the king's own son had been killed. Now he wished to avenge these defeats; what, he asked, did Mencius advise? Mencius told the king that even a very small territory was sufficient to be the starting point for winning control of all of China. He said:

> If your majesty will give benevolent government to the people, lightening punishments and fines, reducing taxes, causing the fields to be plowed deep and weeded carefully, and causing the strong-bodied to use their leisure to cultivate filial piety, fraternal respectfulness, sincerity and faithfulness, so that at home they serve their fathers and elder brothers and abroad they serve their elders and superiors—your people will then be able, at your command, and with nothing more than sticks that they fashion themselves, to beat back . . . soldiers wearing strong mail and armed with sharp weapons.[47]

In this extreme form Mencius' thesis sounds absurd. But his point, which he presents more plausibly elsewhere, is that the morale of an army is even more important than its armament; this is undoubtedly true. Mencius was strongly opposed to war as such. He declared that those who delight in their skill in strategy are, in fact, great criminals.[48] He did, however, leave a loophole in favor of righteous wars. (One wonders whether any ruler has ever believed that he was prosecuting an unrighteous war.)

Mencius pointed out that a ruler who had completely lost the good will of his people could not depend upon them to fight for him in time of war. On the other hand, a ruler who had treated his people well would be supported by them so loyally that he would be invincible.[49] Here the Confucians had a very effective point; the importance of the common people as soldiers was growing, and sometimes they simply refused to fight.

Few philosophers have laid more stress than Mencius did on economics. It is not enough, he insisted, for a ruler to wish his people well; he must take practical economic measures to assure their welfare. Thus he told one ruler that if he wished to practice good government, he must begin by resurveying his lands and laying out the boundaries of the fields anew. A scheme very dear to Mencius' heart was one whereby a sizable square of land was to be divided, like a checkerboard, into nine equal plots. Each of the eight plots on the periphery was to be given to a family, while all the eight families were to cultivate the square in the center in common. The produce of the center square would go to the government and constitute their taxes. At the same time, these eight families would form a community with close relations of friendship and mutual aid. Mencius said that this system had been practiced by virtuous rulers of former times.[50] Scholars are divided as to whether this is really true or whether the scheme is one that was imagined by Mencius, who attributed it to the past in order to gain for it the sanction of tradition.

Some of Mencius' economic measures sound very modern. He advocated diversified farming, with each farm family planting some mulberry trees to raise silkworms and keeping "five brood hens and two brood sows."[51] Even more remarkable, he advocated conservation of fisheries and of forests.[52] If the Chinese people had heeded Mencius' advice in this last connection, their economic position in the modern world would be considerably sounder.

For Mencius, economics was intimately related to ethics. Hungry people cannot be expected, he asserted, to be moral.[53] He did not, however, see the world in purely economic terms. He believed that the people should be given economic sufficiency, but he also advocated that they be taught, so as to raise their ethics above the level of simple response to the needs of the moment. Thus we find Mencius, in the same passages in which he advocates diversified farming, proposing the establishment of a system of public schools.[54] In so far as I am aware, this is the earliest mention of a public school system in Chinese history. Here again Mencius says that this plan was carried out by previous dynasties, but such evidence as we have fails completely to bear him out. It looks as if he is seeking to bolster his argument by manufacturing precedent.

Mencius groups all such precedents together under the term *wang tao*, "the kingly way" or "the way of a true king." By this he denoted the practices of certain good kings of the past, which should be taken as a model by the ages. A ruler who practiced this kind of government would, Mencius said, easily gain control of the whole Chinese world.

In connection with this argument Mencius ingeniously reinforced the Confucian insistence upon the importance of the people. He was firm on this point, asserting that if a ruler fails to bring about the welfare of the people he should be removed.[55] The ideal rulers to whom he most looked up were the legendary emperors Yao, Shun, and Yü. There was, according to tradition, a difference among them. Yao and Shun had each sought out a worthy and virtuous man among his subjects and left his throne to him, but Yü was succeeded by his son, thus supposedly beginning the first hereditary dynasty. One of Mencius' disciples asked him if it were true that Yao gave the throne to Shun. Mencius replied that it was not; that no ruler had the right to give away the throne. What had happened, Mencius said, was that Heaven accepted Shun, and the people accepted him, as Yao's successor. In effect,

Mencius reduced this to the consent of the people, for he quoted the saying, "Heaven sees and hears as my people see and hear."[56]

Later, Mencius said, when Yü died, there was one of his ministers whom Yü had wished to succeed him, but the people would not accept him but adhered to Yü's son instead. Here Mencius makes even the throne of a hereditary monarch the gift of the people. Mencius also explains that if a man other than the hereditary heir is to succeed to the throne, he must possess virtue equal to that of Shun and Yü *and* be designated as his heir by the ruler. It is for this latter reason alone, Mencius explains, that Confucius did not sit upon the Chinese throne.[57] From this we can see how much the exaltation of Confucius had developed in a single century.

It is obvious that tradition played a much greater part in the thinking of Mencius than it had in that of Confucius. A part of the reason was that the Confucian school had by this time developed a large body of tradition suited to its needs. But also important was the seeking for simpler ways to solve problems. Confucius' method, which consisted of incessant hard thinking together with the willingness to re-examine even one's basic premises, is so rigorous that no considerable group of men has ever espoused it for very long. We saw that Mo Tzŭ broke with the Confucian tradition very early and sought refuge in such absolute standards as the will of Heaven and of spirits, expressed through natural phenomena and prodigies. Mencius remained in the Confucian tradition and helped to mold it, but he, too, sought easier touchstones for the truth. Confucius had prescribed a rather difficult formula for judging character. He said: "Look closely into a man's aims, observe the means by which he pursues them, and discover what brings him content. How can a man hide his character?"[58] One of Mencius' statements was evidently an attempt to improve upon this, for he used some of the same words. Mencius said: "No part of a man's body is more excellent than the pupil of his eye. It cannot conceal wickedness. If all within his breast is correct, the pupil is bright; if not, it is dull. Listen to his words and observe the pupil of his eye. How can a man hide his character?"[59]

In line with this same tendency we find Mencius prescribing rules which may be followed in government. It is not enough to be virtuous; one must also model himself after the good kings of old.[60] If rulers and ministers would be without flaw, they need only imitate the conduct of Yao and Shun.[61] In levying taxes, it would be wrong either to tax more or to tax less than Yao and Shun did.[62]

Here we have to do with a philosophy that is presented as a package, labeled "the ways of antiquity," to be accepted or rejected in a piece. Such a philosophy tends to discourage criticism and initiative on the part of the individual and to be inflexible and very difficult to adapt to new situations. Confucian orthodoxy, as contrasted with the thought of Confucius, has had these shortcomings. From the point of view of those who advocate it, however, such a philosophy has the great advantage that its various aspects do not have to be justified individually. If a man can once be convinced that he should follow the ways of antiquity and that those ways are embodied in certain lore, the task of the propagandist is finished.

It was inevitable that books should be written describing the ways of antiquity. It was almost equally inevitable that such books should be attributed to early times, in order that they might profit by the peculiar authority that attaches to documents that are believed to be contemporary with the events they describe. Documents had been forged in China at an earlier time, but the golden age of forgery seems to have begun shortly after the death of Confucius. In the several centuries that followed his death a flood of such materials was produced, and many of them have found a place in the sacred canon of the classics. Most of these works seem to have been

produced under predominantly Confucian auspices, to re-
inforce the views of Confucian orthodoxy. Mencius himself
quotes from a document which, although it was alleged to
be ancient, probably did not exist in the time of Confucius.[63]
There is no indication, however, that Mencius himself was
a forger. On the contrary, he protested against the activities
of the forgers, and said: "Rather than believing in all historical
documents, it would be better to have none at all."[64]

We saw that one of Mo Tzŭ's principal arguments for a
course of action was its utility or profitableness. Mencius
argues against this criterion. The book of *Mencius* begins:
"Mencius had an interview with King Hui of Liang. The king
said: 'Venerable sir, since you have considered it worth while
to journey so far to come here, I assume that you must have
brought with you counsels to profit my kingdom—is it not so?'
Mencius replied, 'Why must your majesty speak of profit?
I have nothing to offer but benevolence and righteousness.
If your majesty asks, "What will profit my kingdom?" then
the great officers will ask, "What will profit our families?"
and the lower officers and the people will ask, "What will
profit our persons?" Superiors and inferiors will contend with
one another for profit, and the state will be endangered.'"
Developing the argument, Mencius points out that such a
condition will place the king in danger of losing his very
life to a subordinate who covets his position and his wealth.
"But," he continues, "there has never been a benevolent man
who neglected his parents, nor a righteous man who regarded
his ruler lightly. Let your majesty then speak only of
benevolence and righteousness. Why must you speak of
profit?"[65]

On this basis it has sometimes been held that Mencius, in
opposition to the Moist position, embraced a nonutilitarian
ethics. Yet it seems perfectly clear that even in the passage
just quoted the argument of Mencius is, in fact, a utilitarian
one. He does not say that one must be benevolent and righteous

because this is a categorical imperative, nor because it will glorify the deity. Instead, he points out that action which has as its sole aim material profit will in the long run not even achieve that, for it will result in anarchy and civil war. What Mencius is preaching here is really a doctrine of enlightened selfishness—which is, of course, quite utilitarian.

Nevertheless, it is true that Mencius does not always talk in such terms. He does speak of the doctrines of Yao and Shun as having authority in themselves. It will be remembered, however, that Shun's title to the throne was ultimately ratified by the adherence of the people to his rule. And it is evident that the people adhered (or rather are supposed to have adhered) to Shun because they believed that his rule would contribute to their well-being. Such thoroughly utilitarian considerations will usually be found to underlie all of the ethics of Confucianism.

This raises a nice philosophical problem. Mencius clearly believes that the doctrines of the sage-kings of old constitute the perfect pattern for men's thoughts and actions. Then how did the sages acquire them? Were they given to them by supernatural revelation? Evidently not. Were the sages themselves men of superhuman endowment? Mencius specifically denies this, saying, "Yao and Shun were constituted just as other men are."[66]

Mencius believed that all men were born with the same kind of human nature, and that human nature is good. This doctrine has been the subject of bitter controversy within Confucianism. One of Mencius' disciples pointed out that in his own day there were those who said that human nature is neither good nor bad, while others said that it could be caused to be either good or evil; still others said that some men are by nature good, while other men are naturally bad. "Now you, Master," the disciple concluded, "say that the nature is good. Are those others all wrong?" Mencius replied:

Man's nature is endowed with feelings which impel it toward the good. That is why I call it good. If men do what is not good, the reason does not lie in the basic stuff of which they are constituted. All men have the feelings of sympathy, shame and dislike, reverence and respect, and recognition of right and wrong. These feelings give rise to the virtues of benevolence, righteousness, propriety, and wisdom. These virtues are not infused into me from without; they are part of the essential *me*. A different view is merely due to lack of reflection. Therefore it is said, "Seek them and you will find them, neglect them and you will lose them." Men differ from one another, some by twice as much, some by five times as much, some incalculably, simply because in different degrees they are unable fully to develop their natural powers.[67]

Obviously, Mencius is on very debatable ground when he speaks of an innate sense of right and wrong. His position is much stronger, however, in regard to sympathy, and he develops this argument admirably. "Suppose," he says, "that a man suddenly sees a little child about to fall into a well. He will, no matter who he may be, immediately experience a feeling of horror and pity. This feeling will not be the result of a desire to gain the favor of the child's parents, or to be praised by his neighbors and friends." It will, Mencius insists, be simply the result of an instinctive sympathy, which is a part of the endowment of every normal human being.[68]

It would seem that this controversy over the goodness of human nature, which has been debated endlessly, has often been approached from the wrong direction. Attention is usually paid to the term "human nature." It might be more fruitful to examine the term "good." It would appear to be the case that for Mencius, as for Confucius, the good is that which is most fully congruent with human nature. Food that gives one a stomach ache is not "good" food. Hay is good food for an ox, but not for a man, because it does not suit his nature. A way of life that allows only two hours out of the twenty-four for sleep is not good, for the same reason. It is possible to go on and develop a whole system of ethics on this basis; this is, to a great extent, what Confucianism does. Thus in his discussion of human nature Mencius points out that men's mouths, ears, and eyes are made alike and have similar likes and dislikes; from this he reasons that their minds should approve similar moral principles.[69]

Thus when Mencius says that human nature is good he is in some degree speaking tautologically, because in the last analysis he seems to mean, by the "good," that which is in harmony with human nature. For Mencius, therefore, the relationship between ethics and psychology is very intimate.

The psychology of Mencius seems never to have been given anything like the study it deserves. I. A. Richards comments that "it is possible that Mencius anticipates some of the educative prescriptions of Freud."[70] I have myself heard a practicing psychiatrist comment, after reading some of Mencius' psychological passages, that he seemed to have anticipated some of the theory of modern psychiatry. It is difficult to feel satisfied that one has really understood the psychological theories of Mencius. He himself said that he found it hard to explain his terminology; and when one translates it into our own psychological language, which is not always entirely clear and precise, the result must be very far from what Mencius had in mind.

As a psychologist Mencius had one great advantage; the idea of a separate soul and body did not hover in the background of the minds of the men of his day, as it broods over much of even our most scientific thinking.* Mencius did, however, have a kind of psychological dualism, between what we may call the "emotional nature" and the "rational faculties"

---

* S. I. Hayakawa has cited a striking instance of the persistence of the "mind" and "body" dualism in a recent book by a physician on psychosomatic medicine. This author, Hayakawa says, "explicitly states ... 'Your body is your mind and vice versa.' In spite of repeated assertions to this effect [Hayakawa continues], the author constantly reverts to the division of body and mind in her text, for example, 'The patient has lost the ability to have his mind maintain control of his body,'—a habit which seriously affects the accuracy of her statements" (S. I. Hayakawa, "What Is Meant by Aristotelian Structure of Language," p. 229).

(these are only very rough equivalents for Mencius' terms). He did not consider one good and the other evil, but he believed that control should rest with the rational faculties. When the rational faculties are firmly knit and unified, they are able to keep the emotional nature under control. If the emotional nature, however, becomes strongly unified, it can take the command away from the rational faculties. Suppose, for instance, that I am walking along with my head in the stars, meditating upon philosophy, and my foot strikes a rock so that I stumble and have to run to regain my balance. In a twinkling my emotional nature has become unified and taken control; my philosophical thoughts have fled, and I am shaken by fear for a brief moment until I can, as we say, "collect my wits" again. When they are collected, or, as Mencius would say, when the rational faculties are again unified, I can resume my meditations.[71]

Although the emotional nature is to be controlled, Mencius says very specifically that it is *not* to be repressed. He considers that if properly channeled the emotions are, far from being immoral, the greatest of moral forces. Thus he says that it is necessary to cultivate one's emotional nature, so that it may attain to its full stature.[72]

Mencius says that one should make his desires few, which is after all only common sense. One who aims at too many goals will not only disquiet his mind but may even fail to achieve any of them.[73] But Mencius does not consider desires as such bad. In a famous interview between Mencius and the king of Liang, the king confesses that he considers himself inadequate to pursue the Confucian ideals, because he is ashamed to say that he has various unworthy tastes— for valor, for music, for wealth, for sex. Mencius assures him, however, that these are perfectly natural tastes and that they will result not in evil but in good if the king will, following his natural tendency of human sympathy, allow his people as well as himself to benefit by them. Thus his cultivation of valor should be to defend his state and his people; he should see that the people as well as himself are able to enjoy music and an economic competence; and, while he himself enjoys sex, he should also make it possible for all the people to marry and do likewise.[74]

We have seen that Mo Tzŭ proposed to get rid of the emotions. The Confucians considered this both impossible and undesirable. For they believed the emotions, properly guided, to be the surest guarantors of moral conduct. They could not conceive that a purely intellectual principle like Mo Tzŭ's "universal love" could be depended upon to make a man act unselfishly in a crisis. This is why Confucius insisted upon the necessity of "discipline by means of *li*" in addition to intellectual training.[75] It is for the same reason that Mencius asserted that only the educated man could be depended upon to remain virtuous in the face of economic privation.[76]

By "education" Mencius seems chiefly to have meant moral cultivation. This cultivation was aimed at preserving one's original nature intact. He said: "That which differentiates men from the birds and beasts is very slight; ordinary men discard it, superior men preserve it."[77] And again: "The great man is he who does not lose his child's-heart."[78] Nevertheless, Mencius recognizes that the innate tendencies to morality, what he calls the "beginnings" of the virtues, must be cultivated and developed in order to reach their full effectiveness. This development does not come suddenly, in a moral rebirth or a flash of enlightenment. Rather it is a result of one's entire conduct, in one's daily life. Thus Mencius says that the proper cultivation of one's emotional nature can be achieved only by the constant "accumulation of righteousness."[79] Mo Tzŭ had said that one must act morally even in the deepest solitude, since everywhere "there are ghosts and spirits who will see one."[80] Mencius would have said that one must always act morally because everything one does will react, for good or ill, on the development of one's own character.

Since all men are good, and equally good, at birth, why do some become evil? Mencius employs a simile like one used by Jesus and points out that if one sows identical grains in different places, that which falls on rich soil and has plenty of moisture will yield an abundant harvest, while that which grows in poor soil or gets too little rain will turn out badly. Men, similarly, differ because of the environment in which they develop.[81] It is important, therefore, to see to it that this environment is as good as possible. If you wish a child to speak the dialect of Ch'i, Mencius said, you had better send him to the state of Ch'i, where he will hear it spoken by all those about him. In the same way, if you desire to cultivate your virtue, you had better associate with virtuous men.[82] A wise ruler who wishes his people to be virtuous will see to it that they have the kind of environment in which virtue can develop.[83] For extreme poverty leaves scars on men's minds and hearts as surely as it emaciates their bodies.[84]

Thus far there is little in Mencius' philosophy of human nature and in his psychology that is not in essential harmony with the ideas of Confucius. It is Mencius' great contribution that he took up and developed much that was merely suggested by, or implicit in, the sayings of the first Master. Confucius, however, seems never to have said explicitly that human nature is good. Perhaps the question did not arise; perhaps Confucius' native caution and sense of balance prevented him from making a statement which, if interpreted in an extreme manner, could lead to undesirable results.

Mencius, undeterred by such inhibitions, carried his theory to, and perhaps even beyond, its logical conclusion. Thus he said: "All things are complete within us."[85] In other words, man's inborn nature not only is perfect but is a sort of microcosm which represents or contains the essence of all things. From this it follows logically that, as Mencius says, "he who completely knows his own nature, knows Heaven."[86] The meaning of these passages has been debated endlessly in Chinese literature for two thousand years, and it is unnecessary for us here to try to determine whether Mencius meant that one may, by introspection alone, learn the nature of the world about him, or whether he merely meant that one can in this way learn the principles of morality, which are all that greatly matters.

In either case, Mencius was here breaking (unconsciously, no doubt) with Confucius, who had explicitly branded meditation as inadequate and urged upon his students the importance of wide observation and critical examination of what went on in the world.

There are a few other passages in the *Mencius* in which he appears to diverge even more widely from the original Confucian doctrine. Certain aspects of the form as well as the content of these passages suggest the possibility that they may not be genuine utterances of Mencius but, instead, have been interpolated into the text.[87] In any case they approach the type of thinking that is called "Taoist," which is the subject of the next chapter.

Chapter VI

The Mystical Skepticism of the Taoists

U P TO this point we have seen, in general, a single attitude toward the problems of the world. Confucius, Mo Tzŭ, and Mencius differed on many things, but they were alike in the great seriousness with which they addressed themselves to the task of making the world a better place to live in. All of them believed that a proper man should be ready to give up his life, if necessary, for the sake of humanity. Confucius, to be sure, did speak of the necessity for recreation and believed that the enjoyment of life is in itself a good; but he was tremendously earnest, for all that. As Confucianism developed, it came to have less and less of the balance and flexibility of the Master and to demand that the individual dedicate himself more and more completely to a fixed code of action on behalf of a world he had not made.

The aristocrats had not, of course, this same kind of earnestness; but they wanted to exercise despotic control over the individual and make all their subjects mere pawns in the games they played for political, military, and economic power. Between the princes and the philosophers, a man had little chance to call his soul his own.

Since human beings are made as they are, it was to be expected that some of them would rebel. They did; and this rebellion was the basis out of which there grew the very remarkable and interesting philosophy we know as Taoism. A Chinese philosopher of the present day has said that Taoism "is the natural and necessary counterpart to the complacent gregariousness of Confucianism."[1]

94

The Mystical Skepticism of the Taoists

It may be that some stirrings of this revolt can be traced back to a time even earlier than that of Confucius. It is very difficult for an individual to achieve independence in a tightly organized feudal society, but there are a few passages in the early literature that may refer to hermits. In the original text of the classic called the *Book of Changes* we find mention of "one who does not serve either a king or a feudal lord, but in a lofty spirit values his own affairs."[2]

We find this revolt in unmistakable form about a century after the death of Confucius. It will be remembered that Mencius referred to a certain Yang Chu as one of the most popular philosophers of his day, saying that all those who were not Confucians or Moists were followers of Yang Chu. About his ideas, Mencius tells only this: "Yang takes the position of selfishness. Though he might benefit the whole world by merely plucking out one of his hairs, he would refuse to do it."[3] A Han dynasty work says that the philosophy of Yang Chu advocated "preserving the integrity of one's personality, holding fast to reality, and not allowing one's self to become ensnared by things."[4]

There is a much more full account, supposedly quoting the words of Yang Chu himself, that appears as a chapter of the Taoist work called *Lieh Tzŭ*. Unfortunately, the *Lieh Tzŭ* is a book that is now generally recognized to be a forgery, probably perpetrated many centuries later than the time of Yang Chu, who is believed to have lived in the fourth century B.C. There are a few scholars, however, who believe that, despite the fact that the book as a whole is a forgery, the portion on Yang Chu may include genuine materials which have survived from an earlier day; they point out that it contains the kind of things we should expect Yang to have said. This is a difficult point. These passages in the *Lieh Tzŭ* may be nothing more than early attempts to reconstruct the kind of statements that Yang Chu might have written, and the kind of sentiments from which the beginnings of Taoist thought originated. Whatever their origins, they are interesting. The *Lieh Tzŭ* tells us:

Yang Chu said: "No man lives more than a hundred years, and not one in a thousand that long. And even that one spends half his life as a helpless child or a dim-witted oldster. And of the time that remains, half is spent in sleep, or wasted during the day. And in what is left he is plagued by pain, sickness, sorrow, bitterness, deaths, losses, worry, and fear. In ten years and more there is hardly an hour in which he can feel at peace with himself and the world, without being gnawed by anxiety.

"What is man's life for? What pleasure is there in it? Is it for beauty and riches? Is it for sound and color? But there comes a time when beauty and riches no longer answer the needs of the heart, and when a surfeit of sound and color becomes only a weariness to the eyes and a ringing in the ears.

"Do we live for the sake of being now cowed into submission by the fear of the law and its penalties, now spurred to frenzied action by the promise of a reward or fame? We waste ourselves in a mad scramble, seeking to snatch the hollow praise of an hour, scheming to contrive that somehow some remnant of reputation shall outlast our lives. We move through the world in a narrow groove, preoccupied with the petty things we see and hear, brooding over our prejudices, passing by the joys of life without even knowing that we have missed anything. Never for a moment do we taste the heady wine of freedom. We are as truly imprisoned as if we lay at the bottom of a dungeon, heaped with chains.

"The men of old knew that life comes without warning, and as suddenly goes. They denied none of their natural inclinations, and repressed none of their bodily desires. They never felt the spur of fame. They sauntered through life gathering its pleasures as the impulse moved them. Since they cared nothing for fame after death, they were beyond the law. For name and praise, sooner or later, a long life or a short one, they cared not at all."

Yang Chu said: "In life all creatures are different, but in death they are all the same. Alive they are wise or foolish, noble or base; dead, they all alike stink, putrefy, decompose and disappear. . . . Thus the myriad things are equal at birth, and again become equal in death. All are equally wise, equally foolish, equally noble, equally base. One lives ten years, another a hundred, but they all die. The benevolent sage dies just as dead as the wicked fool. Alive they were [the sage-kings] Yao and Shun; dead, they are just rotten bones. Alive they were [the cruel tyrants] Chieh and Chou; dead, they are just rotten bones. And rotten bones are all alike;

who can distinguish them? Then let us make the most of these moments of life that are ours. We have no time to be concerned with what comes after death."[5]

These ideas are not unique; we could probably find their counterpart in every literature. Ultimately they boil down to the fact that man is born into a world he did not make and can never completely understand. His life is fettered by duties and harassed by fears, and he makes himself still more miserable by demanding of himself and his mind achievements of which, by their very nature, they are incapable. Justice Oliver Wendell Holmes, in a letter to a friend, made some observations that have remarkable similarities to those of Yang Chu, ending with this reflection: "I wonder if cosmically an idea is any more important than the bowels."[6]

The positive injunctions of such a philosophy are, in general, not to worry but to take life as it comes, not to become entrapped by soaring ambition, and to savor and enjoy as much of one's life as one can, day by day. It may be objected that this is not an exalted philosophy; but it is at any rate consistent, and unless one achieves it to some degree he is likely to develop gastric ulcers.

The philosophy of Yang Chu is interesting, and it resembles Taoism. Yet it lacks one ingredient of Taoism, and that is the most important ingredient of all.

Before we discuss Taoism itself, we must consider the problem of how we can learn anything definite or reliable about early Taoism. This is not easy. The subject is a complex one, about which scholars have wrangled long and sometimes bitterly. It is generally agreed that the oldest Taoist works are the *Lao Tzŭ* and the *Chuang Tzŭ*. And that is about all that is generally agreed upon.

Traditionally it has been supposed that the book of *Lao Tzŭ* was written by a man called Lao Tzŭ. This name should perhaps be translated as "Old Master." Lao Tzŭ is alleged to have been a somewhat older contemporary of Confucius and a keeper of archives at the capital. Confucius is supposed to have met him there, in a celebrated encounter that has been amply shown to be fictitious.

Very few critical scholars any longer believe that Lao Tzŭ, if there was such a person, lived as early as Confucius. The evidence against such a view is overwhelming. There is no mention of Lao Tzŭ in any book until we come to a much later time. The book of *Lao Tzŭ* refers constantly to ideas that were unknown at the time of Confucius and did not become current until much later. Various scholars have tried to establish that Lao Tzŭ lived at some later date; but, even if there was such a man, it seems quite certain that neither he, nor any other single person, wrote the whole book of *Lao Tzŭ*. We shall therefore drop the problem of the man, if there was such a man, known as Lao Tzŭ, as being unprofitable. Instead, we shall consider the book.

The *Lao Tzŭ* is also known as the *Tao Tê Ching;* this may be translated as "The Canon of the Way and of Virtue." This is a small book, consisting of about five thousand characters. It is an interesting and important book. It is a very difficult book, written in a terse style that often seems deliberately obscure. It has often been translated; and if one compares the various renderings, it is sometimes almost impossible to believe that the different translations are based upon the same text. It is sometimes an exasperating book, partly because in different sections it espouses different and sometimes contradictory doctrines. It has been pointed out that different portions of the work employ different rhymes for the same characters, and different grammatical usages. Clearly it is a composite work, the parts of which were written by more than one person. Numerous dates have been assigned to it, varying from the traditional view that it was written as early as the time of Confucius down to opinions that it was put together as late as the second century B.C. I personally believe that it could not have been written earlier than the fourth century B.C.

The Mystical Skepticism of the Taoists

When we turn to the man called Chuang Tzŭ, "Master Chuang," we seem to be on somewhat firmer ground. He is said to have been born in a place in central China that is now in Honan Province, and to have held a minor administrative post there. He is supposed to have died shortly after 300 B.C. We know little of his life, beyond some rather dubious anecdotes. The book of *Chuang Tzŭ* tells us that the ruler of the great southern state of Ch'u sent messengers with costly gifts to Chuang Tzŭ, to persuade him to become his prime minister, but Chuang Tzŭ would have none of it.[7]

When we turn from Chuang Tzŭ the man to the book called *Chuang Tzŭ*, there is considerable confusion. Most scholars seem to believe that not all of the book is by Chuang Tzŭ, but they are not by any means agreed as to which portions are by him and which by others. Some scholars think they detect a multiplicity of authorship even within individual chapters. Here, as in the case of the *Lao Tzŭ*, we find conflicting points of view. Some scholars believe that this text may not have reached its present form until as late as the second century B.C.

There is little point, then, in saying that Lao Tzŭ the man or Chuang Tzŭ the man made such and such statements, for it seems to be almost impossible to be certain that any particular statement was made by either of these individuals. The safer course is to say that the book of *Lao Tzŭ* or the book of *Chuang Tzŭ* makes the statements.

In the earliest Taoism, as we find it represented in the *Chuang Tzŭ* and the *Lao Tzŭ*, there is the same disillusion, not to say disgust, with human life as it is ordinarily lived that we saw in the thought of Yang Chu. In the *Chuang Tzŭ* we read: "To labor away one's whole lifetime but never see the result, and to be utterly worn out with toil but have no idea where it is leading—is this not lamentable? There are those who say, 'It is not death,' but what good does this do? When the body decomposes, the mind goes with it—is this not very deplorable?"[8]

Such pessimistic passages are, however, rather rare. For the Taoists have discovered nature and are amazed and fascinated by it. The *Chuang Tzŭ* asks:

Do the heavens revolve? Does the earth stand still? Do the sun and the moon contend for their positions? Who has the time to keep them all moving? Is there some mechanical device that keeps them going automatically? Or do they merely continue to revolve, inevitably, of their own inertia?

Do the clouds make rain? Or is it the rain that makes the clouds? What makes it descend so copiously? Who is it that has the leisure to devote himself, with such abandoned glee, to making these things happen?[9]

Viewing nature with the eyes of a delighted child, the Taoists found that "every prospect pleases, and only man is vile." Finding the world of men disgusting, they advised that one abandon it. Thus among the persons who figure chiefly in the Taoist writings we find many who are recluses, fishermen, or farmers, living apart, in communion with nature.

In the thoughts attributed to Yang Chu in the *Lieh Tzŭ* there is a good deal of concern about death. The quest for longevity and for immortality came to have a prominent place in the history of Taoism, and the search for an elixir of life led to the development of a considerable Taoist alchemy. There would seem to be some question, however, whether the desire for immortality had any part in the highest phase of early Taoist philosophy.

In any case we can also discern quite another tendency. This type of Taoist thinking recognizes that, to be sure, one must die, and that when one dies this consciousness, this eager insistent "I," will be exterminated. But what of it? Consciousness is a pain and an evil anyway. Will the universe be any different when there is no more "I"? Not one whit!

Thus the *Chuang Tzŭ* tells us: "The universe is the unity of all things. If one once recognizes his identity with this unity, then the parts of his body mean no more to him than so much dirt, and death and life, end and beginning, disturb his tranquillity no more than the succession of day and night."[10] According to the *Lao Tzŭ*, true longevity consists in the fact that, "though one dies, he is not lost" from the universe.[11]

The Taoist philosopher, then, was not merely resigned to such operations of the universe as involve the death of the individual; he delighted in contemplating them, and in identifying himself with the vast cosmic process. To undergo its myriad transformations is, the *Chuang Tzŭ* says, "an incalculable joy."[12] A character in the same work says:

> If my left fore-arm were changed into a cock, I would use it to learn the time of dawn. If my right fore-arm became a crossbow, I'd use it to bring down a bird for roasting. If my buttocks were transformed into wheels and my spirit into a horse, then I would ride; what other carriage would I need?
>
> When life comes, it is because it is time for it to do so. When life goes, this is the natural sequence of events. To accept with tranquillity all things that happen in the fullness of their time, and to abide in peace with the natural sequence of events, is to be beyond the disturbing reach of either sorrow or joy. This is the state of those whom the ancients called "released from bondage."[13]

Taoism is, as Maspero has so well shown,[14] a mystical philosophy. It is a nature mysticism. In the midst of our cities, Taoism may well seem nonsense. But go out to nature, the trees, the birds, the distant view, the placidity of a summer landscape or the savage fury of a storm, and much of Taoism will seem to possess a validity stronger than that of the most intricate logic.

The Christian or Mohammedan mystic seeks communion and union with God. The Taoist seeks to become one with Nature, which he calls the *Tao*.

We have seen that before Confucius the term *tao* usually meant a road, or a way of action. Confucius used it as a philosophical concept, standing for the right way of action—moral, social, and political. For Confucius, however, the *Tao* was not a metaphysical concept.[15] For the Taoists it became one. They used the term *Tao* to stand for the totality of all things, equivalent to what some Western philosophers have called "the absolute." The *Tao* was the basic stuff out of which all things were made. It was simple, formless, desireless, without striving, supremely content. It existed before Heaven and Earth. In the course of the generation of things and institutions, the farther man gets away from this primal state, the less good, and the less happy, he is. The *Lao Tzŭ* says:

> The *Tao* is like a vessel which, though empty,
> May be drawn upon endlessly
> And never needs to be filled.
> So vast and deep
> That it seems to be the very ancestor of all things.
> Immersed in it the sharpest edge becomes smooth,
> The most difficult problem solved,
> The most blinding glare diffused,
> All complexities reduced to simplicity.
> It is as calm as eternity itself.
> I do not know whose child it is.[16]

It will be recalled that the *Lao Tzŭ* is also known as the *Tao Tê Ching*. We have considered *Tao*, but what does *tê* mean here? When this term means "virtue," in the Confucian sense, the Taoists condemn it. But as they themselves use the term it refers to the natural, instinctive, primitive qualities or virtues, as opposed to those enjoined by social sanction and education.

The idea that the primitive is also the good has appealed to men of many lands and many ages. We naturally think of Rousseau, but even Plato in the *Laws* spoke of primitive men in terms remarkably like those of the Taoists, asserting that among them there were neither rich nor poor, and that "the community which has neither poverty nor riches will always have the noblest principles; in it there is no insolence or injustice, nor, again, are there any contentions or envyings. And therefore they were good, and also because they were what is called simple-minded; and when they were told about good and evil, they in their simplicity believed what they heard to be very truth and practiced it."[17]

The Mystical Skepticism of the Taoists

The Taoist ideal is simplicity; the goal, to return to the *Tao*. How can one do this? The *Lao Tzŭ* says:

The ten thousand things come into being,
And I have watched them return.
No matter how luxuriantly they flourish
Each must go back to the root from which it came.
This returning to the root is called quietness;
It is the fulfilment of one's destiny.
That each must fulfil his destiny is the eternal pattern.
To know the eternal pattern is to be illumined.
He who knows it not will be blasted and withered by misfortune.
He who knows the eternal pattern is all-encompassing;
He who is all-encompassing is completely impartial.
Being impartial, he is kingly;
Being kingly he is like Heaven;
Being like Heaven, he is at one with *Tao*.
Being at one with *Tao* he is, like it, imperishable;
Though his body may disappear into the ocean of existence,
He is beyond all harm.[18]

It is a basic principle of Taoism that one should be in harmony with, not in rebellion against, the fundamental laws of the universe. All artificial institutions and all strivings are wrong. That all striving is wrong does not mean that all activity is wrong, but that all straining after that which is beyond reach is a mistake. The *Chuang Tzŭ* says: "Those who understand the conditions of life do not seek to do what life cannot accomplish. Those who understand the conditions of destiny do not seek for that which is beyond the reach of knowledge."[19]

Thus perspective, poise, a judicious understanding of what is and what is not feasible and suitable, are essential. In this connection it is important to recognize that all things are relative. "It is only because everyone recognizes beauty as beauty," the *Lao Tzŭ* tells us, "that we have the idea of ugliness."[20] Although the whole world is tiny in relation to the universe, nevertheless, the *Chuang Tzŭ* asserts, the tip of a hair is by no means insignificant.[21] The same work says:

If a man sleeps in a damp place, he will wake up with an aching back, and feeling half dead; but is this true of an eel? If men tried to live in trees, they would be scared out of their wits; but are monkeys? Of the three, which knows the right place to live? Men eat meat; deer eat grass; centipedes like snakes; owls and crows enjoy mice. Will you tell me, please, which of these four has the correct taste? . . . Men considered Mao Ch'iang and Li Chi the most attractive of women, but on catching sight of them fish dived deep in the water, birds soared high in the air, and deer ran away. Which of these four has the right standard of beauty?"[22]

This same relativism is applied to moral problems. Thus the *Chuang Tzŭ* says:

Concerning the right and the wrong, the "thus" and the "not thus": if the right is indeed right, there is no point in arguing about the fact that it is different from the wrong; if the "thus" is indeed "thus," why dispute about the way in which it is different from the "not thus"? Regardless of whether the various arguments actually meet one another or not, let us harmonize them within the all-embracing universe, and let them run their course.[23]

This relativism is applied to our very existence, so that we read: "And one day there will come the great awakening, when we shall realize that life itself was a great dream."[24]

Since nothing is certain, it would be ridiculous to become so intent on success that one strove with fanatical zeal to attain it. In fact, if one tries too hard, he is certain not to succeed: "One who stands on tiptoe does not stand firm. He who takes the longest steps does not cover the most ground."[25] The *Lao Tzŭ* tells us:

If you would not spill the wine,
Do not fill the glass too full.
If you wish your blade to hold its edge,
Do not try to make it over-keen.
If you do not want your house to be molested by robbers,
Do not fill it with gold and jade.
Wealth, rank, and arrogance add up to ruin,
As surely as two and two are four.
When you have done your work and established your fame, with-
  draw!
Such is the Way of Heaven.[26]

Illustrating the point that one who tries too hard will fail, the *Chuang Tzŭ* notes that an archer who is shooting for a prize no more important than an earthenware dish will non-chalantly display his best skill. Offer him a brass buckle if he hits the mark, and he will shoot cautiously and less well. Offer a prize of gold, and he will become tense, and his skill will desert him entirely.[27]

One should not care, then, for the possession of external things, but only try to achieve self-knowledge and content-ment. Thus the *Lao Tzŭ* says:

> To understand others is to be wise,
> But to understand one's self is to be illumined.
> One who overcomes others is strong,
> But he who overcomes himself is mighty.[28]

Again:

> He who has the greatest possessions
> Is he that will lose most heavily,
> But he that is content is invulnerable.
> He who is wise enough to stop, by his own volition,
> Will endure.[29]

And:

There is no greater misfortune than not to know when one has enough,
And no calamity more blighting than the desire to get more.
If one once experiences the profound satisfaction of being truly content,
He will never again be content to be otherwise.[30]

What, then, shall one do? Do nothing, says the Taoist. "The operations of Heaven and Earth proceed with the most admirable order," the *Chuang Tzŭ* tells us, "yet they never speak. The four seasons observe clear laws, but they do not discuss them. All of nature is regulated by exact principles, but it never explains them. The sage penetrates the mystery of the order of Heaven and Earth, and comprehends the principles of nature. Thus the perfect man does nothing, and the great sage originates nothing; that is to·say, they merely contemplate the universe."[31]

"Do nothing," *wu wei*, is a famous injunction of the Taoists. But does it mean simply to do nothing at all? Evidently not. The sense is rather that of doing nothing that is not natural or spontaneous. The important thing is not to strain in any way. We have already noted the simile of the archer, who shoots badly when he strives to win a gold piece but is relaxed and skilful when nothing of consequence depends upon his hitting the mark. The *Chuang Tzŭ* also includes a famous passage in which the butcher of the king of Liang tells his master how he cuts up an ox. He says that at first he had great difficulty, but that after years of practice he does it almost by instinct; "my senses stand still, and my spirit acts as it wills."[32]

There are many illustrations in the Taoist books of the fact that the highest skill operates on an almost unconscious level, and we can all think of illustrations from our own experience. One cannot skate or ride a bicycle skilfully until he makes the various motions necessary to maintain his balance without ever thinking about them. On the more intellectual plane, a connoisseur, the moment he sees an object of art, immediately "feels" that it is or is not genuine. He does this for many reasons, most of which he will be able to analyze and explain if he takes the time. But if his knowledge and experience have not given him the ability to feel immediately that an object is good or bad, he is no true connoisseur.

Taoism emphasizes this unconscious, intuitive, spontaneous element. There would seem to be little doubt that most of us live too much of our lives on the conscious level, constantly worrying about what to do when it does not really matter, and that this is one reason we keep the psychiatrists increasingly busy. The Taoists point out, for instance, that a drunken man who falls is much less likely to be injured than a sober man, because he is relaxed.

Thus one's path should be nonaction and quietness. The *Lao*

Tzŭ tells us that one should speak as little as possible; this is the way of nature. Even Heaven and Earth cannot make a rainstorm or a hurricane last long.[33] The *Tao* that can be talked about is not the eternal *Tao*.[34] Those who know do not talk and those who talk do not know.[35]

> True words are not flowery,
> And flowery words are not true.
> The good man does not argue,
> And those who argue are not good.
> The wise are not learned,
> And the learned are not wise.[36]

Again: "When we give up learning we have no more troubles."[37] "Discard sageness, get rid of wisdom, and the people will be a hundred times better off."[38]

> He never goes outside his door,
> Yet he is familiar with the whole world.
> He never looks out of his window,
> Yet he fathoms the Way of Heaven.
> Truly, the farther one travels
> The less he understands.
> Therefore the Sage knows without investigating . . .
> Does nothing, yet accomplishes everything.[39]

The *Chuang Tzŭ* says: "There was a time when the wisdom of the men of old was perfect. When? When they were not yet conscious that things existed. Next, they knew that there were things, but did not attempt to distinguish them. Next, they distinguished things but did not try to label some 'right' and others 'wrong.' As soon as such judgments were passed, the integrity of the *Tao* was violated and prejudice came into being."[40]

It is quite logical, in accord with the Taoist views we have considered, that the Taoists should oppose war. Weapons, the *Lao Tzŭ* tells us, are of evil omen,[41] and war horses are reared only in a state that has fallen away from the *Tao*.[42] Oppressive government is similarly denounced. The people starve because their superiors eat too much in taxes.[43] The more laws there are, the more thieves and bandits will multiply.[44] Capital punishment is futile. "The people do not fear death. What is the use, then, of trying to frighten them with the death penalty?" And even if they were afraid, what mortal man is qualified to pronounce this awful judgment against his fellows?[45]

This is, in effect, an anarchistic point of view, and there is a strong element of anarchism in Taoism. "I have heard," the *Chuang Tzŭ* says, "of letting the world go its own way, but not of governing the world successfully." The following passage in the *Chuang Tzŭ* illustrates this attitude and is a good sample of the peculiar flavor of the book:

The Spirit of the Clouds, traveling to the east on a gentle breeze, happened to meet with Chaos, who was wandering about slapping his buttocks and hopping like a bird. Surprised at this, the Spirit of the Clouds stood respectfully and asked, "Venerable Sir, who are you, and why do you do that?" Without ceasing to slap his buttocks and hop like a bird, Chaos replied, "I am having a good time." The Spirit of the Clouds said, "I should like to ask you a question." Chaos looked up at him and said, "Pooh!" The Spirit of the Clouds went on, "The ether of heaven is out of harmony; the ether of earth is confined; the six influences are not in proper relation; the four seasons occur irregularly. Now I wish to harmonize the essence of the six influences so as to nourish all living creatures; how can this be done?" Chaos just went on slapping his buttocks and hopping like a bird. "I don't know," he said, shaking his head, "I don't know."

The Spirit of the Clouds had no opportunity to question him further at that time. But three years later, when he was again traveling in the east, just as he was passing by the wilderness of Sung, he again chanced upon Chaos. Overjoyed, he hurried to him and said, "Have you forgotten me, Heaven?" He bowed twice, touching his head to the ground, and requested instruction. Chaos said, "I drift here and there, with no idea of what I seek; moved only by the impulse of the moment, I have no idea where I am going. I wander aimlessly, regarding all things without prejudice or guile; how should I know anything?" The Spirit of the Clouds replied, "I consider myself, also, a creature of impulse, yet the people follow me about. The people take me as their model; I can't help it. I would like a word from you as to what I should do." Chaos said, "The world's basic principles are violated, the constitution of things is overturned, the mysterious operations of nature are aborted, the herds of animals are scattered, all the birds cry out in the nighttime, plants and trees are blighted, and the harm reaches even to the insect world—all this is because, alas, of the mistake of governing men." "Yes," said the Spirit of the Clouds, "so what shall I do?" "Alas," Chaos said, "this idea of 'doing' is what makes the trouble. Desist!"

"I have had a hard time finding you, Heaven," the Spirit of the Clouds said, "and I would appreciate a word more." Chaos told him, "Nourish your mind. Rest in the position of doing nothing, and things will take care of themselves. Relax your body, spit out your intelligence, forget about principles and things. Cast yourself into the ocean of existence, unshackle your mind, free your spirit, make yourself as quiet as an inanimate thing. All things return to their root, without knowing that they do so. Because they lack knowledge, they never leave the state of primal simplicity. But let them once become conscious, and it is gone! Never ask the names of things, do not seek to spy out the workings of their natures, and all things will flourish of themselves."

The Spirit of the Clouds said, "Heaven, you have bestowed upon me the secret of your power, and unveiled for me the mystery. I have sought it all my life; today it is mine." He bowed twice, touching his head to the ground, took leave of Chaos, and went on his way.[46]

The conclusion of this aspect of Taoist philosophy is negative. "Don't worry." "Do nothing, and everything will be done." Like all true mystics, these Taoist philosophers found their satisfaction in the mystical experience itself. They had no need of the activities and the rewards sought by ordinary men. Thus we are told that when Chuang Tzŭ was invited to become prime minister of Ch'u he refused, with a smile, to leave his fishing.[47] The book of *Chuang Tzŭ* tells us that after Lieh Tzŭ was enlightened, he "went home and for three years did not go out. . . . He took no interest in what went on. . . . He stood like a clod, sealed up within himself despite all distractions, and continued thus to the end of his life."[48]

Such men illustrate the statement that "the perfect man does nothing, and the great sage originates nothing; they merely contemplate the universe."[49] They represent what we may call the "contemplative" aspect of Taoism. Such dedicated mystics are rare, and it is doubtful that there were many of them even among the early Taoists.

The conclusion of contemplative Taoism is clear. One should care nothing for worldly power, position, or honors. One might go into the wilderness as a recluse, or, if one stayed among men, he would be indifferent to their attitude toward himself. Thus the *Lao Tzŭ* says: "Those who understand me are very few; for this reason I am all the more worthy of honor. It is for this reason that the sage wears a garment of coarse cloth, concealing that which is more precious than the finest jade within his bosom."[50]

Now it is all very well to talk of caring nothing for the world's opinion, of not striving, being perfectly quiescent, remaining content with the lowest position in the world, and so forth. But human beings get tired of that sort of thing. And most of the Taoists were human, not matter how much they tried not to be. Thus we find in their works repeated statements to the effect that, by doing nothing, the Taoist sage in fact does everything; by being utterly weak, he overcomes the strong; by being utterly humble, he comes to rule the world. This is no longer "contemplative" Taoism. It has moved to the "purposive" aspect.

The first step in this remarkable transition probably comes from mysticism. The *Tao* is the absolute, the totality of all that is. If one regards himself as simply a part of that, then it is clear that no matter what happens to him, he cannot get out of it. One seeks then to become merged into the *Tao;* the Lao Tzŭ tells us:

This is called the mysterious absorption.
He who has experienced it cannot be treated as an intimate, or rebuffed,
Cannot be helped, or harmed,
Cannot be honored, or humbled.
Therefore, he occupies the first place among all the world's creatures.[51]

This is the transition. One who is absorbed into the *Tao* cannot be hurt because he recognizes no hurt. One who cannot be hurt is impregnable. One who is impregnable is more powerful than all those who would hurt him. Therefore, he is the chief and the most powerful of creatures. This skilful transition is made in many forms. The Taoist sage has no ambitions; therefore, he has no failures. He who never fails always succeeds. And he who always succeeds is all-powerful.

The power of the Taoist sage is, indeed, far beyond the greatest power of which human beings are usually supposed to be capable. For since he is one with the *Tao*, he *is* the *Tao*. Thus he is compared with Heaven and Earth, and described as having the same attributes as are posited of the *Tao* itself.

It should be noted that, even though this reasoning may seem fallacious, the person who is actually convinced that he is "in tune with the infinite" and a channel for all the powers of the universe has great advantages in self-confidence and poise. This is far superior to such autosuggestive devices as telling one's self, "Day by day in every way I am getting better and better." Thus the convinced Taoist would have personal characteristics well calculated to impress others and assure them of his special and sagely character.

The Taoist works tell us of various sages, ancient and contemporary, who refused office as prime ministers and even disdained the offer of thrones; and we should naturally expect the Taoist to be above the vainglory of temporal rule. Nevertheless, we also find a number of passages devoted to telling how one may "get control of the world." Quite evidently the Taoists were human enough to join the competition that was going on among the various philosophies, each of which undertook to point the way to uniting the Chinese world into an empire. Sometimes it appears that a Taoist may act as prime minister to a ruler, but usually the Taoist sage is himself cast in the ruler's role.

Humanly, it was natural for the Taoist to wish to rule. He

knew how the people ought to act to be happy; they should simply remain in a state of primal simplicity. Therefore, the *Lao Tzǔ* says, "the sage, in governing, empties the people's minds and fills their bellies, weakens their wills and strengthens their bones. He constantly keeps the people without knowledge and without desire. When there are those who have knowledge, he sees to it that they dare not act. When he thus enforces nonaction, good order is universal."[52] And in the *Chuang Tzǔ* we read that "the true men of old . . . considering punishments to be the substance of government, were liberal in their infliction of the death penalty."[53]

This has brought us a long way from the Taoist insistence on individual freedom. Here only the Taoist sage has freedom. Still, the sage is governing in the interests of the people as a whole. But there is worse to come. In some passages we are told that the sage is compassionate, but in others both the *Lao Tzǔ* and the *Chuang Tzǔ* tell us that the *Tao*, which is his model, is above such emotion. In the *Chuang Tzǔ* the *Tao* is apostrophized thus: "My Master! My Master! You destroy all things and yet are not cruel; you benefit ten thousand generations, and yet are not benevolent."[54] The *Lao Tzǔ* says: "Heaven and Earth are not benevolent; they treat the ten thousand creatures ruthlessly. The sage is not benevolent; he treats the people ruthlessly."[55]

This conception was capable, if it fell into the wrong hands, of truly terrifying consequences. For the enlightened Taoist is beyond good and evil; for him these are merely words used by the ignorant and foolish. If it suits his whim, he may destroy a city and massacre its inhabitants with the concentrated fury of a typhoon, and feel no more qualms of conscience than the majestic sun that shines upon the scene of desolation after the storm. After all, both life and death, begetting and destruction, are parts of the harmonious order of the universe, which is good because it exists and because it is itself.

In this conception of the Taoist sage, Taoism released upon

humanity what may truly be called a monster. By any human standards, he is unreachable and immovable; he cannot be influenced by love or hate, fear or hope of gain, pity or admiration. Fortunately, this conception has seldom been clothed in flesh; but there is no doubt that some of the more despotic Chinese emperors were inspired, not to say intoxicated, by this ideal. It is ironic that Taoism, at root so completely anarchistic, should have become so greatly associated with government. This connection was so common that a famous Han dynasty work described Taoism as "the method of the ruler on his throne."[56]

In a later chapter we shall consider the philosophy known as Legalism, which proposed a program of unvarnished totalitarian despotism. This would seem to be—and in many ways it is—completely opposed to much that is essential in Taoism. Nevertheless, some Legalists claimed Taoism as the philosophic background for their doctrines. To do this they had to ignore the Taoists' condemnation of war and oppression, but they found a great deal in the "purposive" aspect of Taoism that was very useful to them.

The Taoists condemned the Confucians roundly. This was natural, for more than one reason. In the first place, the Confucians were probably the most successful philosophical school at the time when Taoism developed; this made them a natural target. Furthermore, the Confucians were the chief exponents of a carefully ordered system of government, intended to benefit the people—which the Taoists claimed would only do harm. Thus we find Confucian ideas, as well as Confucius and his disciples, repeatedly made fun of and attacked. Another, and more subtle, method was to assert that Confucius had renounced Confucianism and been converted to Taoism, and then to quote his alleged attacks on his own philosophy at great length. These stories are very obviously fiction, but they were effective propaganda.

One can hardly imagine a world actually governed—or ungoverned—according to the completely laissez-faire program of the Taoist philosophers. If one can imagine it, one would prefer not to. But this is perhaps not a valid criticism. It seems doubtful that they actually expected to be taken altogether seriously. They were poking fun, acting as gadflies, and undoubtedly they performed a useful function. To be sure, what I have proposed to call the "purposive" aspect of Taoist philosophy provided a warrant for despotism. But happily, the Chinese in general seem seldom to have taken this aspect of Taoism very seriously. Perhaps they have regarded it with the proper amount of Taoist skepticism.

The Taoists are fond of paradoxes. And paradoxically this philosophy, so anti-Confucian, so anti-governmental, and in some ways so anti-democratic, has in fact collaborated with Confucianism to produce the very considerable amount of social and political democracy that China has known. While Confucianism has emphasized the worth of the individual and the importance of considering him an end and not merely a means, Taoism has insisted upon his right to call his soul his own. The Taoist emphasis on man's oneness with nature has inspired Chinese art and has given the Chinese people much of the poise that has allowed their culture to endure. By its magnificent assertion of personal autonomy, its universal skepticism, and its doctrine of the relativity of all values, it has contributed incalculably to the development of the individualism and the insistence on compromise which are among the most important ingredients of the Chinese spirit.

Chapter VII

The Authoritarianism of Hsün Tzŭ

CONFUCIUS was in many respects a failure in his lifetime, but today his name is known all over the world. The Confucian philosopher Hsün Tzŭ had an opposite fate. In his own day he was an official and was highly honored as a famous scholar. His influence on the form that Confucianism ultimately assumed was tremendous; Homer H. Dubs has quite properly called him "the moulder of ancient Confucianism." Yet among Confucians, particularly during the last thousand years, he has not enjoyed high favor. Outside China even those who are familiar with the name of Mencius may be quite uncertain who Hsün Tzŭ was.

It has sometimes been said that this lack of high honor is due to the fact that the great arbiter of recent Confucian orthodoxy, Chu Hsi of the twelfth century A.D., condemned Hsün Tzŭ because he disagreed with Mencius' statement that human nature is good. This is important, but it is not the whole story. In considerable measure Hsün Tzŭ brought upon himself the ultimate eclipse of his reputation, by a peculiar limitation in his own thinking.

There was no lack of intellectual power; Hsün Tzŭ was, without qualification, one of the most brilliant philosophers the world has ever produced. But he lacked faith in humanity. This flaw, like the fatal weakness of the hero in a Greek tragedy, went far to nullify his best efforts. It not only blighted his own fame but did much to impose upon later Confucianism a strait jacket of academic orthodoxy.

Hsün Tzŭ was born around 300 B.C. in the northwestern state of Chao. He studied philosophy in the state of Ch'i, where he was highly honored as a scholar and given office at the court. There were representatives of many philosophies at the court of Ch'i, and naturally they disputed about their doctrines. Perhaps as a result of this, Hsün Tzŭ made enemies, and finally he had to leave Ch'i.

He was appointed magistrate of a district in the southern state of Ch'u; apparently he was dismissed from this post, but later reappointed to it. At some time he revisited his native state of Chao; he also made a trip to the western state of Ch'in, which was soon to play such a great role in China's history. During the latter part of his life he spent much of his time in teaching—two of his disciples are famous in Chinese history—and in writing. Upon the death of his superior, he was dismissed from office in 237 B.C. We know nothing more of his life.

There is a book that bears his name, which is our chief source of knowledge of the philosopher. It is supposed to have been written by himself, but some sections of it were apparently written by his students. The last six chapters of the book show considerable differences from the rest, and it has been plausibly argued that these were added to the book by Confucians of the Han period. At other places in the text, briefer interpolations appear to have been inserted.

One of the most important of the Confucian classics, the *Li Chi* or *Records on Ceremonial,* contains long stretches of text that are identical with parts of the *Hsün Tzŭ.* There seems to be no doubt that these passages have been copied into the classic from the work of our philosopher. This is one manner in which he has greatly influenced Confucianism, although he is not credited as the author in the classic that borrows so heavily from him.

As a philosopher, Hsün Tzŭ is perhaps most interesting when he discusses the theory of language. Here he seems remarkably modern. He is dealing with problems that agitate philosophers even today. What are words? What are concepts? How did they originate, and why do people differ so much about them, and in their use of them? These are problems for us, and they were very much problems for Hsün Tzŭ.

We have seen that in ancient China there were philosophers known as "dialecticians" who expounded such propositions as "a white horse is not a horse." Other schools as well used intricate and sometimes paradoxical propositions in their efforts to win men's minds. As the leading Confucian of his day, Hsün Tzŭ had to combat such argumentation. He was not content merely to deal with these problems piecemeal. Instead, he sought to investigate the very nature of language and to lay down rules for its proper use.

Hsün Tzŭ put various questions about language and attempted to answer them. His first question was: "Why do things have names?" His answer is, in effect, that names were needed as a convenience for talking about things and affairs and that they were invented by men to supply this need. We need names, he says, to make it possible to distinguish things that are similar and those that are different, and to distinguish things that are more and less valuable.

To give a simple illustration of this, it would not be very enlightening to say that there were "ten objects" in a field. But if one could use names to group them by similarity and difference, thus saying that there were "five cows, three horses, and two dogs," this would mean a good deal more. One might go even further in classifying them by similarity or difference, saying that there were "two black cows and three brown cows," etc.

Hsün Tzŭ's next question is: "What is the basis of similarity and difference?" At first sight, this may seem a queer or even a foolish question, but in fact it is quite profound. Why *are* dogs dogs, and horses horses? Plato would presumably have said that they are so because they are copies of the ideal dog and the ideal horse, in the same way that he said that all shuttles used in weaving are patterned after "the true or ideal

117

shuttle," an unchanging metaphysical pattern. Similarly, Plato says that beds and tables are what they are because they are copies of the ideal bed and the ideal table. And beautiful things are beautiful only because they "partake of absolute beauty."[1]

This is a kind of problem that has occupied philosophers, especially in the West, a great deal. Are the dachshund and the St. Bernard both dogs because in some ways they look and act alike, so that for convenience we group them under the name of "dog"? Or do they share some mysterious quality of "dogness," that cannot be determined by our senses alone?

Psychologists say that if a person who has been blind from birth suddenly gains the power of sight, he actually sees just the same things that the rest of us see, but at first they mean almost nothing to him. Thus a group of dogs and horses will seem to him, at first, just a series of blurs. But after repeated experiences he will become accustomed to them and will form a "concept" of what a dog is and another of what a horse is. Then, when he sees another dog, although it may not be exactly like any dog he has ever seen before, his mind will immediately catalogue it, and he will say, "That is a dog."

What Hsün Tzŭ has to say on this subject is in some ways quite similar to the findings of modern psychologists. "What is the basis of similarity and difference?" he asks. And he replies, "The testimony of the senses." There is no question here of any such thing as "partaking of absolute beauty," or any other metaphysical process. Things are considered to belong to the same class, Hsün Tzŭ says, when the senses indicate them to correspond to the "mental object" that one has formed to represent that class. In other words, when I see an animal that resembles a dog, I compare it with my concept ("mental object") of a dog, in order to decide whether it is or is not a dog.[2]

Hsün Tzŭ made it very clear that he did not believe that there was anything divinely ordained about the names that are given to things. "Names," he said, "are not inherently suited to the objects they stand for; men have simply agreed that they will use certain names to designate certain things. Once the convention is fixed and the custom established, they are called fitting names. . . . Yet there are names that are inherently good. Names that are simple and direct, easily understood, and not confusing, may be properly called good names."[3]

Hsün Tzŭ used the various principles he laid down concerning language to analyze and demolish the confusing propositions of rival philosophies. He made an excellent plea for the serious, straightforward use of unadorned, direct language to express ideas. Unfortunately, many Chinese and even Confucian writers have paid little attention to his words (which on this point are completely in harmony with the teachings of Confucius). In Chinese as in some other literatures, a premium has sometimes been placed upon obscurity of expression.

The most famous of Hsün Tzŭ's doctrines is his contention that human nature is evil, which he set against the thesis of Mencius that human nature is good. Mencius may have derived his idea partly from observation of the docile Chinese farmers. Many recent observers have been struck by the very remarkable moral soundness of the Chinese common people. On the other hand, some soldiers from other countries, stationed in China during the second World War, who had some of their possessions stolen in a time of the most desperate poverty, concluded that all the Chinese people are dishonest. These judgments have some correspondence to the judgments of Mencius and Hsün Tzŭ, which were also arrived at under somewhat different conditions.

Increasingly, even from before the time of Confucius, there was in each generation a greater degree of social mobility. In the early days of rather sharp social stratification, a farmer's son had almost never become anything but a farmer, or even dreamed that he might do so. But the Confucians had advocated general education and proclaimed that a man might rise even to become a ruler by means of virtue and wisdom, no matter how humble his origin. Furthermore, the old order in which peasants were peasants, and dumbly revered the glorious aristocrats, had begun to pass even before Confucius appeared. As time went on, the favor of the multitude became a factor in the stability of the power of officials and rulers, and we find certain aristocrats becoming demagogues, handing out largesse to the multitude, and thus winning power which enabled them to take over the thrones of states. At the same time, individual plebeians rose to positions of some power, and many others became envious of their success.

Another factor that may have influenced Hsün Tzǔ's view of human nature was the fact that he had seen a considerable variety of cultural patterns—probably more than Mencius had. His native state of Chao was greatly influenced by the nomad barbarians of the north, and he had lived not only in the relatively cultured state of Ch'i but also in Ch'u in the south, which again had its own peculiar customs. Thus Hsün Tzǔ points out that, while the children of various regions make the same sounds at birth, they learn to speak quite differently as a result of training. Furthermore, he says, the states of Lu and Ch'in have widely contrasting customs.[4] He could not, therefore, believe that men were born with a single, normal, "good" pattern of conduct.

Hsün Tzǔ begins his famous chapter called "The Nature of Man Is Evil" as follows:

The nature of man is evil; whatever is good in him is the result of acquired training. Men are born with the love of gain; if this natural tendency is followed they are contentious and greedy, utterly lacking in courtesy and consideration for others. They are filled from birth with envy and hatred of others; if these passions are given rein they are violent and villainous, wholly devoid of integrity and good faith. At birth man is endowed with the desires of the ear and eye, the love of sound and color; if he acts as they dictate he is licentious and disorderly, and has no regard for *li* or justice or moderation [*li*, it will be remembered, was the Confucian code of correct behavior].

Clearly, then, to accord with man's original nature and act as instinct dictates must lead to contention, rapacity, and disorder, and cause humanity to revert to a state of violence. For this reason it is essential that men be transformed by teachers and laws, and guided by *li* and justice; only then will they be courteous and cooperative, only then is good order possible. In the light of these facts it is clear that man's original nature is evil, and that he becomes good only through acquired training.

Crooked wood must be steamed and forced to conform to a straight edge, in order to be made straight. A dull blade must be ground and whetted, to make it sharp. Similarly human nature, being evil, must be acted upon by teachers and laws to be made upright, and must have *li* and justice added to it before men can be orderly. Without teachers and laws, men are selfish, malicious, and unrighteous. Lacking *li* and justice they are unruly, rebellious, and disorderly.

Anciently the sage-kings, knowing this, instituted *li* and justice and promulgated laws and regulations to force and beautify men's natural tendencies, and make them upright. They made them docile and civilized them, in order that they might readily be guided. Then for the first time there was good government, and accord with the right Way (*tao*). At present, men who are transformed by teachers and laws, who accumulate learning, and who act in accord with *li* and justice, are gentlemen. But those who give free play to their natural tendencies, taking satisfaction in doing just what they please without regard for *li* and justice, are small-minded men. In the light of these facts it is clear that man's original nature is evil, and that he becomes good only through acquired training.

Mencius says that the fact that men can learn proves that their original nature is good. But this is not the case. Mencius has not properly understood what human nature is, nor adequately distinguished between the original nature and acquired character. Man's nature is what he is endowed with at birth by Heaven; it cannot be learned or worked for. *Li* and justice were originated by the sages. Men can learn of *li* and justice by study, and incorporate them into their characters by effort. What cannot be acquired by study or effort, but is innate in man, is his nature. But everything that can be learned and worked for is acquired character. This is the difference between nature and acquired character.

It is given, as a part of man's original nature, that the eye can see and the ear can hear; these powers are not things apart from the eye and ear themselves. Nor can the powers of sight and hearing be learned. Mencius says that all men are by nature good, and become evil only because they lose and destroy their original nature. In this, however, he is mistaken. For if this were true it would then be the case [since, in fact, men are *not* born good] that as soon as a person were born he would already have lost what is supposed to be his original nature. In the light of these facts it is clear that man's original nature is evil, and that he becomes good only through acquired training.

The idea that man's original nature is good must mean that his character, without any change from its most primitive state, is admirable and good. If this were true, then the qualities of being admirable and good would be as indissolubly linked to a man's character and mind as the powers of seeing and hearing are bound up with his eyes and ears. In fact, however, man's nature is such that when he is hungry he wants to gorge himself, when he is cold he desires warmth, and when he works he wants to rest. Nevertheless we see hungry men who, in the presence of food, restrain themselves and yield precedence to their elders. We see those who toil without resting, because they are working for the sake of their elders. These latter actions are contrary to human nature, and they violate men's instinctive desires, but they accord with the way of a filial son and with the principles of *li* and justice. Thus if one accords with his natural tendencies he does not yield precedence to others; if he yields precedence to others he violates his natural tendencies. In the light of these facts it is clear that man's original nature is evil, and that he becomes good only through acquired training.[5]

Not only, according to Hsün Tzŭ, are men evil by nature at birth, but all men are born the same. The gentleman and the ordinary man, the most exalted sage-king of history and the most depraved scoundrel, began on exactly the same level.[6] Everyone starts equal in ability, knowledge, and capacity; all alike love honor and hate shame, love what is beneficial and hate what is injurious.[7] The most ordinary man in the world can become a sage by the practice of goodness.[8]

But one cannot practice goodness unless he has a teacher to tell him how. For how, asks Hsün Tzŭ, "can men's mouths and bellies get to know *li* and justice? How are they to learn courtesy and modesty and shame? ... The mouth just munches with satisfaction, and the stomach is pleased at being full. And a man without a teacher or laws is little more than a mouth and a belly."[9]

Obviously, however, there is a difficulty. If one cannot

become good without a teacher, how did the first teacher become able to teach? Teaching and its principles were instituted by the sages, but Hsün Tzŭ specifically denies that the sages were originally different from anyone else. He recognizes this difficulty and tries to deal with it.

"A questioner," Hsün Tzŭ writes, "may ask: 'If man's original nature is evil, then how could *li* and justice ever arise?' My answer is that all *li* and justice were produced by the acquired training of the sages, not by man's original nature. The potter pounds clay into shape so as to make a pot, but the pot is the product of his acquired skill, not of his inherent human nature. The carpenter shapes wood into a vessel, but this vessel is not produced by his innate abilities, but by his acquired training. Similarly, the sages were able to produce *li* and justice, and set up laws and regulations, only as a result of long thought and earnest practice. Thus it is evident that *li*, justice, laws and regulations were produced by the acquired training of the sages, not by man's original nature."[10]

Here Hsün Tzŭ tacitly admits that the sages did, in fact, become good by their own efforts, unaided by teachers. At the same time, however, he steadfastly denies that in his own day this can be done, even though all men have the same innate capacities as the sages.[11] Here we are getting close to the basic weakness of Hsün Tzŭ's thinking. His opponents in argument undoubtedly detected this weak point, and challenged him on it. He tries to reply, as follows:

Someone may say, "The sages were able, by persistent effort, to arrive at sageness; then why cannot everyone do the same?" My answer is that he can, but he does not. The small-minded man can become a superior man, but he is not willing to become a superior man; the superior man can become a small-minded man, but he is not willing to become a small-minded man. It is never impossible for the small-minded man and the superior man to exchange places; nevertheless they do not exchange places. They can do so, but they are not effectively able to do so.

The man on the street can become a Yü [one of the legendary sage emperors of antiquity], but it is unlikely that he ever will.

Nevertheless, the fact that he is not effectively able to be a Yü does not change the fact that he could become a Yü. . . . The laborer, the artisan, the farmer, and the merchant could exchange their callings, yet none of them are in fact able to do so. Thus we see that to have the possibility of doing something is not necessarily to be able to do it.[12]

This is not entirely convincing. Certainly, men do differ in their capacity to discipline themselves, so that whether we agree with Hsün Tzǔ or not we must admit that those who resemble the sages he speaks of are few. This very difference, however, seems to belie his contention that men are originally alike, in ability as well as in morals. What Hsün Tzǔ seems to have believed is that, while there once were men who could find the good and the true for themselves, such men no longer existed in his age.

The fact that in Hsün Tzǔ's day China was in a very discouraging condition goes far to explain, if not to justify, his pessimism. But the result of this belief, that not only the mass of men but all men are incapable of thinking for themselves on fundamental questions, is not merely to inhibit moral and intellectual progress, but even to make moral and intellectual health impossible. For the man, or the mind, that forever follows a track laid out by another is not functioning in a normal manner, and will in time show pathological symptoms. Confucius recognized this when he refrained from laying down any dogmatic basis of authority. Yet we should not blame Hsün Tzǔ too much. The number of philosophers, of any age or nation, who have really been willing to have men think for themselves, and have been so willing even if men should disagree with their own ideas, is not large.

In view of the importance that has been ascribed to the role of the teacher in Confucianism, it is curious to reflect that Confucius himself had no teacher. As early as Mencius' day the teacher was highly honored, but it is Hsün Tzǔ who exalted him to the skies. He said:

If a man is without a teacher or precepts, then if he is intelligent, he will inevitably be a robber; if he is brave, he will be a brigand; if he has ability he will be a troublemaker; if he is a researcher, he will be interested only in strange phenomena; if he is a dialectician his arguments will be absurd. But if he has a teacher and precepts, then if he is intelligent he will quickly become learned; if he is brave, he will quickly become awe-inspiring; if he has ability, he will quickly accomplish whatever he undertakes to do; if he is a researcher, he will quickly push his investigations to their conclusion; if he is a dialectician, he will quickly solve every problem. Thus a teacher and precepts are the most important treasures a man can have; to be without a teacher and precepts is the greatest of misfortunes. The man who lacks a teacher and precepts exalts his original nature; he who has a teacher and precepts emphasizes self-cultivation.[13]

Study, then, is the one means of bettering one's self. The art of study, Hsün Tzŭ says, should occupy the whole of one's life; to arrive at the goal, one cannot stop for an instant. To study in this way is to be a man; to stop is to be like the birds and beasts.[14] The essential thing is industry. Fleet horses that dawdle by the wayside may be outdistanced by a lame tortoise that plods steadily on.[15] Study must not be superficial; the learning of the true gentleman enters his ears, penetrates to his heart, permeates his entire body, and shows itself in his every action.[16] Learning should not stop with mere knowledge but should go on to be embodied in conduct.

Nevertheless, the field of study was to be restricted. Some of the blame for this restriction, which has consistently characterized Confucianism, must be placed upon Confucius himself, even though Confucius did not limit its scope anything like so narrowly as his successors did. But Confucius was seeking to rescue the world, and to teach men who could aid in that rescue by acting as officials. Therefore, he limited his education to what he believed necessary for that task; and the same is true of all the early Confucians. Hsün Tzŭ makes this point clear. He says:

The reason the gentleman is called worthy is not that he is able to do everything that the most skillful man can do. The reason the gentleman is called wise is not because he knows everything that the wise man knows. When he is called discriminating, this does not mean that he is able to split hairs as exhaustively as the sophists. That he is called an investigator does not mean that he is able to examine exhaustively into everything that an investigator may examine. He has his limit.

In observing high and low lands, in judging whether fields are poor or fertile, and in deciding where the various grains should be planted, the gentleman is not as capable as a farmer. When it is a matter of understanding commodities, and determining their quality and value, the gentleman cannot vie with a merchant. As regards skill in the use of the compass, square, plumb line, and other tools, he is less able than an artisan. In disregarding right and wrong, truth and falsehood, but manipulating them so that they seem to change places and shame each other, the gentleman cannot compete with Hui Shih and Têng Hsi [these men were dialecticians].

However, if it is a question of ranking men according to their virtue; if offices are to be bestowed according to ability; if both the worthy and the unworthy are to be put in their proper places; . . . if all things and events are to be dealt with properly; if the chatter of Shên Tzŭ [a philosopher who combined Taoist and Legalist tendencies] and Mo Tzŭ are to be suppressed; if Hui Shih and Têng Hsi are not to dare to put forth their arguments; if speech is always to accord with the truth and affairs are always to be properly managed—it is in these matters that the gentleman excels.[17]

The discussions of the dialecticians are unprofitable, and even a sage could not set them all out; therefore, the gentleman does not talk about them. Furthermore, no one can explore the entirety of what there is to be known, and if one "wishes to exhaust the inexhaustible and reach the end of the limitless, then even if he breaks his bones and destroys his sinews in the effort till the end of his days, he will not succeed."[18] But if he sets a reasonable goal for his effort, it can be attained. What limit should the wise man set for his investigations? It is the knowledge of the sage-kings.[19] And this knowledge may be acquired, Hsün Tzŭ tells us, especially by studying the classics.

This is a new term. Confucius considered books only a part

of the subject matter of education, and Mencius was distinctly skeptical even of the authenticity of some of the books current in his day. But now, with Hsün Tzŭ, we find the beginning of that attachment of supreme value to certain books that has characterized Confucianism ever since. Exactly what were the classics to which Hsün Tzŭ referred is such a difficult problem that it cannot now be solved completely. He names certain books, but some of them seem to have been lost, and others were almost certainly not the same as the books of the same names that we have now. Whether, when he speaks of *li*, he is speaking of a particular book on *li*, is not wholly clear.

Hsün Tzŭ says: "Where should study begin, and where should it end? The art begins in reciting the classics, and ends in learning the *li*. Its purpose begins with making the scholar, and ends in making the sage."[20] "Scholarship means to study with singleness and intentness of purpose. . . . It is only when there is completeness and exhaustiveness that there is scholarship. The gentleman knows that when his knowledge is not complete or refined it is inadequate to be classed as excellent. Therefore he repeatedly recites in order to penetrate, reflects deeply in order to comprehend, and practices in order to embody it in his life."[21]

Although Hsün Tzŭ was even more outspoken against hereditary privilege than Confucius was, he did not think that everyone was capable of understanding the classics; he said specifically that they were beyond the comprehension of the "ordinary man."[22] Nevertheless, he believed that study was the open door through which, if they would walk in and make the effort, the humble might become noble, the ignorant wise, and the poor rich.[23] This was partly true in his own day, as some of the aristocrats lamented bitterly. Even more, these words were prophetic of what was to come. But Hsün Tzŭ gave them a meaning beyond the mere grasping for wealth and power, by pointing out that what is attained through study is the self-cultivation that is its truest reward, beside which recognition or the lack of it is unimportant. He said:

> Therefore the true gentleman is noble though he have no title; he is rich though he have no official emoluments; he is believed in though he does not vaunt himself; he is impressive though he does not rage; he is honored though poor and living in retirement; he is happy though he live alone. . . .
>
> Therefore it is said that an honored name cannot be striven for by forming cliques, nor acquired by bragging, nor taken by force. It can be attained only by devoted study. To strive for it is to lose it, but if one declines it it comes unbidden. If one is modest, his fame will accumulate; if he boasts, it will be in vain.
>
> Therefore the gentleman pays attention to developing his inner capacities, but effaces himself in external matters; he cultivates his virtue, and lives modestly. Thus his fame arises like the sun and the moon; the whole world responds to him as though to a clap of thunder. Therefore it is said: The gentleman, in obscurity, is yet known; though he seems insignificant, his fames shines forth; he contends with no one, yet conquers all.[24]

This last statement is remarkably similar to what the *Lao Tzŭ* says that the Taoist sage attains through *not* studying.

In spite of his great emphasis on study, Hsün Tzŭ was not merely an intellectualist. He recognized the importance of the desires and the emotions and of regulating them with *li*. He agreed with Mencius that the means of coping with desire is not to banish it—that is death—or even to diminish the desires, but rather to guide them into the proper channels.

One of his best passages discusses the importance of directing one's desires toward spiritual, rather than purely material, things. His words are worth considering today, when we simultaneously enjoy the highest general level of material prosperity and also, very probably, the highest incidence of nervous and mental disease that the world has ever known.

> Those who regard moral principles lightly always attach great importance to material things. And those who externally attach great importance to material things are always inwardly anxious. Those who act without regard for moral principles are always externally in a dangerous position. And such persons are always inwardly afraid.
>
> When the heart is anxious and afraid the mouth may hold fine

food, but it will not taste it; the ears may hear bells and drums, but they will not hear the music; the eyes may behold fine embroidery, but they will not see its pattern; one may wear the most comfortable clothing and sit on an even mat, but his body will be oblivious of them. Even if all the pleasant things in the world were offered to one in this state, he could not be content. If someone were to ask him what he wanted, and give him everything he asked for, he would still be dissatisfied. And so, when every pleasant thing has been given him, sorrow is still abundant; and when all beneficial things have been added to them, harm is still plentiful. Such is the lot of those who seek material things.

Is food life? Is porridge old age? Wishing to satisfy their desires, men give free rein to their instincts instead. Desiring to foster their natures, they endanger their bodies instead. Wishing to enjoy themselves, they do violence to their minds instead. Seeking to enhance their reputations, they bring disorder into their conduct instead.

Such persons, though they be enfeoffed as nobles or called rulers, are no different from common thieves. They may ride in carriages and wear caps of ceremony, but they are no better off than paupers. This is what is called making one's self a servant of material things.

When a man's mind is peaceful and happy, then even sights below the ordinary will satisfy the eye; even sounds below the ordinary will content the ear; coarse rice, vegetables, and soup will be enough for the mouth; clothing of coarse cloth and sandals made from rough cords will give comfort to the body; a hut of straw, with a mat on the floor and a battered stool to lean against, will suffice for the form.

Such a man, lacking all the fine things in the world, is yet happy; though he has neither power nor position, his name becomes known. If he were appointed to rule the empire, this would mean much for the empire, but it would make little difference in his peace of mind and contentment. This may indeed be called giving due weight to one's self, and making material things one's servants.[25]

Here again the resemblance to Taoism is striking. Hsün Tzŭ lived in a day much like our own, characterized by moral breakdown, frequent wars, and a sense of impending doom. Then, as now, men were seeking a way to get rid of their fears. Taoism offered an easy way: simply be content. Hsün Tzŭ too offered contentment, but he did not believe that it is easy to attain. It could be achieved, he held, only by educating the desires and the emotions by means of *li*.[26]

Li, it will be recalled, originally denoted sacrifice, and was

connected with religion. Hsün Tzǔ almost completely eliminated the religious factor, not only from his conception of *li*
but from all of his thinking. He was a tough-minded rationalist.
Ghosts, he said, are just imagined by confused people; they
don't really see them. Beating a drum to cure rheumatism will
wear out the drum, but won't cure the rheumatism.[27] "If men
pray for rain and get rain," Hsün Tzǔ asks, "why is it? There
is no reason," he replies. "If they hadn't prayed it would have
rained anyway."[28]

Mo Tzǔ, it will be remembered, had said that good harvests
and prosperity were signs that Heaven approved the virtue of a
good ruler, while natural catastrophes were divine warnings
against the misrule of wicked sovereigns. Hsün Tzǔ laughs at
such ideas and says that there is no reason to fear the working-
out of the natural processes of the universe. There are indeed
bad omens, he says, but for these examine the way in which the
government is conducted, see whether it has the confidence of
the people, and whether the people enjoy plenty or are starving.
It is these things, and not the appearance of comets and eclipses
of the moon, that should engage men's anxious attention.[29]

Hsün Tzǔ does not say that men should not sacrifice; on the
contrary, he declares that the proper conduct of sacrificial ceremonies is the very highest expression of refinement. Yet what is
sacrificed to has, he says, "neither substance nor shadow."
These are simply ceremonies that are prized for their social
value and provide for the expression of emotion in a recognized
and beneficial manner. The common people consider them to be
a matter of serving the spirits, but the gentleman is aware that
they really have to do only with the living.[30]

Hsün Tzǔ does not discard the idea of Heaven, the highest
deity, but he redefines it. Heaven is simply the order of nature;
our "Nature" with a capital *N*. But, like the God of the Deists,
Heaven as Hsün Tzǔ conceives it never interferes with its own
laws to perform a miracle.[31] Heaven is the order of nature, and
one should learn Heaven's laws and act in conformity with

them. Quite literally, Heaven helps those who help themselves—intelligently.

To return, then, to *li:* Confucius had extended this concept far beyond its original religious sense, and Hsün Tzŭ seems to extend it still further. One's conduct in every situation whatever, no matter what one undertakes to do, should be governed by *li;* and if it is not, it will be wrong.[32] It was invented, according to Hsün Tzŭ, by the sages, but it is not an arbitrary thing. Even the birds and beasts mourn for a dead mate; how much more should man do so?[33] *Li* gives beauty, interest, rhythm, and control to all of man's actions.[34]

In Hsün Tzŭ's day the stratification and even the organization of society had broken down to a considerable degree. Therefore, he was worried about the fact that men coveted the power and the possessions of others, and he advocated *li* as a corrective. He wrote:

> If all men were equal in power, the state could not be unified; if all stood on the same level, there could be no government. As soon as heaven and earth existed, there was the distinction of superior and inferior. When the first wise king assumed the throne there were classes.
>
> Two nobles cannot serve each other, and two commoners cannot give each other orders—this is a law of nature. If all men were equal in power and position, and all liked and disliked the same things, since there would not be enough to go around the inevitable consequence would be strife. The result of this would be disorder, and the impoverishment of all.
>
> To forestall such disorder the ancient kings established *li* and justice to divide the people into the classes of rich and poor, noble and plebeian, so that all might be under control. This is the fundamental necessity in caring for the empire.[35]

Hsün Tzŭ did not regard this division into classes as primarily a hereditary one. A man of sufficient learning and character should be made prime minister, no matter how plebeian his origin. On the other hand, an unworthy scion of royalty should be relegated to plebeian status.[36] The worth and glory of the true gentleman exceeds that of an emperor.[37]

Hsün Tzǔ's ideas on government are essentially similar to those of Confucius. Government is for the people, not for the ruler.[38] To impoverish the people and mistreat scholars is to court disaster.[39] No ruler can win success in war whose people are not in harmony and attached to him.[40] War is an evil, but armies are necessary for police purposes.[41] The function of the ruler is to select virtuous and capable ministers and advance them on the basis of performance, without regard to relationship to himself and without favoritism.[42] A ruler who is evil should be managed as one manages a wild horse or cares for an infant.[43] To disobey the ruler's commands, in order to benefit him, is loyalty.[44] A virtuous ruler is impregnable; a wicked ruler is no longer a ruler and should be dethroned.[45]

Although Hsün Tzǔ was aware of Taoism, he was not greatly influenced by it. Another current of thought that was abroad in his time made a deeper impression on him. It was widely believed that the cure for the disorders of the day was "discipline." And Hsün Tzǔ, although he had been nurtured in the Confucian tradition that emphasized the consent of the governed, thought that more discipline would be an excellent thing. Undoubtedly he had had difficulties, as an administrative official, which had convinced him that men in general were a rascally lot, evil by nature and in need of stern control. The wise rulers, he says, did not discuss fallacious doctrines or seek to give the people the reasons for all their actions. Instead, they "went before the people with authority, guided them with the Way, repeatedly admonished them by their decrees, instructed them by their proclamations, and restrained them by punishments. Thus the people were turned into the right way as if by magic."[46]

Nevertheless, although Hsün Tzǔ sometimes talked in this way, he was no totalitarian. A totalitarian regime was being developed in the far western state of Ch'in. The philosophy that inspired it was Legalism, which will be discussed in the next chapter. Hsün Tzǔ did not like everything about it; in fact, he condemned its basic doctrine. But at the same time he could not help admiring some aspects of this regime.

Hsün Tzŭ visited Ch'in, and afterward he was quite lyrical about the strict discipline that he found there. No one dared, he said, to do anything except what was prescribed for him by the state. The people were "deeply afraid of the officials, and obedient."[47] This is a far cry from the ideal state of Confucius, in which men would co-operate altogether voluntarily.

The two most famous students of Hsün Tzŭ were both Legalists. One of them provided much of the philosophy that inspired Ch'in's government. The other was a high official in Ch'in, and helped that state clamp a totalitarian despotism on all of China in 221 B.C. This has had much to do with the relatively low esteem in which Hsün Tzŭ has been held in Confucian circles.

Yet the real harm that Hsün Tzŭ did to Confucianism was not this. It lay rather in his divergence (not for the first time in the history of Confucianism, but perhaps most influentially) from the willingness of Confucius himself to trust something to the intelligence and the initiative of mankind in general. Confucius had said, "Men can enlarge the Way, but the Way cannot of itself enlarge the man."[48] But Hsün Tzŭ did not trust men to think for themselves. He wanted to put morality on a guaranteed basis, obliging each generation blindly to follow the classics as expounded by its teachers. He said: "Not to consider right the ways of one's teacher, but to prefer one's own ways, is like using a blind man to distinguish colors . . . there is no way to get rid of confusion and error."[49] Thus, as Dubs has said, "Hsüntzŭ developed Confucianism into an authoritarian system, in which all truth was to be derived from the sayings of the sages."[50]

Because he distrusted men and was willing to risk nothing, Hsün Tzŭ lost, for Confucianism, a great deal. "Nothing ventured, nothing gained," is as true in philosophy as in business. Hsün Tzŭ, and others who thought as he did, condemned Confucianism to a considerable measure of sterility. By making it an authoritarian system they also laid it open to the danger of being perverted, by whomever might succeed in convincing men that he possessed authority.

Hsün Tzŭ meant exceedingly well. Precisely because he meant so well—because, as the Taoists would say, he tried too hard—he did a great deal of harm. Such was the tragedy of one of China's most brilliant minds.

Chapter VIII

The Totalitarianism of the Legalists

ALL the philosophies we have considered thus far, from that of Confucius through Taoism, have had one point in common. They have been concerned at the unfortunate plight of the people of ancient China, crushed by poverty and oppression and torn by war. They have all criticized the rulers, sought to prohibit or mitigate their exactions and oppression, and tried to end war.

The philosophy we must now discuss was also concerned by conditions. It was alarmed, however, not because the people were regimented but because they were sometimes disobedient; not because they were poor but because they did not work hard enough to enrich their rulers; not because there were wars but because the people lacked enthusiasm for war. It blamed these conditions, in very large measure, on the fact that the people had been made discontent and corrupted by the Confucians and the Moists.

The philosophy known as Legalism was, in considerable degree, a philosophy of counterrevolution, seeking to defend the authority of the ruler against the increasing insistence that government exists for the people, not for the ruler, and that any government that fails to satisfy the people stands condemned.

Many scholars have claimed, and some still claim, that the Legalists were not counterrevolutionists at all. The Legalists themselves claimed that they were bold innovators, proclaiming a new doctrine for a new age. They branded the Confucians and the Moists as stick-in-the-mud traditionalists, clinging to outworn theories and unwilling to see the world benefited by modernization.

This question, as to who were the true moderns and who were the true reactionaries, has been clouded by several factors. Confucius himself had some tendency to talk like a conservative, although his program was fundamentally revolutionary. The later Confucians became, or believed they became, true traditionalists, but their traditionalism took a very peculiar form. Legend filled the past with all sorts of institutions and practices that in fact had never existed on land or sea, but were the fanciful expression of what the Confucians thought the ideal world should be. These legends were written down in books and accepted as genuine, and many of them entered the corpus of the classics. Thus the Confucians themselves believed that they were advocating a return to the practices of antiquity, when in fact they were proposing complete innovations. The Confucians agreed with those who branded them as traditionalists, even when this was not true.

Confucianism opposed rule by force rather than by persuasion. The Legalists advocated strong centralized government which should exercise absolute power by the threat of harsh punishments. This policy was repugnant not only to the Confucians but also to the subordinate feudal lords, who would have lost their power and even their thrones under it. On the theory that those who have a common enemy must be friends, it has therefore been supposed that the Confucians were, by principle, upholders of feudalism.

It is true, moreover, that many of the Confucians were dependent upon minor feudal lords, and therefore no doubt favored their interests. We have seen that Mencius had a certain sentimental attachment to feudalism. Nevertheless, it is not true, as is sometimes said, that Confucianism as a philosophy favored the continuance of the hereditary transmission of feudal positions and power. On the contrary, its insistence that offices should be filled on the basis of merit alone was clearly opposed to this.

On the other hand, the Legalists were not wholly wrong in

their contention that they were innovators. Many of their methods were new. They sought to break up the patriarchal family, which was an age-old institution. They advocated private ownership of land (but it must be noted that they also advocated such rigid state control of all activities that the private proprietor would have had only a narrow choice as to what he could do with his land). And they also favored strongly centralized government, functioning by means of fixed and rigid laws, which was something new.

The objective of the Legalists, however, was not wholly new. They sought, for the ruler of the whole state, much the same kind of absolute power over his subjects as each feudal lord had exercised in the "good old days," before the people had begun to get notions about rights and freedom, or to be corrupted by having these things talked about by the Confucians.

It is significant in this connection that the actual practice of Legalistic theory took place chiefly in the state of Ch'in, which lay on the western frontier of the Chinese world. We are told that as late as 361 B.C. Ch'in was looked upon, by the Chinese in general, as in effect a barbarian state.[1] Repeatedly we find it said that the Confucian concepts of *li* and justice were unknown in Ch'in.

In the previous chapter we noted that when Hsün Tzŭ visited Ch'in, sometime after 300 B.C., he reported that he found its people simple and rustic, standing in fear of the officials and quite obedient. As for the officials, they too attended strictly to business, going from their homes to their offices and from their offices straight home, having no personal concerns. Both people and officials, Hsün Tzŭ said, were of "antique type," having no modern foolishness about them.[2] Clearly this was a people that would not be hard to bring under totalitarian regimentation. In fact, the regimentation that had anciently been the rule had never been entirely abandoned.

Not only was Legalism practiced chiefly in Ch'in. The three most famous Legalists were all born, and seem to have spent most of their lives, in peripheral states, away from the central states which were generally recognized to constitute the most cultured and at the same time the most Confucian part of China. It is not surprising, then, that they saw things in a different light from that of the Confucians, and even of the Moists.

There is another difference between the Confucian and the Legalist philosophers. Confucius grew up in humble circumstances. Mencius is said to have been a scion of a noble family, but even this is not clear; if he was, the family seems to have been in reduced circumstances by his day. But the two most influential Legalist philosophers were members of families that actually ruled the states of Wei and Han, respectively, in their own times. It is natural, then, that they should have argued the case for the rulers and not for the people.

While nearly all critics are agreed that the point of view of the Legalists is, in fact, that of the ruler, we are not to suppose that they proclaimed their policies as a system of tyranny. On the contrary, they tell us that it is they and they alone who are genuinely working for the interests of the people.[3] It is true, they say, that they advocate stern government; but government must be stern for the sake of the people, just as soldiers must die for the common good or the putrid flesh about a wound must be injured in order to cure the disease. The ruler punishes the people, the Legalists assert, only for their own benefit.[4]

Although the Legalists were outspokenly critical and contemptuous of Confucianism, the two philosophies nevertheless had some points in common. Confucius had deplored the chaotic disorganization of the times as much as the Legalists did, and had advocated centralization, although he would have condemned the Legalist method of achieving it. Although the Legalists attacked Confucius, they had enough respect for his reputation to pretend in some of their books that he had been converted to Legalism, and even went so far as to put Legalist speeches into his mouth.[5] Furthermore, Legalist thought ultimately infiltrated Confucianism to a considerable degree, so that we find Legalist ideas in some of the Confucian classics.

Even the *Analects* contains some Legalistic speeches which have been attributed to Confucius and inserted into this most sacred of the Confucian classics.[6]

Hsün Tzŭ forms a kind of bridge between Confucianism and Legalism. Although he opposed Legalist ideas as such, his doctrine that human nature is evil and his authoritarianism tended in the Legalist direction. His two most famous students were Legalists; one of them was the greatest Legalist of all.

Mo Tzŭ hated war, while the Legalists gloried in it. Nevertheless, his doctrine of "identification with the superior," holding that "what the superior thinks to be right all shall think to be right; what the superior thinks to be wrong all shall think to be wrong," has obvious overtones of totalitarianism. Mo Tzŭ also advocated a system of enjoining people to "report good and evil" done by others in their groups to the superior, in a manner that has some similarity to the system of informers that was later used in Ch'in.

It is with Taoism, however, that the affinities of Legalism are clearest. At first sight this is most surprising, for the basic purpose of Taoism, it will be remembered, was to assert the autonomy of the individual. Furthermore, the Taoists bitterly condemned war and oppressive government. How, then, could Taoism have any connection with a philosophy that considered war to be man's natural destiny and advocated complete totalitarian despotism?

This is incomprehensible unless we remember that Taoism had two aspects, not easy to reconcile with each other. In the second aspect we find the Taoist sage undertaking to rule the world by means of his vast powers, like those of the *Tao* itself. We are told that he "empties the people's minds and fills their bellies, weakens their wills and strengthens their bones."[7] The appeal of such ideas to the Legalists is obvious. They took Taoism as a sort of metaphysical background for their system and conveniently suppressed or altered whatever did not suit their purpose.

Legalism as a philosophy is somewhat difficult to deal with.

In the first place, the name "Legalism" (which is a close translation of the Chinese *fa chia*) is not very apt. The Legalists do emphasize law, but only as a means, and not the only means, of achieving their ends. Furthermore, the Legalists were not "legalistic" in the sense of being mainly concerned with the letter of the law and its interpretation. Fung Yu-lan points out quite correctly that "it is wrong to associate the thought of the Legalist school with jurisprudence."[8]

For such reasons some scholars have come to speak of these philosophers as Realists. By this it is meant that they were unsentimental, "hardheaded," and thus realistic. But this name has its difficulties, too. The Legalists would have agreed that they were realistic, but it is not certain that we can agree. They certainly saw a part of reality, but did they see it all? There is, as we shall see, good reason to question that they did.

The most descriptive term by which these philosophers might be called is "authoritarians," or, still better, "totalitarians," since they taught that every individual must be compelled to live, work, think, and on the ruler's demand die, wholly for the state, without any regard for his individual desires or welfare. But, since "totalitarian" is a long and clumsy word, we shall save three syllables and respect convention by continuing to refer to them as Legalists.

But we cannot properly speak (although it is done) of the "Legalist school," because there was none. This doctrine, which emphasized authority like no other, was alone among the philosophies in having no recognized founder. It is significant that Han Fei Tzŭ, the greatest Legalist of all, had as his teacher not a Legalist but Hsün Tzŭ, a Confucian. There were simply various men and various books that in different ways and varying degrees espoused the kind of thought we call "Legalism." What makes it rather confusing is that some philosophers and some books are classed as Legalist by some scholars but not by others. Furthermore, some of the books called Legalist are extremely composite, containing some parts that do not set forth Legalist philosophy at all.

The Totalitarianism of the Legalists

It is significant that most of the men who are considered Legalists were officials who wielded actual administrative power. This was not true, it will be remembered, of either Confucius or Mencius; while both held offices, they seem to have served merely in "consultative" capacities. Hsün Tzŭ, alone among the leading Confucians, was a practical administrator, and in some respects he veered toward Legalism.

Probably the earliest individual who has been called a Legalist is Kuan Chung, a famous prime minister of the seventh century B.C. He has not always been classed as a Legalist, however, and the accuracy of the label is doubtful; while we have not a great deal of information about his ideas, some of them sound more nearly Confucian. A book known as the *Kuan Tzŭ* has been attributed to his authorship, but in fact it is a collection of essays by later writers. Some of them are Legalist in tone, while others are not.

Shên Pu-hai, who died in 337 B.C., was a minister of the state of Han for fifteen years; during this time, it is said, the state was well governed and its armies strong. A book bearing his name had considerable influence in Han times but is now lost. He stressed the importance of administrative methods, *shu*, for government.

Shên Tao lived at the same time as Mencius, around 300 B.C. He was born in Chao, but held office in Ch'i; it seems probable, however, that he was not actually an administrator. He was a Taoist as well as a Legalist, and he emphasized *shih*, power and position, which we shall have to consider at more length later. The work attributed to him is considered a forgery.

The list of names of Legalists and reputed Legalists could be expanded a great deal, but to little purpose. Perhaps the most important and by all odds the most interesting of the early Legalists is Shang Yang (also called Wei Yang or Kung-Sun Yang), who died in 338 B.C. He was closely related to the ruling house of another state but served as an official under the prime minister of the state of Wei. It is said that this prime minister, knowing that he was fatally ill, asked his ruler to appoint Shang

141

Yang as his successor. If he did not do that, the minister warned, he should put Shang Yang to death, since he would be a dangerous enemy if permitted to enter the service of another state. But, according to the story, the ruler of Wei did neither, to his subsequent sorrow.

Shortly after this, Shang Yang heard that the duke of the western state of Ch'in was seeking for capable men to help him strengthen his state and enhance its military power. Shang Yang went to Ch'in, and soon found favor with the duke and was given office. He proposed sweeping reforms, which were opposed by other ministers but ultimately adopted. The *Historical Records*, written in the Han dynasty, tells us:

His decree ordered that the people be organized into groups of families, which should be mutually responsible for each other's good behavior and share each other's punishments. Anyone who did not denounce a culprit would be cut in two at the waist; anyone who denounced a culprit would receive the same reward as if he had cut off the head of an enemy soldier; anyone who harbored a culprit would receive the same punishment as if he had surrendered to the enemy. A family including two adult males would have to be divided, or pay double taxes. Military prowess was to be rewarded by the ruler with titles of nobility, according to a definite schedule. Those who fought each other because of private quarrels would be punished according to the severity of their offense. All, great and small, would be compelled to work at the fundamental occupations of farming and weaving; those who produced a large quantity of grain or silk would be exempted from forced labor. Those who sought gain through the secondary occupations [trade and crafts], and the lazy and indigent, would be made slaves. Members of the ruling family were to be considered as not belonging to it unless they showed military merit.

The decree set out clearly the differences between high and low, and between the various ranks in the hierarchy. It also stated precisely what lands, male and female servants, and clothing were to be permitted to various families, according to their place in this scale. Persons having merit were to be highly honored, but those without merit, even though they might be rich, were to be permitted no distinctions.

After the decree was drawn up Shang Yang did not at once publish it, fearing that the people did not have confidence in him. He therefore had a pole thirty feet long placed near the south gate of the capital. Assembling the people, he said that he would give ten measures of gold to anyone who could move it to the north gate. The people marveled at this, but no one ventured to move it. Shang Yang then said, "I will give fifty measures of gold to anyone who can move it." One man then moved it, and Shang Yang immediately gave him fifty measures of gold, to demonstrate that he did not practice deception.[9]

The mention of the giving of titles for military merit emphasizes what was, in fact, the prime purpose of this reform. We have noted that a great contest was on, among the various states, to get control of all China. The Confucians said that such control might be secured by virtue. The Legalists replied that this was sheer foolishness and that the way to get the country was to conquer it; in order to do this, one had first to make one's state rich and well-disciplined, and one's people into soldiers.

The people of Ch'in found the new regulations harsh, and criticized them. The crown prince broke the law. In order to make an example, Shang Yang punished the tutor of the crown prince and had his teacher branded. Thereafter the laws were obeyed. Some people then praised the laws; Shang Yang had *them* banished for daring to say anything at all about the laws. Ch'in became very orderly.

The reforms of Shang Yang had, if our records are trustworthy, several aims. Ch'in was altered from a group of small feudal territories to a strongly centralized state with a bureaucratic organization. The aristocratic families were greatly reduced in power, and a new hierarchy of men distinguished by military merit was created. At the same time the use of arms in brigandage and in private quarrels (that is, not in the service of the state) was severely penalized. An attempt was made to break up the patriarchal family, both by forcing its members to live apart under the threat of increased taxes and by setting members of families to spy and act as informers against one another. Agriculture and weaving were encouraged, while trade (which was considered unproductive) was discouraged. The system of taxation was changed, and weights and measures were standardized.[10]

It has also been said that Shang Yang introduced private ownership of land, as over against the feudal situation in which those who cultivated the land did so for a lord, who in turn held it from his overlord. This change probably did come about in Ch'in; but some scholars have recently held that this was a gradual development that took place all over China, as a result of the breakdown of the feudal system.

Shang Yang made Ch'in rich and its armies strong. On its eastern borders certain lands had long been in dispute between Ch'in and Wei. In 341 B.C., after Wei had been defeated by another state, Shang Yang led a Ch'in army to invade Wei. It will be remembered that Wei was the state in which Shang Yang had originally held office; he was therefore personally acquainted with the prince who led the army of Wei against him. Shang Yang proposed to the prince that they meet and settle their difficulties, as befitted old friends. The prince agreed, and fell into an ambush that Shang Yang had arranged. The prince was captured, his army was destroyed, and Ch'in got the disputed territory.

Shang Yang was ennobled and given a large fief. Nevertheless, he was not generally liked in Ch'in; it is said, indeed, that his harsh laws had made him so unpopular that he did not dare go out without a small army of bodyguards. When the reigning duke of Ch'in died and was succeeded by the crown prince whose teachers Shang Yang had punished, Shang Yang had to flee. Ultimately he was killed, it is said, by being torn to pieces by chariots.

A work called *The Book of Lord Shang*, supposedly written by Shang Yang, has come down to us. Duyvendak, who has studied and translated it, does not believe, however, that any of it was written by him. It is a compendium of writings by various Legalist authors, of considerable interest and value even though it is difficult to date them exactly.[11]

The Totalitarianism of the Legalists

From an intellectual point of view the most important of all Legalists is Han Fei Tzŭ, who died in 233 B.C. He was a member of the ruling family of the state of Han, which lay to the east of Ch'in. An impediment in his speech caused him to turn to writing as a means of expression. He became an avid student especially concerned with the study of law and government. He was well acquainted with his predecessors in the development of Legalist theory, but he studied with the Confucian, Hsün Tzŭ. His fellow-student under Hsün Tzŭ was a certain Li Ssŭ, a man of about his own age who had started life as a government clerk in the southern state of Ch'u. It is said that Li Ssŭ recognized that he was less able than Han Fei Tzŭ; this is very probable, for there was actually no comparison between them.

Han Fei Tzŭ was seriously concerned over the weakness of his native state, and he repeatedly urged the ruler of Han to strengthen it. Although his program was somewhat similar to that of Shang Yang, Han Fei Tzŭ had his own ideas and did not follow any model uncritically. No attention was paid to him. Frustrated and incensed, he poured out his thoughts in several long essays. Two of these came into the hands of the ruler of Ch'in, who exclaimed: "Ah, if I could only see this man and get to know him, I would not regret dying." This opportunity came in 233 B.C., when Han Fei Tzŭ was sent to Ch'in as an envoy of Han. The ruler of Ch'in liked the man as well as his writings and considered offering Han Fei Tzŭ a place in his government.

The former fellow-student of Han Fei Tzŭ, Li Ssŭ, had already been in Ch'in for some fourteen years and was one of its ministers. He was probably disturbed by the prospect of having the brilliant Han Fei Tzŭ as a rival, and he may have genuinely feared that he would not be loyal to Ch'in. In any case he pointed out that Han Fei Tzŭ could not well be expected to collaborate in plans for the conquest of his own state, and got the philosopher thrown into prison. Once there, Li Ssŭ managed to cause him to commit suicide.[12]

The book called *Han Fei Tzŭ* gives us our most complete and mature picture of the Legalist philosophy. It includes, in something at least close to their original form, a number of the essays of Han Fei Tzŭ. But this is not all it contains. These are mixed with a great mass of other Legalist writings and some material that is not even Legalist at all. The book must therefore be used with care.

Like the advocates of other philosophies the Legalists had their own version of history, but in many respects it was remarkably similar even to that of their chief opponents, the Confucians. The Legalists did not (as they well might have) deny that the sage emperors Yao and Shun ever existed, or that they had abdicated their thrones, or that men were generally virtuous during their reigns. But they put a different interpretation on these things. Han Fei Tzŭ wrote:

In antiquity men did not till the soil, but were able to gather their food from the plants and trees. Women did not weave, for the skins of birds and animals were sufficient for clothing. Without working they enjoyed plenty, since the people were few and goods were abundant. Thus there was no rivalry. Neither liberal rewards nor heavy punishments were employed, and yet the people kept themselves in order. Now, however, a family of five children is not considered large, and each of them has five more. Thus a grandfather, while still alive, has twenty-five grandchildren. For this reason commodities are scarce and people many, so that although they work hard they still get only a poor living. Therefore, the people contend with each other. Even though rewards were doubled and punishments multiplied, it would be impossible to get rid of disorder.

When Yao ruled the empire, he lived in a hut of untrimmed thatch, with roof-beams of unhewn oak. He ate coarse millet porridge and soup made only of vegetables. In winter his clothing was of deerskin, in summer of coarse cloth. His clothing and food were no better than those of a gatekeeper. When Yü was emperor he set the people an example by personally toiling at farm labor. He worked his thighs thin and wore all the hair off his shins. No slave labors harder than he did.

In the light of this, it is clear that those who abdicated the throne in antiquity were in fact only giving up the living of a gatekeeper, and relinquishing the labors of a slave. Their conduct can hardly be called worthy of extravagant praise. Today, however, a mere district magistrate amasses so much wealth that for many generations after his death his descendants can keep carriages. For this reason such offices are valued. This is why it is that in antiquity emperors lightly abdicated the throne, while today even district magistrates cling to their posts. It is simply a matter of the change in value of such offices.[13]

In ancient times, Han Fei Tzŭ tells us, men could afford to be kind and polite, because there were not too many of them. In antiquity, therefore, it was profitable for rulers to be benevolent and just, and in those days one might hope by this method to become king.[14]

In one respect Han Fei Tzŭ bitterly criticized the rulers whom the Confucians idolized; he accused them, in fact, of corrupting the world. Yao and Shun, by yielding their thrones to plebeians, had treated subjects like rulers. The founders of the Shang and Chou dynasties, whom the Confucians praised as having fulfilled a divine mission by rescuing the people from tyranny, had in fact simply murdered their sovereigns. Thus they had undermined respect for constituted authority.[15] Here we clearly see Han Fei Tzŭ the prince, alarmed at the inroads that had been made upon the prestige of the class to which he belonged.

Even in antiquity, Han Fei Tzŭ says, different methods were found necessary at different periods, and how much more is this true when times have radically changed? He tells the story of a farmer who, having once seen a hare run into a tree and knock itself unconscious, spent the rest of his life waiting behind the same tree in the hope that more hares would do the same thing. This, he says, is just like the Confucians who expect the conditions of antiquity to return.[16]

Han Fei Tzŭ lays a large share of blame for the disorder of the world on such "useless scholars," who slander their rulers by praising antiquity, and waste time in useless discussion.[17]

The larger the number of citizens that study, the less there will be to raise food, to make the state strong and the ruler rich. Even the study of the art of warfare is harmful, Han Fei Tzŭ holds. The more numerous those who study strategy, the fewer the soldiers who can be thrown into the line of battle.[18]

Thus scholars ought, he declares, to be punished, made to give up their harmful vocation, and put to useful work. But instead of doing this, he complains, the rulers vie with one another to pay honor to such men, and this naturally causes others to emulate them. When it is possible to become wealthy and powerful merely by studying, without having to undergo either toil or danger, who would not become a student? Thus more and more men are withdrawn from productive pursuits, weakening the state and the economy and causing general distress. Furthermore, Han Fei Tzŭ warns, rulers who honor the learned and virtuous, even though they are of plebeian birth, are in fact undermining the prestige of their own class and thus endangering their own positions.[19] He goes so far as to denounce literature altogether, declaring: "In the state of an intelligent ruler there are no books, but the laws serve as teachings. There are no sayings of the former kings; the officials act as the teachers."[20]

Han Fei Tzŭ frequently classes the Moists together with the Confucians in his denunciations. He also condemns, as corrupters of the age, specious talkers, bravos, merchants and artisans who reap great profits at the expense of the farmers, and public officials who betray their trusts for their own profit.[21]

The Legalist view of human nature was very different from that of the Confucians. Mencius, as we have seen, said that man's nature was good, while Hsün Tzŭ asserted that it was bad. But, although Hsün Tzŭ believed that all men were born "selfish, vicious, and unrighteous," he also believed that by teaching they could be made into thoroughly virtuous and trustworthy beings. In our discussion of Hsün Tzŭ we noted that this transformation is a little mysterious, since the teachers are themselves human and therefore originally bad, and Hsün Tzŭ expressly rules out the intervention of any extra-human agency.

Hsün Tzŭ, like most of the Legalists, was a practical administrative official, and he probably spent part of his time being a superior kind of police officer. There are policemen who take an optimistic view of human nature, but they are rare; their experience causes them to regard mankind in general with a skeptical eye. Hsün Tzŭ was skeptical, but as a Confucian he found a formula to resolve the difficulty, with some sacrifice of logic. His pupil Han Fei Tzŭ was, in this respect, unswervingly logical. Like the other Legalists, he accepted the view that men are self-seeking and did not try to mitigate it in any way. He said:

> The empire can be ruled only by utilizing human nature. Men have likes and dislikes; thus they can be controlled by means of rewards and punishments. On this basis prohibitions and commands can be put in operation, and a complete system of government set up. The ruler need only hold these handles [rewards and punishments] firmly, in order to maintain his supremacy. . . . These handles are the power of life and death. Force is the stuff that keeps the masses in subjection.[22]

Even within the family, Han Fei Tzŭ believed, self-seeking is the rule. "When a boy is born," he wrote, "the father and mother congratulate each other, but if a girl is born they put it to death. . . . The reason for this difference in treatment is that the parents are thinking of their later convenience, and calculating what will ultimately bring them profit. Thus even the attitude of parents toward their children is marked by the calculation of gain. How much more must this be the case with relationships which are not characterized by the affection that exists between father and child?"[23]

If human nature is of this sort, it is obviously foolish and dangerous to rely on such virtues as gratitude and loyalty in the sphere of political action. Han Fei Tzŭ asserts, in fact, that subjects and ministers are so constituted that they will all, without exception, murder their superiors and supplant them in the enjoyment of their power and wealth, if they are able to do so with impunity. Only stern surveillance by the sovereign and strict repression of these tendencies, which Han Fei Tzŭ asserts are present even in his most trusted advisers, will make it possible for the ruler to retain his position or even his life.[24]

This Legalist psychology sounds much like the analysis that a trainer of lions and tigers might make of his charges. It is said (the author of this book has no firsthand knowledge of lion training) that the big cats cannot be really tamed but must always be regarded with suspicion and controlled by means of rewards and punishments. This is the Legalist technique with human beings. Are the analysis and the technique valid?

Certainly it is true that, if self-interest is understood in the broadest terms, everyone acts from self-interest. I once knew a woman who said that she would never do anything dishonest because she wanted to go to heaven. Others refrain from acting unethically because they value the respect of those around them more than they value what might be gained by such action. Some people will do what they think is right even if no one else will ever know of their actions, because they value self-respect; such persons sometimes say, "I couldn't sleep at night if I did that."

All these ethical motivations can be interpreted in terms of self-interest, but in these instances self-interest has come to be calculated in special and complex ways. Those who study animal psychology recognize that such factors as conditioned reflexes and substitute stimuli make even the psychological processes of animals by no means simple. Those of human beings are far more complex.

The Confucian criticism of Legalist psychology would be, therefore, that it is far too simple. It does not take account of what was stressed by every Confucian: the tremendous power of education to transform and to socialize human beings. Neither does it recognize that, while it is perfectly true that men are motivated by desire, they may desire all sorts of things. They may desire to be trusted, for instance, even more than they desire money. Thus, the Confucians would say, a sincere leader who makes his subordinates feel that he depends on them may be served more faithfully than a much more clever leader who employs only the promise of great rewards and the threat of dire punishments to gain his ends.

Legalist theory listed three things which the ruler must employ in order to govern the world properly. One was *shih*, which means both power and position. The second was *shu*, methods. The third was *fa*, law. Some Legalists laid special stress on one of these, and some on another.

The importance of *shih*, power and position, was demonstrated by pointing out that even the sage emperors were unable to make the people obey them until such time as they occupied the throne, while even the most unworthy of rulers had secured obedience. Thus, it was concluded, virtue and wisdom are of no account as compared with power and position.

In their insistence that the conduct of government requires administrative techniques, *shu*, the Legalists were on their firmest ground as opposed to the Confucians. Although Confucius had insisted that mere learning was of no value unless its possessor could use it in the proper conduct of government, he had laid primary emphasis on virtue as the chief requisite for a good administrator. The Confucians had preserved the letter of his teaching but forgotten much of its spirit, until they finally came to insist that all an administrator needed was virtue and a knowledge of certain classical books. But as states became larger and more centralized and economic activity became increasingly complex, the administration of government came more and more to demand specific technical knowledge and skills. The Legalists recognized this, and that is probably the chief reason why Chinese government continued to be strongly influenced by Legalism, long after Legalism as a developing philosophy had virtually ceased to exist.

In connection with the third point, law, the difference between the Legalists and the Confucians was no less sharp. Here the Confucian position undoubtedly grew out of the situation that had existed under feudalism, where the landed proprietor exercised almost unrestricted legal authority over the peasants of his domain. If he were oppressive, it would obviously be desirable that his authority be limited by a precise code of laws. But if he were good and wise, such a man, presiding over the welfare of a small number of people all personally known to him, might be able to administer sounder justice if he were permitted to take full account of all the special circumstances and pronounce judgment on the basis of his own good sense, limited only by custom. This is the view of legal procedure that the Confucians have regularly taken. They have therefore placed the stress on putting the administration of justice into the hands of good and wise men rather than on limiting its administration by codes of law.

As political units became larger, officials were not, in fact, personally acquainted with all those under their jurisdiction, and the existence of codes of law became a necessity. The Confucians accepted this fact grudgingly, but still placed primary emphasis on government by men rather than by laws.

Chinese courts, up to the end of the Manchu dynasty, functioned in a manner quite different from ours. A trial was not a contest between lawyers for the prosecution and the defense, refereed by a judge who rendered his decision according to the code. Instead, it was in theory an investigation by the court into the facts of the case, including every mitigating or aggravating circumstance, followed by a decision rendered in the light of law, custom, and all the circumstances. If this system seems totally different from our own, it is well to remember that many of our Western courts have recently added to their personnel probation officers, whose function is precisely to examine into all the circumstances of the case and recommend action in accord with them. This is hailed as a great modern advance.

It has often been charged that the traditional Chinese courts were incompetent and corrupt. But the distinguished French jurist, Jean Escarra, who spent some years in study of the Chinese legal system, questions this charge. In some cases, he says, it grows out of the fact that the Chinese courts have placed equity and social justice above the letter of the law. He finds the traditional Chinese judicial system (which is basically Confucian) to merit "more of admiration than of criticism."[25]

Hsün Tzŭ, as we would expect, has more good to say of law than other early Confucians had. But even Hsün Tzŭ points out that laws cannot enforce themselves, and he asserts that they are far less important than good men to administer them. Furthermore, he says, if all the circumstances of particular cases are not considered carefully, then "those cases for which the law does not provide will certainly be treated wrongly."[26]

The Legalist conception of law was in some respects much more similar to that of the West than the Confucian one, but its objective was very different from what we commonly think of as the objective of law. To us "the safeguards of the law" mean protection for the individual against unlimited exactions by the government. The Legalists, however, regarded law as an instrument for the complete control of all citizens by the government. They wanted precise laws set forth and known to all. In effect, this constituted the posting of an exact schedule of rewards and penalties, so that citizens would know just what would happen to them if they did what. "Rewards," Han Fei Tzŭ wrote, "should be generous and certain, so that the people will value them. Punishments should be severe and inevitable, so that the people will fear them. Laws should be uniform and definite, so that the people can understand them. Therefore the ruler should reward without stint, and punish without mercy."[27]

It is said that the law of Shang Yang provided that anyone who threw ashes into the street should have his hand cut off. He is quoted as having said, "Small faults should be punished severely; then, if small faults are inhibited, great crimes will not appear. This is called using punishment to get rid of punishment."[28] If this seems a little hard on the individual who loses his hand, we should remember that, as Han Fei Tzŭ tells us, rewards and punishments are not concerned primarily with the individual to whom they are applied but are designed to have an exemplary effect upon the whole people.[29]

By means of law and the other techniques of Legalism the intelligent ruler compels men to act as they should; he places no value at all, Han Fei Tzŭ says, on the spontaneous virtue of individuals, which is accidental and unreliable. Nor does such a ruler himself act in the manner which scholars call "virtuous," being kind to the people and helping them in adversity. To help the poor by giving them aid derived from taxing the rich is merely to penalize industry and thrift, and to encourage extravagance and idleness.[30] Han Fei Tzŭ says:

The strict household has no unruly slaves, but a doting mother is sure to have a spoiled son. From this I know that only awe-inspiring power can suppress violence, while kindness and magnanimity cannot possibly deter the rebellious. The sage, in governing a state, does not trust men to do good of themselves; he makes it impossible for them to do wrong. In an entire state you could not find ten men who can be trusted to do good of themselves, but if you make it impossible for the people to do wrong the whole state can nevertheless be kept in order. A ruler must concern himself with the majority, not with rare individuals. Thus he takes no account of virtue, but concerns himself rather with law.[31]

It is a mistake, therefore, to compare a ruler to a father; the ruler does not (or at any rate should not) feel affection toward his people. The story is told of a duke of Ch'in, who, recovering from an illness, heard that some of his people had sacrificed an ox for his recovery. He thereupon punished them, because love between ruler and subject would spoil government and must therefore be nipped in the bud.[32]

Nor must the ruler indulge in any foolish liking for even his closest ministers. The more able they are, the more likely it is that they will murder him. They must have the capacity to do their jobs, and they should be given high rank and generous emolument, but they must not be given power or influence, and the ruler should not pay too much attention to their advice.[33] Ministers should not be too wise, or they will cheat the ruler; they should not be pure, for pure men are likely to be stupid. It is totally unnecessary to seek virtuous and upright men as officials; you could not find enough such men to staff the government anyway. If the ruler simply makes the law uniform and overawes them with his power, they will not dare to be wicked, no matter how much they may wish to do so.[34]

Power, force, is the only thing that counts, Han Fei Tzŭ said.[35] He was concerned with making the ruler rich, and powerful for war. *The Book of Lord Shang* lamented the fact that the people disliked war, but it proposed a practical remedy: make the people's ordinary life so hard that they will welcome war as a release from it.[36] If we examine history, war and totalitarianism are found together so frequently that their association can scarcely be accident. Totalitarianism seems rarely to thrive except during war and under the threat of war. If these conditions do not exist, totalitarian states often create them artificially in order to survive.

In the state of Ch'in, after Li Ssŭ had brought about the death of Han Fei Tzŭ he made constant use of the ideas of his former fellow-student. Ch'in had long been growing in power, and the rest of China regarded its rise with mingled fascination and horror. In a series of events reminiscent of our own twentieth century, the other states formed an alliance that stood firm for a time, but which Ch'in succeeded in destroying by a variety of means.

The *Historical Records* says that the ruler of Ch'in, in accord with the advice of Li Ssŭ, "secretly sent out agents well supplied with gold and gems, which they were to use to persuade the various feudal lords to ally themselves with Ch'in. Thus they bought the adherence of those rulers and statesmen who could be bribed. Those who could not be bribed were cut down by the assassin's sword. Thus they divided the rulers and their subjects. After these conspirators had done their work, the king of Ch'in sent his excellent generals to reap the harvest."[37]

Ch'in got control of China by a series of conquests that seem rather bloody even by modern standards. On one occasion, it is claimed, 400,000 soldiers who had surrendered to Ch'in were massacred in a body. No doubt the figure is exaggerated; but, divide it as one likes, it remains large. A huge number of lives were lost, but finally, in 221 B.C., all of China was subject to the ruler of Ch'in, who assumed the title of emperor.

All over China the people heaved a sigh of relief. It was centuries since a single strong ruler had controlled all of China and enforced the peace. The emperor took as his title simply the appellation "First Emperor" and directed that his descendants should be named "Second Emperor," "Third Emperor," and so on, up to ten thousand. He made, as he proclaimed in an inscription he set up, a new beginning.

With his Legalist prime minister, Li Ssŭ, he set out to create a brave new world, unshackled by precedent. History tells us that "laws and regulations were made uniform, weights and measures standardized, the gauge of all vehicles made the same, and the forms of written characters made uniform."[38] In order that the peace might not be disturbed, weapons were gathered in from all over the empire. A hundred and twenty thousand wealthy and influential families were transported to live in the neighborhood of the capital, where they could easily be prevented from making trouble. In place of the old feudal system, China was divided into a number of administrative districts, each headed by one of the emperor's officials, thus producing a centralized government.

Such changes could not have been brought about rapidly without the Legalist system of autocratic government and severe punishments visited upon those who opposed the ruler's decrees or broke the laws. The government was harsh, but it achieved its objectives. There were at least two difficulties, however.

Totalitarian states commonly suffer from the fact that, since full initiative is permitted to no one but the dictator, all affairs must wait for his decision. The First Emperor toiled late every night, but could hardly get through all the documents that demanded his personal attention. He died at the age of fifty, probably from overwork.

Furthermore, not everyone appreciated the advantages of the new regime. Many of the scholars, who specialized in knowledge of the past, did not look with favor upon the wiping of all precedent from the boards. Some of them were killed because they were suspected of having criticized the First Emperor personally. Others certainly did criticize the regime, so that Li Ssŭ charged them with "spreading doubt and disorder among the people." It was decreed that all books in public circulation, except those on medicine, divination, and agriculture, should be burned, and that all persons who dared to cite the Confucian classics in order to criticize the government were to be executed.

The multiplication of punishments did not always have the effect that the Legalists had hoped for. It was very easy to become liable to the death penalty, quite accidentally and with the most submissive of intentions. Since according to Legalist principles there was no possibility of clemency, no matter how extenuating the circumstances, those offenders who could do so naturally fled to the mountains. They were joined by all those who did not wish to live under a totalitarian dictatorship and had the courage to take to the wilds. A number of bands of men, of very considerable size, thus lived as outlaws. Despite all the First Emperor's raging, his armies seem to have had little success in tracking down these elusive foes.

Eleven years after he had consolidated the Chinese world, the First Emperor died. Li Ssŭ plotted with a eunuch to do away with the First Emperor's eldest son (who is said to have favored the Confucians) and made a weakling emperor in his place. Two years later the eunuch caused Li Ssŭ to be executed.

In the meantime the dynasty, set up to last for ten thousand generations, had been collapsing like a house of cards. A peasant had raised the banner of revolt. Immediately Confucians, Moists, and all sorts of men who hated the house of Ch'in flocked to his banner. After a few months he was killed; along with him there died the direct heir of Confucius, in the eighth generation, who had been one of his closest advisers. But this did not stop the revolt, which was spreading like a prairie fire.

By 207 B.C. the house of Ch'in was nothing but an execrated memory. The son of a farmer, who had turned outlaw when he unintentionally violated one of the Ch'in laws, and who subsequently became a general in the revolution, founded the Han dynasty. Legalism, as the avowed philosophy of the Chinese state, was dead.

Chapter IX

The Eclectics of Han

IN THE West we do not usually think of government and philosophy as being intimately related. In China, however, they have commonly been linked quite closely. Most of the Chinese philosophers we have considered held government offices of some sort, and those who did not were very much interested in the way government was carried on. The connection between government and philosophy became especially apparent in the last centuries before the Christian Era.

In 213 B.C., under the short-lived Ch'in dynasty, almost all the philosophical literature was proscribed, and discussion of the classics that were particularly in vogue among the Confucians was forbidden. Legalism was in the saddle. A few years later, after the founding of the Han dynasty, the situation as regards philosophies was fluid. When we come to the time of the Emperor Wu, who reigned from 140 to 87 B.C., students of Legalist writings were barred from official positions, an imperial university was established for the study of the Confucian classics, and considerable strides were made in the development of the examination system. Since that time, a large proportion of Chinese officials have normally been appointed on the basis of examinations in the Confucian classics.

Thus, in the space of less than a century, the full swing was made from the situation under Ch'in, in which Legalism was the officially sanctioned doctrine, to that under the Han Emperor Wu, in which we have what is commonly called "the triumph of Confucianism."

The nature of Confucian orthodoxy, and the position that it has occupied in China during the last two thousand years, were profoundly affected by its so-called "triumph" in Han times. Many attempts have been made to explain this event. Some scholars have sought to interpret it as solely the consequence of the political and economic circumstances of the age, moving along inevitable lines to a predictable result. Others have gone to the other extreme and tried to explain it as due simply to the predilections of certain rulers and their close advisers. Still others—and there are many of these—have said that the Emperor Wu adopted Confucianism as the official philosophy of his government because Confucianism emphasized the subservience of subjects to the ruler, and enhanced the power and prestige of the emperor and the ruling class.

Whatever else may be right or wrong about them, all these generalizations are much too simple. If we are really to understand what took place, we must try to forget preconceived theories and examine with care what actually happened. We must of course consider the political and economic circumstances, for they are an important part of the data. Particular attention needs to be paid, however, to three human factors: the rulers, the scholars, and last but not least the mass of the people.

Anciently the aristocrats could almost ignore the ignorant masses. But the masses had become far less ignorant. The founder of the Han dynasty was so poor as a young man that his wife—later a reigning empress of supreme and terrible power—worked in the fields with her own hands. But at the same time his younger brother studied philosophy with a disciple of Hsün Tzŭ.[1] We have already noticed that as early as the days of Confucius and Mencius the common people of eastern China had come to enjoy such importance that certain great families cultivated their favor, and found it useful in promoting their political ambitions.

This was not equally true in the relatively uncultured state of Ch'in. We have some evidence that its people did not enjoy the severe repression that their government exercised, any more than a horse likes to be beaten, but like the horse they were used to it and made little protest. One of the greatest mistakes that the First Emperor of Ch'in made was to suppose that the whole Chinese people could long be confined within the strait jacket of savage discipline to which the people of his native state submitted meekly.

Only a few years passed before a peasant began the rebellion, in the east, and he was immediately joined by all sorts of men, including a number of Confucians and Moists. As one of his chief advisers he had the direct heir of Confucius in the eighth generation. The peasant leader seems to have believed that Confucianism had propaganda appeal to the masses. He and the descendant of Confucius were killed together after a few months, but this did not stop the revolution, which had spread like wildfire. The Ch'in imperial regime virtually collapsed of itself as the result of palace intrigues; but after it had been overthrown, it was still necessary to decide who should found a dynasty to replace it. War continued for several years, between the two most able of the revolutionary generals.

One of these generals, Hsiang Yü by name, was the very type of the hereditary aristocrat. His ancestors had held fiefs, and had been distinguished as generals, for generations. In the field he was so skilful that it is said he never lost a battle of which he was personally in command. His manner was so imposing that, it is reported, men instinctively fell to their knees at his approach, and even the war horses of his adversaries neighed and fled in terror when he bent his piercing gaze upon them. As befitted one so highly bred, he had a very low regard for humanity in general, and enjoyed nothing so much as to boil or burn a captured enemy alive, or order his soldiers to slaughter every man, woman, and child in a captured area.

Since Hsiang Yü was always successful in battle, it may seem a little surprising that he lost the war. He himself was completely baffled by the fact that, although he led his men to victory after victory, his armies slowly melted away until finally he had to commit suicide.

His adversary, who founded the Han dynasty, was the first

man of plebeian birth to sit on the Chinese throne. For convenience we may call him by the name that history has given him, Han Kao Tsu. The son of a farmer, he accidentally broke one of the Ch'in laws and had to flee for his life. He became a bandit chief, and when the revolution came emerged as one of the leading generals. It was not as a strategist that he excelled, however, but as a leader of men, one who could select capable strategists and men with other skills and get them to exert themselves in his service.

His self-control was almost incredible. On one occasion, when his army was drawn up opposite that of his enemy, he met Hsiang Yü in full sight of both armies for a parley. Hsiang Yü drew a hidden crossbow and shot him in the chest. Han Kao Tsu was seriously wounded. If his soldiers, who were looking on, had realized this, they would have been dangerously discouraged. Without a moment's hesitation Han Kao Tsu picked up his foot and cried out, "Oh, this villain has shot me in the toe!"[2]

He was ruthless. He fought by every means, fair or foul, that promised success. He pledged his word and violated it as served his purpose. He was capable of sacrificing the lives of thousands of men and women, and even the lives of his own children, to save his own life.

If this were all, he would have been only another intelligent and ruthlessly ambitious man. But Han Kao Tsu was far more. He was a profound student of psychology. He knew that he could not afford to appear ruthless. Therefore, whenever he could do so without injuring his cause, he was conspicuously generous. He gave his subordinates full credit for all his accomplishments and said that his only merit was that he had appreciated and used their abilities. When some of his followers plotted rebellion he first had them arrested, then pardoned them and restored them to posts of honor. He even treated his common soldiers well, which was unheard-of.

Once Kao Tsu was emperor, a genealogy was of course

made for him, proving that he was descended from the mythical emperor Yao. We might expect that he would have disowned, if not disposed of, all those who had known him as a common man. On the contrary, he gave offices to some of his early associates and exempted his home town from taxation. Furthermore, he returned there on one occasion and feasted all his old friends and acquaintances for some days, personally singing and dancing to entertain them.[3]

Kao Tsu was no snob. In this he was sincere, but it was also policy. Homer H. Dubs has written: "Kao-tsu's generous and kindly treatment of the people thus brought to him the fellow-feeling of the people. They realized that he was one of them. More than once the leaders of the people came to him with important advice. His lack of manners and use of churlish language towards even his most distinguished followers probably accentuated the kindly feeling of the people to him. He won because he manipulated public opinion in his favor; that feeling was so strong two centuries later that, at the downfall of his dynasty, only another Han dynasty with the same surname could gain the throne."[4]

Kao Tsu not only sought to win the people's favor by proclaiming amnesties, remitting taxes, freeing slaves, and so forth. He also, early in his struggle for power, gave the people a very limited voice in the government, by arranging that his officials should regularly consult with representatives of the people to ascertain their wishes. When he was made emperor, he said that he was accepting the title only "for the good of the people."[5] Even after he was emperor he did not act arbitrarily, but only with the advice and consent of his ministers.

Gradually this practice achieved the force of unwritten law, so that decisions of his successors, if not ratified by their ministers, were considered illegal. Dubs says that "the accession of Kao-tsu marks the victory of the Confucian conception that the imperial authority is limited, should be exercised for the benefit of the people, and should be founded upon justice, over the legalistic conception of arbitrary and absolute sovereignty. While Kao-tsu and his successors technically remained absolute sovereigns, in practise their powers were much limited by custom."[6]

Here, then, we have a government that to some extent agrees, in theory, with Confucius' idea of what a government should be: a government run *for* the people, *by* ministers selected by a ruler who leaves the administrative authority in their hands. Obviously, it was still far from Confucius' ideal, but it is surprising that a burly ruffian like Han Kao Tsu should have even approximated it.

Kao Tsu was no partisan of the Confucians. He considered them pompous bookworms and liked nothing better than to humiliate them with very vulgar practical jokes. Nevertheless he had some Confucians, including his own younger brother, among his intimate advisers, and they did all they could to Confucianize him, even writing a book for the purpose. Becoming disgusted with the rowdy manners of his rough companions in the court, Kao Tsu called upon a Confucian to devise a simple court ceremonial to be followed. Beyond doubt, however, what chiefly moved this shrewd statesman in favor of Confucianism was its popularity among the people.

It is often supposed that in Han times Confucianism was primarily the doctrine of aristocrats and wealthy landed gentry. This was not the case. Even as late as the first century B.C., after many of them had been made more prosperous by government subsidies, their enemies described the Confucians as a class of poverty-stricken scholars living on poor farms and in mean alleys, wearing plain clothing and torn sandals.[7] As a group, they seem to have remained in economically depressed circumstances throughout the Han period. This very fact, however, kept them in touch with the people, and therefore influential with them.

Han Kao Tsu recognized this and exploited its propaganda

value. During his struggle for power he preached a "crusade" against his adversary, Hsiang Yü, in Confucian language, with gratifying results. Later we find Confucian language appearing frequently in his edicts. In 196 B.C. he ordered that his officials throughout the empire should recommend all virtuous and capable men to the throne, so that they might be honored and given positions.[8] This practice, continued and elaborated by his successors, developed into the characteristically Confucian institution that we know as the Chinese examination system.

Nevertheless, Kao Tsu's court was neither exclusively nor predominantly Confucian. Taoism, with its large ideas and sweeping generalizations, naturally appealed to adventurers. Increasingly it was becoming amalgamated with the popular superstitions, which caused it to appeal to the masses. Since many of Kao Tsu's followers were adventurers of plebeian birth, it is not surprising that Taoism attracted them.

Neither was Legalistic thought by any means dead. Although the Confucians firmly believed that they should hold the principal offices in the government, they were too much occupied with questions of ritual, metaphysics, and literature to be bothered with the mundane problems of keeping house for the empire; they thought that such matters were unworthy of gentlemen anyway. But the Han state was a huge political and economic organization, that imperatively demanded complex administrative techniques and officials able to use them. Only the officials left from the Ch'in empire possessed these skills, and the Han emperor had to employ them. They were essentially Legalist in outlook.

The fourth Han sovereign, Emperor Wên, who reigned from 179 to 157 B.C., conformed in many respects to the ideal of what a Confucian ruler should be. He considered the imperial office a stewardship, having for its purpose the welfare of the people. He reduced taxes to the minimum, freed government slaves, discouraged official corruption, reduced the severity of the law until capital punishment became a rare occurrence, and set up pensions for the aged. He repealed the laws forbidding criticism of the emperor, saying that he wished to hear about his faults. He proposed that he should, in accord with Confucian principles, not leave his throne to his son but, instead, seek out the most virtuous man in the empire and make him his heir; his officials persuaded him, however, that this would not benefit the empire, but endanger it. He lived frugally, and when he died he asked that mourning be limited to the absolute minimum, in order not to trouble the people.

This was not hypocrisy; Emperor Wên was a genuine paragon of Confucian virtue and one of the most benevolent monarchs in all history. Nevertheless he was very superstitious, and was repeatedly imposed upon by adventurers who claimed to possess magic powers. Among the scholars at his court who were officially appointed to study philosophy, all the various doctrines were represented; at first there was only one Confucian among them. Furthermore, when Wên came to choose a tutor for his heir, he chose a man who was a Legalist.[9]

Despite this fact, the Confucians were again dominant at court when the Emperor Wu, the sixth ruler of the dynasty, succeeded to the throne in 140 B.C. It is rather generally held that Emperor Wu was a sincere if perhaps misguided patron of Confucianism, that Confucians were influential at his court, and that Confucianism "triumphed" during his reign.

Yet if we look carefully at the facts that history has preserved for us, it is difficult to avoid the following conclusions: First, while Emperor Wu may have been a Confucian when he first inherited the throne, as a boy of fifteen, he quickly outgrew this phase; during his long adult life he was in fact a Legalist, who made an elaborate pretense of being a Confucian for reasons of policy. Second, the advisers who carried real weight in framing the policies of his government were outspokenly Legalistic and anti-Confucian. Those nominally Confucian officials who held high office at Wu's court were

in fact not very good Confucians, and in any case Wu paid
almost no attention to their advice on matters of real importance. Finally, if we agree that Confucianism "triumphed"
in the reign of the Emperor Wu, this can be only in a very
limited sense. The fact is that in the process Confucianism was
perverted and distorted in a manner that would have horrified
Confucius, Mencius, and Hsün Tzŭ, as in fact it horrified
genuine Confucians of Emperor Wu's own day.

It has often been remarked that if we look at the overt acts
of Emperor Wu, they correspond remarkably well with the
prescriptions of such Legalists as Han Fei Tzŭ. Confucian
scholars complained that he used the totalitarian method of
registration of the population that had been devised by Shang
Yang. The severe laws of the Ch'in dynasty had never been
wholly repealed, and under Wu they were expanded into a
strict and detailed legal code that was enforced without mercy.
For trifling crimes men were compelled to pay heavy fines,
condemned to serve in the army, or made slaves of the government, so that merchants and the middle class were ruined.
Wu's Legalist advisers urged that he confiscate the more profitable industries; he did so, and the manufacture of salt, iron,
and fermented liquors was made a government monopoly. To
provide labor for these monopolies alone, it appears that more
than one hundred thousand persons were condemned to slavery.
To pay for his military adventures he taxed heavily and
debased the coinage. Punishments were so frequent and severe
that men feared to hold government office; a plan was then
devised whereby those appointed to office might make a
payment to buy themselves free of the dubious "honor"; this
further enriched the treasury.[10]

The Legalists emphasized warfare, and so did Wu. At the
beginning of his reign there was a genuine threat from the
neighboring barbarian tribes; but after this had been removed,
his taste for conquest became boundless. His armies pushed
far into Central Asia; on one occasion he sent more than one

hundred thousand men to Ferghana in order to secure a rare breed of horses. It is impossible to calculate how many tens of thousands of lives were lost in these incessant expeditions, but we know that they ruined the country economically. Nevertheless, Wu greatly expanded China's territories; this fact undoubtedly helped to make his repressive measures slightly less unpalatable to the people at large.

Emperor Wu no longer left the administration of government in the hands of his ministers, as Confucius had long ago recommended and as had been the practice, generally speaking, since the founding of the Han dynasty. Instead he held the reins of government himself, and seems to have refrained from confiding really effective power to any of his ministers or advisers, exactly as Han Fei Tzǔ had recommended. No longer was it lawful, as it had been under the Emperor Wên, to criticize the emperor; such impertinence was punished severely. Nevertheless there was much criticism, especially in Confucian circles, and in 99 B.C. a rebellion broke out. Significantly, it centered around the region of Confucius' birthplace. When it was suppressed, more than ten thousand persons were executed.[11]

Not only did Emperor Wu act like a Legalist and have Legalists as his most influential advisers. As more than one scholar has noted, there is considerable reason to believe that he consciously modeled himself after the First Emperor of the Ch'in dynasty. And in his edicts he occasionally quoted from Legalist works, including the *Han Fei Tzǔ*, showing that he was acquainted with them, although he was too prudent to name his sources.[12] How, then, did such an emperor ever get the reputation of being a sincere, if perhaps somewhat misguided, patron of Confucianism? In a very interesting manner.

When he became emperor at the age of fifteen, the court was dominated by certain Confucian ministers. Since the boy ruler's studies had inclined him toward Confucianism, these ministers had no difficulty in getting him to sign a decree barring from office students of certain Legalist works, including those of Shang Yang and Han Fei Tzŭ. Apparently this decree was never formally rescinded, but the young emperor's genuine enthusiasm for Confucianism was short-lived. His grandmother, the powerful Grand Empress Dowager, was an ardent Taoist, and she quickly curbed the power of his Confucian advisers.

The emperor soon found that Confucians were not to his liking. They had not enough respect for his august position and criticized him quite impertinently. Furthermore, he complained (and here the emperor was quite right), they were utterly impractical. They not only opposed needless war but even argued against any reasonable preparedness against the incursions of the savage nomad hordes that ravaged the borders. If the emperor would only meet them with virtue, the Confucians asserted, these barbarians would submit of their own accord. In government too, they said, only virtue and a knowledge of the classics were necessary. Such vulgar trivia as arithmetic and administrative methods were, in their opinion, utterly unworthy of gentlemen.

These men could not possibly have successfully administered Wu's vast and complex empire. Yet they believed themselves entitled to do so, and they were popular with the people. The fate of the Ch'in dynasty had shown that it was dangerous to offend them. Wu had started his reign with the reputation of being a friend of Confucianism, and he was careful never to lose it. He constantly referred to the Confucian classics in his edicts. He gave positions of high honor—but no power—to two descendants of Confucius. While multiplying the laws and making punishments more savage, he asserted: "My endeavor is to decrease punishments that evil may become less." While wringing the last ounce of tribute from the people, he repeatedly issued edicts proclaiming the anguish which he felt for their sufferings. For his most predatory schemes he alleged ingeniously plausible motives of the purest benevolence.[13]

For some time it had been the practice for scholars, recommended from their home districts, to go to the court and be examined by the emperor. A famous Confucian named Tung Chung-shu took such an examination early in Wu's reign. In his examination paper he accused the emperor point-blank of using the Legalistic methods of the Ch'in dynasty, and asserted that his officials were grinding down the people.

The Ch'in First Emperor would have made a martyr of Tung Chung-shu, but Emperor Wu was much more clever. He appointed him as a high minister at the court of a swashbuckling vassal who hated pedants and had the habit of executing ministers who annoyed him. However, Wu's reasonable expectations were disappointed, for Tung Chung-shu became a favorite of his new master. The emperor tried again, sending him to the court of a still more murderous vassal. This time Tung Chung-shu resigned, as he said, "for reasons of health," and spent the rest of his life in retirement. During his later years the emperor would from time to time send one of his courtiers to Tung Chung-shu "to ask his advice." In this way Wu obtained, and still enjoys, the reputation of being a patron of the Confucian scholar, Tung Chung-shu.[14]

A little later than the examination of Tung Chung-shu, another was held in which one of the hundred scholars examined was a certain Kung-Sun Hung. As a young man he had been a jailer; possibly this gave him the interest in Legalism that he showed later. Discharged for some fault, he became a swineherd, and late in life studied one of the Confucian classics. He was in his sixties when he wrote an examination for the emperor. His reply, although it had the necessary Confucian façade, was in fact distinctly Legalistic. He said that the emperor must energetically set forth the laws, and use *shu*, "methods" (it will be recalled that this is a Legalist term). Further, the emperor must "monopolize the handles that control life and death" (this paraphrases a passage in the *Han Fei Tzŭ*) and keep strong personal control of the government.

The scholars who graded the papers were scandalized at this and graded Kung-Sun Hung's paper last among the hundred. When the papers reached the emperor, he moved it up to first place.[15] Here at last was the "Confucian" he needed. He heaped Kung-Sun Hung with honors and soon made him prime minister. The emperor kept him in this position until he died of old age. The government was actually run by the emperor and a small group of Legalistically inclined advisers. The prime minister provided, as another official of the emperor's court tells us, a convenient Confucian façade for the Legalistic operations of the government.[16]

Look up Kung-Sun Hung in almost any history, and you will read that he was a Confucian scholar, a former swineherd whom Emperor Wu honored so greatly for his knowledge of the classics that he made him his prime minister and ennobled him as a marquis. We may be quite sure that the emperor planned that history should read in this way.

He richly rewarded those nominal Confucians who applauded him and punished those who criticized. Thought control was strict; Tung Chung-shu was once condemned to death for writing a "stupid" book, but the emperor pardoned him. Wu made co-operation with the government attractive by founding the imperial university, in which fifty Confucian students were supported by the state. Offices in the government were increasingly awarded to scholars who performed satisfactorily in the government examinations on the Confucian classics; these examinations gave the emperor a matchless opportunity to influence the direction of Confucian thought and studies.

Because much of the literature had been destroyed in the Ch'in period, scholars were greatly interested in recovering old books, especially the classics. The emperor encouraged this interest in texts, which from his point of view was greatly preferable to the accent that Confucius and Mencius had placed on the criticism of social and political practices.

Around this time there began the great period of the production of commentaries, to explain the ancient books. In these explanations, Han scholars interpreted all the classical literature in terms of the thought of their own day. It is largely in terms of these commentaries that the classics are still studied and translated in the twentieth century, despite the fact that the Han thinking they set forth is very different from that of the time when the early classics were written.

It is human to want to do things in the easiest way. Few of us will add a column of figures when an adding machine is at hand or think out a difficult problem when a satisfactory short cut makes this unnecessary. We saw that Confucius believed that each individual must think things out for himself, but that almost immediately after his death Confucians began to rely more and more on authority, and to seek easier ways to solve problems.

One such method, divination, had been used in China from remote antiquity. An ancient diviner's manual, the *Book of Changes*, came in Han times to be considered one of the Confucian classics, despite the fact that Confucius and all the great early Confucians had scorned the practice of divination. Ten appendixes to the *Book of Changes* were also written; they set forth a method of understanding and even controlling events by means of a mystical science of numbers. These appendixes were probably written by Confucians who were deeply influenced by Taoism. The appendixes pretended, however, to quote Confucius and were even ascribed to his authorship.

Another idea, which possibly began its rise in the fourth century B.C., was that all things may be classified as partaking of the *yin* or negative principle, or the *yang* or positive principle. Everything was classified under these categories. *Yin* is female, *yang* is male. Heaven, the sun, and fire are *yang;* earth, the moon, and water are *yin*. If you want proof, a burning-glass will draw fire from the sun, while a mirror left out at night will collect dew, that is, water, from the moon. It should be noted, however, that this was not a dualism of the Occidental sort, like that between good and evil or spirit and matter. On the contrary, *yin* and *yang* complemented each other to maintain the cosmic harmony, and might transform into each other; thus winter, which is *yin*, changes into summer, which is *yang*.

Another very important conception that appears to have arisen about the same time is that of the so-called "Five Elements." The Chinese term might better be translated as the "Five Forces." They were: wood, fire, earth, metal, water. With these were correlated five directions, the center being added to the four cardinal points. Five seasons were also found to correspond to them, by adding a center season between summer and autumn and calling it "earth," the name of the center force. There were also added five colors, flavors, odors, numbers, organs of the body, etc., almost ad infinitum.

In philosophy the sequences of these forces are very important. Wood produces (that is, can support) fire; fire produces earth (that is, ashes); earth produces metal; metal produces water (dew deposited on a metal mirror); water produces (that is, makes possible the growth of) wood. The order of their destruction is: water extinguishes fire; fire melts metal; metal cuts wood; wood penetrates earth (either by the roots of trees or by the wooden plow); and earth soaks up or dams the course of water; thus the cycle is again completed.

By means of such divination techniques as those of the *Book of Changes*, and the theories of numerology, *yin* and *yang*, and the five forces, there was developed a vast and intricate system for the analysis and control of phenomena. If the theories had been stated tentatively and checked by experiment, they might well have developed into true science. But since this theorizing was almost completely dogmatic and nonexperimental, it never rose above the level of an elaborate pseudo-science.

We have already noted that Taoism early took over a great deal of popular superstition. These pseudo-scientific ideas were also adopted and cultivated in Taoist circles. The First Emperor of the Ch'in dynasty heavily subsidized Taoist magicians, who undertook to obtain for him the elixir of immortality. In the Han dynasty Emperor Wu married his eldest daughter to a magician who promised to obtain for him this elusive drug; when the magician failed to deliver, Wu had him cut in two at the waist.

During the reign of Emperor Wu a certain prince, who studied various philosophies but inclined chiefly toward Taoism, had a book compiled by philosophers whom he supported as his guests; it has come down to us under the name of *Huai Nan Tzŭ*. It is generally Taoistic in nature but shows the strong tendency to eclecticism that is characteristic of Han thought. Its first chapter says: "Unfold the *Tao* and it fills the universe; and yet it can be contained in a tiny scroll that does not fill the hand! ... It is the very axle of the universe, and the vessel that contains the *yin* and the *yang*. It binds all space to all time, and illumines the sun and moon and stars."[17] A later chapter says:

Heaven has the four seasons, five forces, nine cardinal points, and three hundred sixty-six days. Man similarly has four limbs, five viscera, nine apertures, and three hundred sixty-six joints. Heaven has wind, rain, cold, and heat, and man has the activities of taking and giving, joy and anger. Thus the gall bladder corresponds to clouds, the lungs to air, the liver to wind, the kidneys to rain, and the spleen to thunder. In this way man forms a trinity with Heaven and Earth, and his heart is master. For this reason his ears and eyes play the parts of the sun and moon, and the blood and breath of the wind and rain. There is a three-legged bird in the sun, and a three-legged toad in the moon. If the sun and the moon get off their courses, the result is an eclipse and darkness. If wind and rain occur unseasonably, there is destruction and disaster. If the five planets get off their courses, whole states and even continents suffer calamity.[18]

Chapter 13 begins by saying that anciently emperors did not display pomp, nor inflict punishments, nor collect taxes.

Instead, they treated the people kindly and bestowed wealth upon them. The people responded by appreciating their virtue. "At this time the *yin* and the *yang* were in harmony, wind and rain were seasonable and moderate, and all things flourished. Crows and magpies were so tame that men could reach into their nests and handle them; wild animals could be led on the leash." This passage is obviously Taoist, but with Confucian overtones. The chapter goes on to develop the point that practices have been changed and, indeed, must be changed with changing times. It ascribes the fall of the Hsia and Shang dynasties to an obstinate "refusal to change their methods." This is, of course, thoroughly Legalist.

There follows a lengthy discourse that is both Taoist and Legalist, which criticizes both Confucians and Moists by name. Yet at the same time the First Emperor of Ch'in is criticized for his repressive methods and his excessive militarism. And the same chapter includes some very Confucian sentiments, of which neither a Legalist, nor a Taoist in the early sense of that term, could possibly approve. For instance: "If the ruler of a badly governed state seeks to enlarge his territory but neglects humanity and justice, and seeks to enhance his position but neglects the Way and virtue, he is discarding that which could save him and paving the way for his downfall."

The fact that the *Huai Nan Tzŭ* includes ideas chosen from various schools does not, of course, prove that its authors were necessarily confused. On the contrary, they sometimes seem uncommonly level-headed, seeking to strike a balance between the militarism and despotism of the Legalists on the one hand and the pacifism and too complete trust in the power of virtue of the Confucians on the other.

The Confucians were not less eclectic. In fact, it is difficult to find what we may call a "pure" Confucian in Han times. One of the longest and most important of the so-called Confucian classics, the *Records on Ceremonial*, was compiled during the first century B.C. from documents of varying age. Although it has always held a high place of honor in Confucianism, it contains much that is transparently Legalist and Taoist, as well as incorporating the theories of *yin* and *yang* and the five forces. One lengthy section of this work explains what activities must be carried on (especially by the emperor), what colors must be used, and so forth, during each month of the year, and what dire calamities would befall if this were not done. Punishments, for instance, such as the death penalty, should be inflicted in autumn; if they were inflicted in spring, "there would be great floods and cold waves, and attacks by plundering raiders."[19] Something more than a century after the publication of the *Records on Ceremonial* it was ordered, by imperial decree, that such punishments must henceforth always normally be carried out in the autumn.[20]

This same work quotes Confucius as having made various statements involving the mystical significance of numbers and as saying that a true ruler must be able to predict the future.[21] Some parts of this sacred Confucian text quote Confucius as speaking like a complete Taoist and attacking the very cardinal principles of Confucianism.[22] Nor do its various portions agree; in one section we find it prescribed, in the Confucian manner, that one should make antiquity his sole study, while elsewhere we find this principle condemned in the manner of the Legalists.[23] There is a good deal of Legalist influence. Whereas Confucianism commonly deplored harsh punishments, we find here many crimes that are said to have been punished, in the ideal times of old, by death without mercy; they include using licentious music, being hypocritical, studying false doctrines, and wearing strange clothing.[24] If one studies the *Records on Ceremonial* closely, he is compelled to conclude that the Confucians of Han times must have been somewhat confused.

Tung Chung-shu has frequently been called the greatest Confucian of the Han period. A number of examples of his thought have come down to us; the chief of these is the work called *Luxuriant Dew from the Spring and Autumn Annals*. The following passage from its forty-second chapter illustrates the manner in which he used Taoist and other conceptions in developing his moral and political philosophy:

Heaven has five forces, namely, wood, fire, earth, metal, and water. Wood is first and water last, with earth in the middle. This is their Heaven-ordained sequence. Wood gives birth to fire, fire gives birth to earth [ashes], earth gives birth to metal, metal gives birth to water, and water gives birth to wood. This is their father-son relationship. Wood occupies the left, metal the right, fire the front, water the rear, and earth the center. This is the order in which, as fathers and sons, they receive from and transmit to each other. Thus wood receives from water, fire from wood, earth from fire, metal from earth, and water from metal. As transmitters they are all fathers, as receivers, sons. Constantly to rely upon one's father in order to provide for one's son is the way (*tao*) of Heaven. Therefore wood, living, is nourished by fire;* metal, when dead, is buried by water. Fire delights in wood and nourishes it by means of the *yang* [solar?] power; water overcomes metal [its "father"], yet mourns it by means of the *yin* power. Earth, in serving Heaven, shows the utmost loyalty. Thus the five forces provide a pattern of conduct for filial sons and loyal ministers. . . .

The sage, by understanding this, is able to increase his love and lessen his severity, to make more generous his support of the living and more respectful his performance of funeral rites for the dead, and so to conform with the pattern established by Heaven. Thus as a son he gladly cares for his father, as fire delights in wood, and mourns his father, as water overcomes† metal. He serves his ruler as earth reverences Heaven. Thus he can be called a man of "force."‡ And just as each of the five forces keeps its proper place according to their established order, so officials corresponding to the five forces exert themselves to the utmost by employing their abilities in their respective duties.[25]

Three centuries earlier Mo Tzŭ had declared that natural calamities were the expression of Heaven's displeasure at improper conduct on the part of the ruler. This same idea appears, as we have seen, in the *Records on Ceremonial.* Tung Chung-shu reduced it to a science. He based his system on the

---

* "Fire" here probably means the warmth of the sun.

† This "overcoming" probably refers to the way in which the older generation is replaced by the younger.

‡ There is an untranslatable pun here, based on the fact that the character *hsing* that means "force" in "five forces" also means "conduct."

Spring and Autumn Annals, one of the classics which is a skeletonized history of Confucius' native state for the years 722–481 B.C. and which was erroneously attributed to the authorship of Confucius.[26] Tung made an exhaustive analysis of natural phenomena occurring in that work, together with political events that preceded them. On this basis, he said, whenever in his own day there was a large fire, a flood, a famine, or any such phenomenon, it was only necessary to search the *Spring and Autumn Annals* to find the reason and the remedy.

Thus in the Han period a great variety of pseudo-scientific and even magical practices were grafted onto Confucianism. And this new kind of Confucianism became, as Hu Shih has said, "a great synthetic religion into which were fused all the elements of popular superstition and state worship, rationalized somewhat in order to eliminate a few of the most untenable elements, and thinly covered up under the disguise of Confucian and Pre-Confucian Classics in order to make them appear respectable and authoritative. In this sense, the new Confucianism of the Han Empire was truly the national religion of China."[27] In some Han works we find Confucius described as a god, the son of a certain mythical Black Emperor. At his birth, it is recounted, spirits and dragons hovered in the air over the scene of the nativity.

All this is different enough from the teachings of the scholar of Lu, but there is another aspect of Han Confucianism that would have disturbed Confucius, if he could have known of it, even more. We saw that in the Confucian authoritarianism of Hsün Tzǔ there was already an insistence upon the stratification of society, although the strata were not fixed by heredity. The scholars, Confucian and otherwise, had a strong tendency to consider themselves an elite composed of something far better than common clay. Thus Tung Chung-shu, in arguing against Mencius' idea that human nature is good, says that this is obviously not the case, for otherwise the masses of the people would not be called "the blind," by which he apparently means "the stupid."[28] "Heaven," he says, "endowed the common people with the raw material of goodness, but they could not make themselves good. For this Heaven established the king, to make them good; this was Heaven's intention. . . . The king is charged by Heaven with the duty of teaching the people to bring out the potential goodness that is in them."[29] Having been given this responsibility by Heaven, the ruler looks upon Heaven as his father, and thus it is most fitting that he is called the "Son of Heaven."[30]

It was almost inevitable that Han metaphysics, as an ideology tailored to fit the centralized Han empire, should thus have given to the emperor this supernatural support for his position, which Confucius had been careful to withhold from the ruler. It was equally inevitable that this should have played into the hand of monarchical despotism. Thus we find a non-Confucian official of Emperor Wu's court declaring that it is the Confucian doctrine that the emperor must take the lead, and his ministers must follow.[31] It is not unnatural, therefore, that some scholars have concluded that Emperor Wu favored Confucianism because it was an aristocratic doctrine favorable to autocratic rule.

Certainly, from this time forward, Confucianism was often exploited by despots, seconded by complaisant ministers, to forward their selfish designs. But this is not the whole, or the most important part, of the story. Despots always find, or distort, or create, an ideology to condone their tyranny. And although Confucianism was misused in this manner, its total effect has been far more to eliminate or at least to modify despotism. Tung Chung-shu's method of arguing from analogies in the *Spring and Autumn Annals* was devised as a check on the autocracy of the emperor, and it was actually used in this way by later Confucians. Tung also advocated that taxes should be lightened, that the amount of land which might be held by a private owner should be limited, and that slavery should be abolished.

We do find, in fact, that in Han times even very high nobles were punished for mistreating slaves, and the circumstances leave no doubt that this was in large measure the result of Confucian humanitarianism. From Han times onward, Confucianism has sometimes been dragged at the chariot wheels of despotism, but can hardly be said to have been its willing handmaiden. The best Confucians have always spoken out fearlessly for what they believed to be right, whether the cost might be exile, prison, or death.

By Han times, ideas peculiar to each of the major philosophies may be said to have won a certain triumph. Beyond doubt, the Han imperial system was in very large degree the child of philosophy, or rather of the various philosophies. Yet the situation was such that the philosophies must have found themselves in the position of the man who, having at last attained success, wonders why he valued it so highly.

Certainly Legalism had triumphed in large measure, for the actual administration of the state was Legalistic. But it was not nominally so, and after Wu many emperors were to a large extent Confucian in fact as well as in name. Ministers were selected, in theory at least, on Confucian principle, for their learning and virtue. Most abhorrent of all to Legalism, these ministers were given power. In fact, both the Former Han and the Later Han dynasties were terminated by supremely powerful ministers who supplanted their rulers.

Taoism had come far. Indeed, the so-called Confucianism of Han times was in large part Taoism. Taoism itself was greatly in favor in aristocratic circles, and much of the time at the court. But the emphasis on military aggression under Wu, the oppression of the people, and the downright stupidity of much that was called Taoism in Han times would not have pleased the authors of the *Lao Tzŭ* and the *Chuang Tzŭ*.

It might seem that Moism had been forgotten. Yet there was a considerable sense of hierarchy in Han times, which would have pleased Mo Tzŭ. Furthermore, the ideas propounded by Tung Chung-shu, that natural phenomena are the warnings of Heaven and that the emperor is Heaven's vice-regent on earth, became increasing popular, and it will be remembered that Mo Tzŭ had preached both of them. It is obvious, however, that the state of the world would have pleased him no more than it would the Taoists.

And finally, Confucianism. It had triumphed, but at the cost of such transformation that one wonders whether it can still properly be called Confucianism. The very fact that the Han political system was called Confucian caused Confucianism to be held responsible for the repressive despotism that functioned under the cover of its name. The criticisms of its enemies—and they were many—make it clear that Confucianism was increasingly thought of as a system of hidebound traditionalism, meaningless ritualism, and abject subservience to despotic authority.

If we may generalize concerning Han thought from around 100 B.C. up to the time the Later Han dynasty fell in A.D. 220, it appears that it was often disturbed, frequently apathetic, but seldom vigorous in the sense of being forward-looking and original. Of the Confucians of the time of Emperor Wu, Hu Shih has said: "They were groping in the dark for some means whereby to check the absolutism of the rulers of a united empire from which there was no means of escape."[32] Étienne Balázs describes the thought of the second century A.D. as characterized by "a certain uneasiness, an irresolution, an uncertainty among the best minds." And he analyzes this as being due to the fact that Chinese philosophy, no matter how metaphysical it may seem, is at base a social and even a political philosophy, so that Chinese thinkers find it difficult to be at ease in a world that is manifestly out of joint.[33]

The Confucians in particular found it impossible to ignore the distress of the world, partly because most of them were poor and shared in it. Finally, in the latter half of the second century A.D., the Confucians became so open in their attacks upon the aristocracy and the eunuchs, who had pushed them from power, that many of the Confucians were exterminated by their enemies. Yet, although the Confucians took up the cudgel to right the wrongs of the people, they had become too much identified with the oppressive government to be able decisively to control popular favor.

In a sense the dream of the philosophers had come true. China was united, under a sovereign who ruled in the *name* of the good of the people and repeated the slogans beloved of the philosophers. But the dream proved a nightmare, and the sage emperor, at his worst, a Frankenstein's monster. What could be done? Unless one had influence at court, very little. In the days of Confucius and Mencius and Han Fei Tzŭ, if one did not like one state he could go to another, but now there was nowhere to go. In those days philosophers had rebuked rulers with impunity, but now one might be put to death if he merely acted discourteously toward some worthless favorite of the emperor. We need scarcely be surprised that men's minds were not very creative or if they took refuge in such pastimes as a kind of elaborate and abstruse repartee, and in what Balázs calls "nihilism," an attempt to flee from reality.

We have noted that for a long time there had been a tendency to seek easier and easier formulas to solve problems. This reached a high point in the sort of magical procedures proposed by men like Tung Chung-shu. There was a reaction against his ideology which took various forms, and some of them were remarkably refined and subtle. On the whole, however, the critics were not very original, and they themselves proposed easy formulas.

The Confucians said, in words that sound like those of Mencius, that it was only necessary to return to the ways of antiquity and to restore the reign of *li* and justice. The Taoists said that all would be well if everyone would just be natural; they sometimes seem almost to be reciting from the *Lao Tzŭ* and the *Chuang Tzŭ*. Some thinkers turned, to find the way out, to Legalism, but they seem to have considered its practice to be a far easier thing than Han Fei Tzŭ ever did; some of them conceive of "law" as almost a metaphysical principle which, if espoused, will solve all problems as if by magic. These latter-day Legalists insist that the trouble is that men look to the past and do not recognize that new times need new measures; but in making this very point they often seem to be content to parrot Han Fei Tzŭ almost verbatim.

These are generalizations, to which there are always exceptions. An outstanding exception was Wang Ch'ung, who lived from A.D. 27 to about 97. Unlike most scholars of the day, he did not merely study and memorize one or a few classical texts but read widely. Being a poor boy he could not buy books, but browsed constantly in bookshops, and it was said that he could repeat from memory whatever he had read. Being given a small official post he tried, like the very bright young man that he was, to instruct his colleagues and superiors concerning their mistakes. Very soon he had to resign. He wrote several books, of which one long work called the *Lun Hêng* or *Critical Essays* has survived.

They certainly were critical. If we consider the environment in which they were produced, it may be doubted whether any other literary work in human history shows a more independent spirit. Wang attacks the entire mode of classical study, saying that it is too narrow. In writing, he says, one should not just comment on the classics, nor imitate what has been done before, but should express one's own ideas, in clear and understandable language. Although he considers history important, he asserts that modern times are quite as worthy of study as antiquity, and declares that much of what is accepted as history is manifestly false.[34]

Although Wang apparently considers himself a Confucian, he does not fear to criticize even Confucius himself, accusing him of speaking obscurely, vacillating in his opinions, contradicting himself, and even acting improperly. Much of the trouble sprang, he says, from the fact that Confucius' disciples did not question him or criticize him enough. All students ought to argue with their teachers, he says, and to accept nothing that the teacher does not prove.[35]

Wang makes a detailed attack on thousands of the superstitions that were believed even by the learned. It was believed—and is to this day believed by the ignorant—that the bore in the Ch'ien-t'ang River was caused by the spirit of a minister who had been put to death and thrown into the river in the fifth century B.C. Wang makes fun of this and correctly explains that the bore is caused by the entrance of tidal waters into a constricted channel; he also says that tides are correlated with the phases of the moon.[36]

To a large extent Wang is a tough-minded mechanist, and therefore a determinist. Heaven and Earth do not produce man purposely, but accidentally. Heaven has no intelligence or will power, and it cannot bless the good or punish the evil. Natural phenomena are just that, not warnings from Heaven. Neither divination as to the future nor pills to prolong life have any effect. Men die when the circumstances cause them to do so, and when they are dead that is the end; there are no ghosts.[37]

All this sounds astonishingly modern. Yet since Wang Ch'ung was not superhuman he could not entirely escape the beliefs of his age. Although he refuted many superstitions, he solemnly averred that a variety of miracles recorded by tradition had indeed taken place.[38] His criticisms are often as pedantic and ill-grounded as the propositions he attacks, and he is often inconsistent. Furthermore, as Fung Yu-lan has well said, he is so predominantly a destructive critic, and offers so little of his own that is constructive, that in fact his thought is not as important as many contemporary scholars suppose it to be.[39]

What was his influence on Han thought? A number of scholars of the present day have held that he strongly affected the reaction against the traditional Confucianism in the second century A.D. But this seems doubtful. The very fact that much of Wang Ch'ung's thought appears so reasonable to us indicates that it would probably have seemed absurd, if not incomprehensible, to many of his contemporaries. There seems to be no evidence that the *Critical Essays* was even known in scholarly circles until long after Wang was dead. The book was discovered in Wang Ch'ung's native district on the southeast coast, about a century after it was written, by a scholar who did not publish it but, instead, kept it secret and used it to embellish his conversation, pretending that the ideas he borrowed from it were his own. Again in the third century the book is said to have been discovered in Wang's native district by an official who used it in the same way, but did at length make it public.[40] This does not sound as if Wang Ch'ung's book was well known at an early date.

The great new influence on Chinese thought, which began to make itself felt in Han times, was Buddhism. And it pointed in a direction almost diametrically opposed to that of the thought of Wang Ch'ung.

Chapter X

Buddhism and Neo-Confucianism

UNTIL around the beginning of the Christian Era, Chinese civilization was probably more isolated than any other great culture. This is not to say that, despite difficult seas, lofty mountains, and barren lands inhabited by inhospitable peoples, certain cultural influences did not seep in from outside. They did, and they were important—how important only future study can tell us.

Nevertheless, speaking generally we can say that Chinese thought, until around the beginning of the Christian Era, bears a peculiarly Chinese stamp. The student of Western philosophy who studies Indian thought finds much that is new, but by no means everything is totally unfamiliar. The metaphysical subtleties to which he is accustomed are there—if anything, in forms of even greater complexity. But the Western philosopher who studies early Chinese thought may be inclined to deny that it is philosophy at all. Certainly one has to admit that it is a very different kind of philosophy, which usually stays very close to the ground of human life here and now and to human problems.

We have reached a point in history when this will no longer be the case. Around the beginning of the Christian Era, Buddhism spread to China from India. This meant far more than the mere coming of a religion. For some Chinese it meant a new way of life. For all Chinese, whether they accepted Buddhism or rejected it, it meant that henceforward the world would be looked at in new ways, and the universe conceived to be quite a different thing from what it had been. The whole Chinese manner of thinking was to some extent changed, so gradually and so universally that very few people knew what was happening. For roughly a thousand years the Chinese mind was largely dominated by Buddhism.

If the Buddhist view of the world is different from the Chinese, it is also different from our own. To understand it we must look briefly at the way it came into being and at the history of the people who created it.

Our earliest knowledge of Indian history comes from the hymns that make up the Vedas. They were written by a people known as the Indo-Aryans, who were related to the Iranians. Their language, called "Vedic Sanskrit," belonged to the Indo-European family of languages and thus was related to all the principal languages of Europe. These people are believed to have moved into India from the northwest, at some time perhaps in the neighborhood of 2000 B.C. They are thought to have been tall and fair-skinned; as they spread down into India, they came into contact with the short, dark Dravidian people of the region. The earliest culture that we know from the Vedas is one in which men lived heartily and joyously, without the weariness of life that came to dominate Hinduism a little later. Yet even in this early day we find certain attributes that are to persist. These Indians put tremendous emphasis on their religion. And even the earliest Veda asks whether in the beginning there was being, or not being.[1]

As Hinduism developed, several characteristics became prominent. Perhaps the most basic idea of all is that of reincarnation. It was (and still is) generally believed in India that the life that one now lives is only one in a great series of lives that extends far back into the past. One may formerly have been, and may again be in the future, incarnated as an animal or even as a god, or at least a godlike being.

Since one may be reborn in various forms and places, there must be a cause for these differences. There is; and quite fairly and logically the Hindus say that this cause is the sum total of one's deeds in his past existences. Since the Sanskrit word for "deed" is *karma*, this idea is known as the doctrine of karma.

What one is, whether an animal, an angel, or a man, and whether of high or low caste, depends upon his accumulated karma, the balance of the account of the good and bad deeds that he has performed in previous existences.

The techniques of salvation to be found in Hinduism are many, but the goal, at least for the more intellectual, is one. We might suppose that it would be to cause one's self to be born as a man of the highest caste or as a god. But it is not. It is called by many names—the Buddhists call it "nirvana"—and it may be interpreted in various ways, but the goal is essentially a state in which *one is not born again at all.*

Why? Because even the best life is characterized by a great deal of suffering and because, moreover, this ceaseless round of rebirths keeps one in a constant state of change, giving nothing to satisfy the craving for permanence which, to the Indian at least, is imperative. Is this release from rebirth extinction? It is not usually so understood. Sometimes it is explained as identification with the supreme soul of the universe and as a condition of unchanging bliss. In any case, however, it must be so different from anything that we know that it is a virtual extinction of all that we are now, even if it can be said that we continue in another state.

How can the Indians desire this? On first consideration it seems incomprehensible, pessimistic, even morbid. Why should people not want to live any more? We must remember, however, what the Indians believe to be the alternative—an endless succession of rebirths, lives, and deaths. One Indian philosopher took the relatively optimistic view that all, fools and the wise alike, would find release after wandering through eight million four hundred thousand births.[2] That prospect is a little staggering. How many of us would be willing to live over again the painful years of adjustment that we went through in adolescence, in this single life? Multiply that by infinity, and it is easier to understand the Indian point of view.

Much, though not all, of Hindu thought asserts that the only true reality is the supreme being, with which the individual soul is actually identified if it could only realize that fact; it follows that the world as we know it is merely an illusion. Whether agreeing with this idea or not, Hinduism in general has a strong tendency to regard life in this world as unimportant, as being, as one scholar has put it, "a shadow play without even a plot."[3]

As means of salvation, sacrifice and ritual have been important since the time of the Vedas. Asceticism, self-mortification, is also mentioned in those early hymns and has continued important ever since. This is not merely a matter of doing penance for past sins; asceticism is conceived as having a positive value in itself. The ascetic is believed to acquire power by his austerities, and it is even related that certain deities produced the world by means of asceticism. The highest path to salvation, however, is that of knowledge. But this knowledge is not the sort that is taught in most universities, but knowledge of the highest things. It comes not merely through study but also, and especially, through meditation. By meditation you are supposed to come to realize that you—even you—are identical with the supreme reality of the universe. This is the idea expressed by the famous statement of one of the Upanishads: "That art Thou."

To describe Hinduism at all is extremely difficult, because variety and toleration of differences are among its principal characteristics. If this thumbnail sketch of a few of its attributes has made it appear either absurd or naïve, the fault lies in the description. Hindu metaphysics is so sophisticated that it makes one dizzy; it would seem to have explored every possible position, from pantheism to complete atheism and materialism. An Indian agnostic is not content simply to assert that we have no certain knowledge. One of them refused to say, as regards the question of whether good and bad actions bring consequences, either that they do, that they do not, that they *both* do and do not, *or* that they *neither* do nor do not.[4]

It is against the background of Hinduism that we must understand the rise of Buddhism. It is generally agreed that the individual known as "the Buddha" was a man who really lived, although there is much difference of opinion even among scholars about some of the facts of his life. The tradition of southern Buddhism dates his birth in 623 B.C., but most scholars seem to agree that he lived from about 560 to about 480 B.C. If so, he was a slightly older contemporary of Confucius; but it is most unlikely that either man ever heard of the other. Scholars differ even as to what were the essentials of his teaching. All we can do is to pick our way carefully among those portions of the tradition that most scholars seem to accept as valid. For our present purpose the nature of the tradition itself is important.

The family name of the Buddha, by which he is often called, was Gautama. He was the son of the ruler of a small state in northern India. He married and had a son; but at the age of twenty-nine, according to tradition, he gave up his ordinary life and left home to pursue a religious life. This was not an unusual thing to do in India at that time; many members of the upper classes became religious wanderers. He studied with two teachers successively, practicing meditation and asceticism, but was not satisfied that the way of either would certainly lead to salvation. He wandered on, seeking the true path. He fasted until he was nearly dead, but to no avail. Finally, while sitting under the famous "tree of enlightenment," he went through several stages of meditation, at the end of which he could say: "Rebirth has been destroyed. . . . I have no more to do with this world." He had become "the Buddha," that is to say, "the Enlightened One." He had apparently entered nirvana even in this life, and in any case would not be born again.

At first he despaired of being able to communicate to others the truth that he had discovered. At length, however, he became convinced that it was his duty to try to enlighten others, and he did so.

His doctrine, as it is set forth in various scriptures, is based on the law of causation. Existence is an evil to be got rid of. What causes existence? Desire, the clinging to life and the things of sense. Exterminate this desire and clinging, and one will be free from the round of existence. To the end of one's life, then, one is simply to practice celibacy, good deeds, and contemplation, and at death (if not before) one will enter nirvana. Those who embarked upon such a life and became members of the order were monks; Gautama later permitted women to become nuns, though he did this with great reluctance. The laity were not members of the order but acquired merit by supporting monks and nuns. Laymen had a much simpler code of conduct to follow; they must not take life, drink intoxicants, lie, steal, or be unchaste. While the layman may hope for nirvana, it is also right for him to aim at rebirth in a temporary heaven.

It is not to be supposed that Buddhism was long, if ever, without those trappings of mythology that are seldom lacking from any religion. The Buddha was early, and perhaps from the start, regarded as a miraculous being. Nevertheless, if one accepts the basic postulate of reincarnation, early Buddhism was a relatively simple and rational doctrine. This kind of Buddhism is often called (for reasons we shall consider shortly) "Hinayana Buddhism." There is some reason to believe that this is the kind of Buddhism that was first known in China.

We do not know how and when Buddhism first reached China; we do know that the traditionally accepted account of this event is incorrect. It has often been pointed out that there are similarities between the Taoist thought of the *Lao Tzŭ* and the *Chuang Tzŭ*, and ideas to be found in some Indian works. Passages in Buddhist books can be cited which show great resemblances to them. It is quite possible that Indian ideas did enter China early enough to influence these Taoist works, but for detailed proof on this score we must await future investigation. We have evidence, however, that Buddhism was known in China by about the beginning of the Christian Era.

There is a very interesting work called *Mou Tzŭ*, after its author, which was probably written around A.D. 200.* Mou Tzŭ was a Chinese scholar who knew the Confucian classics extremely well. He also studied Taoism, and finally became a Buddhist. But Mou Tzŭ himself tells us that Buddhism was not well considered in China in his day by men of the world and scholars at the court. Mou Tzŭ felt that he himself was looked upon as a heretic. For this reason he wrote his book, in dialogue form, to explain and defend Buddhism.

He lists the current Chinese objections to it: It is a barbarian doctrine. Reincarnation is improbable. Filial piety requires that one leave one's body intact and have posterity, but Buddhist monks shave their heads and are at least supposed to be celibate (Mou Tzŭ admits that not all of them are really so). If Buddha is really the greatest teacher, why did not the sages, Yao, Shun, and Confucius, follow him? Mou Tzŭ parries these and many other objections with great skill, showing himself adept at quoting the Confucian classics for his purpose. He has not abandoned Confucius, he insists, by becoming a Buddhist. The Confucian classics are the flowers, but Buddhism is the fruit.

What is most remarkable is Mou Tzŭ's constant quotation from the *Lao Tzŭ* in support of Buddhism. For the Buddhist "nirvana" he uses the term *wu wei*, which as we saw earlier is a Taoist expression meaning "nonaction." He uses other Taoist terms, too, in his exposition of Buddhism. In fact, Mou Tzŭ seems to regard Buddhism as simply an older and ampler form of the Taoist doctrine.

Taoism and Buddhism were commonly associated in the Chinese mind. Many Taoist terms were used in translating Buddhist scriptures, and many Chinese studied Taoism and

* Paul Pelliot wrote an Introduction to this work and translated it under the title "Meou-tseu ou les doutes levés," in *T'oung Pao*, XIX (Leyden, 1920), 255–433. There is some difference of opinion concerning the date of this work (see *ibid.*, pp. 258–66 and 429–33). Pelliot, although admitting the possibility that it may be a forgery, thought that it was probably a genuine work of the end of the second century A.D.

Buddhism together. The Buddhists were often quite tolerant of Taoism and sometimes even included Taoist deities in their temples.

Taoism, which in late Chou and Han times had absorbed a vast amount of Chinese magical practices and popular religion, copied Buddhism by establishing temples, monks, nuns, scriptures, and doctrines which in many respects are astonishingly similar. The Taoists, however, were not so tolerant of the Buddhists as the Buddhists were of them; perhaps their extensive borrowing from Buddhism left them with a bad conscience. The Taoists said that Lao Tzŭ had gone to India and taught the Buddha, so that Buddhism was nothing more than an offshoot of Taoism. The Buddhists and the Taoists were commonly rivals for influence at the Chinese court, and Taoists were very often the instigators of moves by the government to curb Buddhism in China.

We have seen that early Buddhism is sometimes called "Hinayana Buddhism." This name was given to it by the advocates of a variety of Buddhism developed later, which they called "Mahayana." This means "great vehicle"; they patronizingly called the earlier form "Hinayana," "lesser vehicle," to distinguish it. The Mahayana was developed in India, possibly around the beginning of the Christian Era. Its most essential difference is the place it gives to the *bodhisattva*, literally, "being of enlightenment." A bodhisattva is a being who has qualified to enter nirvana and become a Buddha, but who voluntarily renounces this privilege in order to remain among the still unenlightened beings of the universe and work for their salvation. He is a heroic figure, reverenced and even worshiped for his suffering, toil, and compassion for others. The Mahayana Buddhists consider the striving for personal attainment of nirvana that characterized the Hinayana to be selfish.

In general, Mahayana Buddhism caters to the popular tastes, developing to the highest degree those superstitious and mythological elements which were not pronounced in early Buddhism.

We also find in the Mahayana a great deal of metaphysical speculation, dealing with the sort of subjects that the Buddha refused to discuss because, he said, they were unprofitable. The embarrassing problem of the difference between the two teachings is dealt with openly in one of the most famous Mahayana scriptures. It quotes the Buddha himself as saying that he had at first taught only the Hinayana doctrine because men were not yet ready for the superior truth of the Mahayana.[5]

It appears that the first Buddhist scriptures translated into Chinese were Hinayana, but some Mahayana materials were translated as early as the second century A.D., and most of the translations after the fifth century were Mahayana.

Although Buddhism was known in China by the beginning of the Christian Era and perhaps even earlier, it appears to have had little influence in Chinese scholarly circles for several centuries. In Chinese literature it seems to have been mentioned very little until the third century. Among the masses, however, it was spreading. An especially fertile field for propagation of the new faith was provided by the peoples from the north and west who invaded China and carved out states over which they ruled as conquerors. Some of their rulers became devout converts, and it is said that by 381 nine-tenths of the people of northwest China were Buddhists.[6] The famous Indian monk Kumarajiva was made a government official at Hsian shortly after 400; he organized a bureau, numbering hundreds of monks in its personnel, which translated ninety-four Buddhist texts under his supervision. At about this same time a Chinese emperor, whose domain was now limited to southern China, became a Buddhist.

A century later Emperor Wu (reigned 502–49), the founder of the Liang dynasty, began his reign as a Confucian, but after a few years he was converted to Buddhism. He publicly lectured on Buddhist scriptures, collected the first Chinese Buddhist canon, wrote on Buddhism, and three times retired to a monastery. He also issued edicts forbidding the sacrificing of animals, which is against the Buddhist doctrine of noninjury.

In later Chinese history a number of emperors and empresses were Buddhists.

Temples and monks multiplied rapidly, and the faithful deeded over a vast amount of land to the temples. This withdrawal of large numbers of citizens from production and of large tracts of land from the tax rolls caused severe misgivings in official circles. In 845 an emperor devoted to Taoism decreed that more than 40,000 Buddhist temples be demolished, 260,000 monks and nuns be secularized, 150,000 temple slaves be set free, and a tremendous acreage of land belonging to the temples be confiscated. These figures may be exaggerated, but they emphasize that Chinese Buddhism had achieved huge proportions. Neither this nor occasional other attempts at repression succeeded in destroying it.

It was not only the humble and the emperors who became Buddhists. As the movement gained momentum, during the first millennium of the Christian Era, the best minds turned more and more to Buddhism. In the eleventh century the famous reformer statesman Wang An-shih (whose tablet was placed in the Confucian temple next to that of Mencius after his death) deplored the fact that scholars turned to Buddhism and Taoism for ideas; nevertheless, his own son wrote books on both Taoism and Buddhism.[7] In the twelfth century Chu Hsi, who is considered the fountainhead of recent Confucian orthodoxy, asserted that educated men had found themselves compelled to turn to Taoism and Buddhism for religious and ethical conceptions.[8]

Perhaps the most striking indication of the influence of Buddhism is the fact that, while a few Confucian scholars continued to deprecate it as a foreign superstition, Confucian temples from the eighth to the sixteenth centuries contained images of Confucius, his disciples, and other worthies in an arrangement remarkably similar to that of the images in a Buddhist temple. John K. Shryock says of this similarity that it is "difficult to assume it as a coincidence."[9]

This rapid and extensive success of Buddhism is surprising.

There are many things in Buddhism that one would expect to have been distasteful to the Chinese. They were; even the book by the Buddhist scholar Mou Tzŭ tells us so. But there were even more compelling attractions. Some of them are fairly obvious.

It is not mere coincidence that the period of the tremendous growth of Chinese Buddhism was one in which the Chinese world was exceedingly troubled. We have seen that the later days of the Han dynasty, in the second century A.D., were anything but placid. Intellectuals took refuge in a sort of nihilism or in Taoist mysticism. The common people, ground between the oppression of the officials and that of the great landed proprietors, fell more and more into the ranks of the landless proletariat, if not of slaves.

These miserable masses were swept together in a Taoist movement that preached the advent of an age of prosperity and equality. They were organized into rustic communities with common meals and public confession of sins, and were prepared for military action. In 184 these "Yellow Turbans," as they are called, took up arms and gained control of a large proportion of China. In a single year a half-million persons are said to have been killed. The revolt was quelled, but it plunged the country into civil war that lasted for a generation and transformed China, as one scholar has said, "from a powerful empire into one vast cemetery."[10] China was divided into three states, and a century later the barbarian invasions began. Between A.D. 220 and 589, there was only one brief period of twenty-four years in which China was united; at some times it was divided into a number of states, all mutually hostile.

It is not remarkable that in such a world many sought refuge in Buddhism. Mou Tzŭ, the Chinese Buddhist author whom we considered earlier, tells us that in late Han times, after the rebellion of the Yellow Turbans, many persons who could fled to southwestern China, which was relatively calm, and there many immersed themselves in Taoism. Mou Tzŭ was one of these refugees, and he says frankly that he turned to Buddhism in fleeing the evils of this world.

The Buddhist monastery must have seemed a divine haven in such times. There one did not need to worry about the world's insoluble problems, but only to read the scriptures, perform the ritual, and meditate. One did not even have to work, since support would be provided by the laity. If one were a sincere believer, he was certain of peace of mind, and one could hope that his monastery would remain an island of peace even while wars raged about it.

Only a few could become monks or nuns, but everybody could be a lay Buddhist. This was rather a new thing. To get much satisfaction from Confucianism one needed to be able to read fairly well. In Taoism the goal was to become an immortal, but only a few rare spirits could attain this. In Buddhism, however, and especially in its Mahayana aspects, absolutely everybody could win a very satisfying degree of salvation. Of course, one would have to wait until after death for it, but traditional Chinese thought had been almost silent on life after death. Buddhism offered at least a hope, and at times when men were living in a hell on earth it was much to be able to hope for heaven after death. In any case, it was something that even the humblest individual could hope to win *for himself.*

Powerful bodhisattvas stood ready and even anxious to help him. One of them, male in India, has been transformed in China into a feminine figure, whom Lewis Hodous has called "the most popular goddess in China." He says of this bodhisattva (Kuan Yin, commonly called "the Goddess of Mercy") that "her image is found in almost every household and her temples have a place in every part of China."[11] (I confess that some of the small representations of this goddess, exquisitely rendered in wood, ivory, or porcelain, are so beautiful and appealing as almost to convert me to Buddhism.)

Then there is Amitabha, one of the many Buddhas, who was so compassionate that he refused to become a Buddha except on condition that he could apportion his vast store of accumulated merit to others as he chose. For this reason those who live righteously, or meditate properly on Amitabha, or even (according to the most optimistic interpretation) make a single invocation of his name, will be born after death into his paradise, which is called "the Land of Pure Delight."[12]

This is not nirvana, of course, but only a stage toward it. However, the time spans in Buddhism are so inconceivably long that most people do not worry about this point. Another interesting figure is the Buddha who is to come, whose image holds a bag containing future happiness for all. He laughs because he knows, no matter how bad things may look now, how wonderful everything will be in the blessed future.

Buddhism in China has not only offered salvation to the good and the faithful but has also portrayed in graphic terms the tortures that await the wicked in the multiplicity of Buddhist hells. But here again it offers a way out. These torments are not permanent, but only a series of purgatories; by an elaborate series of ceremonies it is possible to help those one loves to pass through them quickly. Services for the dead have been important in China from time immemorial; Buddhism succeeded in making for itself a large place in the performance of this age-old function.

Buddhism appealed not only to men's minds and hearts but also to their eyes. Towering pagodas and temples of noble proportions impress even the unbeliever. We are likely to think of "idols" as gross representations designed only to impose upon the credulous, but historians of art tell us that the best Chinese Buddhist sculpture was much more than this. J. LeRoy Davidson writes that "it is only in China in the fifth century that conventional restraint and religious fervor blended to produce a perfect balance between the human representation and the Buddhist idealization which conveys with a minimum of distraction and a maximum of power the generalized spirit of the most profound concepts of the teaching. . . . The icons are as human as they must be for mass recognition. They are dehumanized in repeated rhythms so that the worshipper is carried beyond them to the abstractions they represent."[13]

The Chinese are tolerant. They see nothing wrong in taking part in ceremonies in a Buddhist, a Taoist, and a Confucian temple on the same day. Buddhists are tolerant too. We have noted their attitude toward Taoism. They said that a certain bodhisattva was an incarnation of Confucius, and Lewis Hodous reports that there was at one time "a Buddhist temple to Confucius" in Shantung.[14] The Chinese deity "Heaven" is honored in certain Buddhist ceremonies.[15] The virtue of filial piety was not wholly lacking even in Indian Buddhism;[16] but in China it was accorded a special emphasis in keeping with the customs of the country. Buddhist temples have been built to accord with the Chinese system of magical ideas, involving the five forces and so forth, known as *fêng shui*.

It would be a great error to suppose that all Chinese Buddhists have been ignorant folk ensnared by talk of magic and naïve superstitions. I have had the privilege of being rather intimately acquainted with a Chinese scholar who was a devout Buddhist, a most intelligent man who was by no means without a sense of humor. He never talked about his religion, but it gave him a serenity and a gentleness that were as impressive as they were unobtrusive.

The ethical code of Buddhism is one which, with slight exception, would win the approval of moral men everywhere. The ethics of Buddhism, quite as much as its spectacular promises, has been important in winning over the Chinese.

Even among the different sects of Christianity there are numerous doctrines that appeal to a variety of temperaments. In Buddhism this is even more true. One strain of thought in Indian Buddhism, which was brought to China by a famous monk in the seventh century, attained a highly rarefied plane of metaphysical reflection. As Clarence H. Hamilton explains it, it taught that "the universe is mental representation only," and sought "to prove that the seemingly external, substantial world is but the fabrication of our own consciousness, the purpose being to free us from the fear of it and from attachment to it."[17] Its technique was, at least in part, that of meditation.

Such subtle metaphysics seems to have had only a limited appeal in China. Another strain of thought, which also gave the primary emphasis to meditation, came to have a more pervasive influence not only upon Buddhism but upon all Chinese thought. Its name comes from a Sanskrit word meaning "meditation," translated into Chinese and then into Japanese; in the West it is almost universally known by the Japanese term as "Zen Buddhism."

Even to begin to explain Zen properly would require an entire book and far more wisdom than the author of this one can command. The history of Zen in China is disputed and need not concern us. A part of its background would seem to lie in teachings like those of a Chinese monk who flourished around 400, who declared that the world of Buddha is not some distant "Pure Land," but the world around us; that all sentient beings possess the Buddha-nature; and that all, even opponents of Buddhism, may attain Buddhahood by sudden enlightenment, if they only realize this fact.

As Zen developed it was believed that enlightenment could be attained by practices of meditation learned from India, such, for instance, as contemplating a blank wall. One influential school taught that no special technique was necessary; one need only act straightforwardly and intelligently. If a disciple of a Zen master asked the meaning of the Buddhist Trinity, he might be told, "Corn, wheat, and beans," or he might be given a box on the ear. He was expected to think things out for himself. There was a tendency to discard externals, even the scriptures. Zen monks participated in the manual labor of the monastery. Hu Shih writes: "The Zen

monasteries were the great centres of philosophical speculation and discussion throughout the 9th and 10th centuries.
It was not until Zennism had superseded practically all the
other sects that the Zennist monasteries came to take up the
older rituals and worships which they, as publicly supported
institutions, were now expected to perform."[18]

Iconoclasm sometimes went far. A monk is said to have entered a temple and spat on the image of Buddha; when reproached, he said: "Please show me a place to spit where
there is no Buddha." Another, one cold night, chopped up
a wooden image of Buddha for firewood. Here are some
of the pungent sayings of a famous ninth-century monk, as
translated by Hu Shih:

"The wise seek not the Buddha. The Buddha is the great murderer who has seduced so many people into the pitfall of the pros-
tituting Devil." "The old Barbarian rascal [the Buddha] claims that
he had survived the destruction of three worlds. Where is he now?
Did he not also die after 80 years of age? Was he in any way different from you?" "O ye wise men, disengage your body and your
mind! Give up all and free yourself from all bondages."

"Here in my place, there is not a single truth for you to take
home. I myself don't know what Zen is. I am no teacher, knowing
nothing at all. I am only an old beggar who begs his food and clothing and daily moves his bowels. What else have I to do? But allow
me to tell you: Have nothing to do; go and take an early rest!"[19]

Karl L. Reichelt says that the leaders of the most famous
school of Zen in China "have constantly maintained that man
in himself has the powers which are needed to attain sanctifica-
tion, and can himself create his own happiness and overcome
his difficulties, if only he has the right view of the true
character of his human nature."[20]

It is perfectly obvious that all this is remarkably similar
to early Taoist philosophy, as we find it for instance in the
Lao Tzŭ and the *Chuang Tzŭ*. It is perhaps even more striking-
ly similar to some Taoist philosophy that we find in late Han
times. There is general agreement that at least some degree
of Taoist influence is apparent in Zen, and it has been alleged

that Zen is not really Buddhism at all, but a revolt against it. Can we say, then, that the Chinese reply to the challenge of Buddhism came within this very influential Buddhist school itself? There may be some truth to this. But it is also true that, while Zen discards many of the trappings of the Mahayana, much of what is left is remarkably like early Indian Buddhism. Indeed, it seems probable that the original teaching of Gautama, who said that each man must find nirvana for himself, was in many ways extraordinarily similar to Zen.

We have seen that by late Han times Confucianism had become thoroughly impregnated with Taoist metaphysics, and that it strongly emphasized tradition and antique ritual. It had not completely lost its historic role as champion of the common people. But it fulfilled it so ineffectively that the oppressed masses turned for relief rather to the kind of Taoist doctrine that was preached by the Yellow Turbans, who promised an era of unheard-of peace and happiness. When this dream of heaven on earth proved illusory, most Chinese, during the troubled centuries that followed, accepted the Buddhist promise of happiness after death. This, at least, could not be proved false. From the third through the sixth century A.D. Buddhism was the dominant intellectual force in China, followed by its Chinese imitator, Taoism. Even those scholars who continued to study the Confucian classics seem to have become deeply tinged with Taoism and Buddhism.

Some study of the classics did continue, however, and when China was again unified under the T'ang dynasty (618–906), the official bureaucracy came to be recruited in considerable part by competitive examinations based principally on the Confucian classics. In this period, while Buddhism was enjoying its peak of influence and official favor, Confucianism began the remarkable resurgence that was ultimately to eclipse, in intellectual influence, the imported doctrine.

By the compensatory process that often operates, the very

success of Buddhism caused it to become identified with various political and economic abuses. Powerful monks, enjoying favor at court and controlling vast properties, sometimes found it quite unnecessary to be bound by the moral code of the order. These things naturally brought Buddhism into ill repute. At the same time the Confucians, almost shorn of prestige and influence, could no longer bask in the complacency that had characterized their predecessors of Han times. Confucianism gradually acquired a new standing as the doctrine of those who sought reform, not only in philosophy but also in the realm of practical affairs.

Despite the tremendous success of Buddhism in China, it would seem that in a sense it was always somewhat alien to the Chinese mind, which is normally practical, a bit skeptical, and eminently this-worldly. We have seen that in Zen even Chinese Buddhism discarded much of the trappings of the Mahayana and came to be much like early Taoism. Nevertheless, the wholly devoted practitioner of Zen had to become a monk, though it is a little hard to see why, on its philosophical premises, this is so.

In T'ang times we find a famous Confucian scholar asserting that by means of such techniques as meditation one may attain enlightenment and become, not a Buddha, but a Sage. While doing this, however, one does not retire from, but continues fully to participate in, the family, the government, and the usual activities of a moral man. Here we have Zen carried to what would probably seem to most Chinese minds its logical conclusion. This did not lead to the attainment of nirvana, but an essential characteristic of nirvana was freedom from rebirth, and traditional Chinese thought had never believed in rebirth anyway.

If Gautama, the Buddha, had ever crossed the mountains and preached his doctrine to Confucius, Confucius would probably have replied somewhat as follows: "What you say is interesting, and may be true. But your doctrine of reincarnation would require a great deal of proof, which I do not see how you can provide. A part of your ethics is admirable, but taken as a whole your program offers little or nothing to remedy the grave political, social, and economic problems by which men are oppressed. On the contrary, it would probably make them worse."

To the Chinese of Confucius' day this argument would have carried conviction. By the T'ang dynasty, however, the Chinese in general had become so accustomed to the complexities of Buddhist—and Taoist—cosmological theories that a simple and matter-of-fact philosophy seemed to them to lack something. One could not hope to wean them away from such doctrines except by a bold frontal attack on the whole metaphysical system. The time came, as we shall see, when a few Confucians made such an attack, but the time was not yet.

During the Sung dynasty, which lasted from 960 to 1279, there arose what is commonly called "Neo-Confucianism." Its beginnings quite clearly go back to the T'ang period. Neo-Confucianism sought to show that Confucianism could offer everything desirable that Buddhism could, and more. Specifically it undertook, first, to match the Buddhist cosmology; second, to explain the world and the Confucian ethics metaphysically; and finally, while doing these things, to justify social and political activity and to vindicate men's right to find happiness in the ordinary pursuits of the normal life.

Cosmology and metaphysics could not easily be derived from the statements of Confucius in the *Analects*. A few Neo-Confucians even said, as some practitioners of Zen did within Buddhism, that the authority of the scriptures was not of crucial importance. In general, however, it was found possible to read everything necessary into the words of Confucius by rather elaborate interpretations.

In dealing with the philosophy of Mencius we noted that certain of his ideas diverge considerably from the matter-of-fact attitude of Confucius and embody an almost mystical element that points toward Taoist thought. It was to Mencius and to works that show the influence of his thinking that the Neo-Confucians appealed especially. This tendency was already present in T'ang times, and in the Sung period it led to the establishment of the so-called "Four Books" as the peculiarly sacred scriptures of Neo-Confucianism. These consisted of the *Analects*, the *Mencius*, the *Great Learning*, and the *Doctrine of the Mean*. The latter two works had previously existed simply as two chapters in the classic called the *Records on Ceremonial*. We do not know exactly when they were written, but it has been plausibly suggested that at least parts of each of them were inspired by the ideas of Mencius. Just as the Zen Buddhists claimed that their doctrine was an esoteric teaching of the Buddha, not imparted to the common herd, so certain Neo-Confucians maintained that the *Doctrine of the Mean* embodied the esoteric teaching of Confucius.

Compelled to offer a cosmology that could compete with that of the Buddhists, the Neo-Confucians took over bodily some of the ideas of their rivals. Thus we find them echoing the Buddhist idea that the universe is ceaselessly destroyed and re-created. This is interpreted in Chinese terms, however, as a function of the operation of the *yin* and *yang*, the five forces, mystic numerology, and the diagrams which are the basis of the *Book of Changes*.

We have seen that this fortune-teller's manual, alien in its whole purport to the thought of Confucius and to early Confucianism, was probably first espoused and expanded in circles heavily tinged with Taoist thought. But as Confucianism was infiltrated by a type of complex metaphysical speculation, more and more Confucians took up the *Book of Changes*, and by Han times Confucius was even believed to have written its appendixes. Such a work, sanctified by tradition with the blessing of Confucius himself, was of course a godsend to the Neo-Confucians. For many of them it became a virtual bible.

Later Taoism, especially after it was influenced by Buddhism, had developed an elaborate cosmology based on the *Book of Changes,* and there is no doubt that this influenced those Neo-Confucians who developed a very similar cosmology based on the same book. In fact, Fung Yu-lan has shown that the very *Diagram of the Supreme Ultimate,* which was accepted as a fundamental exposition of cosmology by all Sung Neo-Confucians (even though they might differ about its meaning), is almost identical with a diagram published in a Taoist work of earlier date.[21] One school of Neo-Confucianism accused its principal rival of deriving inspiration from Taoism; the rival school retorted that the doctrine of its accuser had more resemblance to Zen Buddhism than to Confucianism. In fact, both schools were influenced by both Taoism and Buddhism.

There were many varieties of Sung Neo-Confucianism, but two schools predominated. The leader of one of these schools, the most famous of all Neo-Confucians and the most influential single Chinese philosopher during the last thousand years, was Chu Hsi, who lived from 1130 to 1200.

Chu Hsi came of a literary family, and even as a boy he was a serious student. While quite young he studied Taoism and Buddhism; it has been alleged, though there is doubt of this, that he once became a Buddhist monk. In any case he early became a firm Confucian. He held official posts of considerable importance, and in these he made a special point of strengthening education in the colleges. He had many students, and his recorded conversations with them reveal a strong, versatile intelligence and an attractive personality. He wrote extensively. His commentaries on a number of the most important classics were officially approved, as embodying the interpretations to be considered as correct in the government examinations, from 1313 until the examinations were abolished in 1905.

Chu Hsi brought together ideas developed by a number of predecessors in the Neo-Confucian movement, combined them with his own genius, and elaborated a philosophic system.

Probably its most central conception is that of "principle," *li*. Although in modern Chinese this is pronounced identically with the *li* meaning "ceremony," the characters, 理 and 禮, are quite different, and the terms should not be confused. The term *li* which means "principle" appears to have been taken over from the *Book of Changes*.

All existent things are made up, Chu Hsi affirmed, of "principle" plus *ch'i*. The term *ch'i* cannot really be translated, but is somewhat like our idea of "substance." Thus a leaf and a flower are different because their *ch'i* is governed by different *li* ("principles"). All things (even bricks) consist both of *ch'i* and of the *li* which give them their form; yet in a sense the *li* are prior, since they existed before any objects had come into being. Relationships, such as that between father and son, have their *li* also.

Principles or *li*, Chu Hsi says, are "without birth and indestructible." They never change in any way. They are all really part of the one great *li*, the Supreme Ultimate, which Chu Hsi sometimes equates with the *Tao*. Chu Hsi conceived of *li* as composing a kind of world of its own that is "pure, empty, vast, without form ... and unable to create anything."[22] Western thought has often conceived of matter as being inert, but Chu Hsi believed that *ch'i* (which most nearly corresponds to our idea of matter) was alone responsible for the production of existent things and for change. In this he was undoubtedly influenced by the Indian idea that only that which is permanent and unchanging is good in the highest sense.

Man's nature, according to Chu Hsi, is his *li*, which is a part of the Supreme Ultimate. Thus the *li* of all men is the same, but unfortunately their *ch'i* ("substance") is not. If one's *ch'i* is impure, one is foolish and degenerate, as if a pearl (one's *li*) lay concealed in muddy water (the impure *ch'i*). One must get rid of the impediment of this cloudy *ch'i* and recapture one's original nature, in which (as Mencius said) there are present the four fundamental virtues of benevolence, righteousness, the *li* that means ceremony or courtesy, and wisdom. Of the beclouding of the pearl which is man's nature Chu Hsi said: "If one could but realize that it is human desire that thus obscures his true nature, he would be enlightened."[23] In some respects this is remarkably similar to the doctrines of Gautama and of Zen Buddhism.

The reader will also have noticed the resemblance between Chu Hsi's conception of *li* or "principle" and the doctrine of "ideas" or "forms" in the dialogues of Plato. At some points the similarities are remarkable, as, for instance, in the *Phaedo*, where Socrates is quoted as saying that the mind best perceives absolute truth "when she takes leave of the body, and has as little as possible to do with it, when she has no bodily sense or desire, but is aspiring after true being."[24]

There is a famous passage in the *Great Learning* which was considered important as early as T'ang times and has continued, variously interpreted, to be emphasized in Neo-Confucian philosophy up to our own day. It reads:

Those who anciently wished to exemplify illustrious virtue to the whole world, first ordered well their own states. Wishing to order well their states, they first regulated their families. Wishing to regulate their families, they first cultivated their own characters. Wishing to cultivate their characters, they first rectified their hearts. Wishing to rectify their hearts, they first made their thoughts sincere. Wishing to make their thoughts sincere, they first extended their knowledge to the utmost. This extending of their knowledge to the utmost lay in the investigation of things.[25]

Chu Hsi laid great stress on "the investigation of things" as the means of attaining moral understanding. "When one has worked at this for a long time," he wrote, "a day will dawn when suddenly everything will become clear . . . and the mind and its operations will be completely enlightened."[26] The resemblance of this to Zen is, of course, considerable.

In the political sphere there is, Chu Hsi said, a *li* or principle that establishes the ideal type of political conduct. This is the *Tao*, the Way. When the actual government corresponds to this ideal government, it is good; when it differs from it, it is bad. But although this *Tao* was not made by men and is eternal and indestructible, Chu Hsi declared that it had not been permitted to operate in the world for the last fifteen hundred years, which would mean since about the time of Confucius. The ruler ought to extend his knowledge by the investigation of things until he becomes a sage. An esoteric doctrine explaining how to be a proper ruler was handed down, Chu Hsi said, by the sage-kings of old, but more recent rulers have all become fettered by human desire.[27]

So much of this philosophy seems quite alien to early Chinese thought that it would be easy to conclude that the Neo-Confucians have been converted to Buddhism in everything but name. Yet have they? Where is reincarnation? Where are the Buddhist heavens and the Buddhist hells? Where is the conviction that this life is only a relatively unimportant incident, if not in fact an illusion? None of these things, so fundamental for Buddhism, has any place in Neo-Confucianism. Its tone is not ascetic and pessimistic, but moderate and optimistic. It does not preach withdrawal from life and from the business of the world, but confident participation in them.

Unlike the Taoists, the Neo-Confucians do not seek immortality or fear death. For them death is a normal occurrence; when it comes, at the end of a long and full life, one recognizes that it is time to rest. Nor do they, like the Buddhists, consider life in this world to be an evil thing. Like Confucius himself, they believe that life is or ought to be a happy thing, for all men.

Chu Hsi's greatest rival, the leader of the other principal school of Sung Neo-Confucianism, was a man only a few years younger than himself. Chu Hsi gave systematic form to that current of Neo-Confucian thought which emphasized investigation of the objective world. Lu Hsiang-shan (1139–93) was the champion of the view that laid the chief stress on meditation and intuition. Although this emphasis resembles that of

Zen Buddhism, it already had a long history in Confucianism.

Confucius, with his characteristic balance, had warned against overemphasizing either study or thought. "Study without thought," he said, "is a waste of time. But thought without study is dangerous."[28] He reported that he had tried meditation as a means of seeking the truth, but found it to be useless. Instead, he recommended broad inquiry and experience, supplemented by a rational testing and arrangement of the facts that experience yields.[29]

Mencius, however, placed less emphasis on study and experience. He stated flatly that man is good by his very nature, and that if one desires to be virtuous he needs only to cultivate his original nature. Even the knowledge of right and wrong, Mencius said, is innate.[30] In the *Mencius* we read: "All things are complete within me." "By exhaustively examining one's own mind, one may understand his nature. One who understands his nature understands Heaven."[*]

It is evident that such ideas would be very useful to anyone who wished to erect, upon an orthodox Confucian foundation, a system of thought resembling that of Zen Buddhism. As early as the T'ang dynasty it was asserted that the pure Confucian tradition had ended with Mencius;[31] this of course excluded Hsün Tzŭ, who during Han times had been rather more highly esteemed in Confucian circles than Mencius. The emphasis was placed on meditation by the famous T'ang Confucian Li Ao, who quoted the *Book of Changes* to prove that one may attain enlightenment by a process of quiescent meditation in which one does not think.[32] His philosophy was based partly on the ideas of Mencius, and had a remarkable resemblance to Zen Buddhism.

Lu Hsiang-shan, who carried forward this stream of thought, was born in 1139, nine years after the birth of Chu Hsi. At

---

[*] *Mencius* 7(1)4.1, 7(1)1.1. As was indicated earlier, I feel uncertain whether this first portion of Book 7 really represents the thought of Mencius. But in any case it has been very generally accepted and quoted as genuine.

the age of thirty-four he passed the highest state examination, receiving the degree that is often translated as "the doctorate." His official career was passed in the Imperial Academy and later in minor government posts. As a magistrate he was so honest and effective that he was recommended for promotion, but he refused it. His greatest interest was always in teaching. When not in office he lectured at his native place, where a lecture hall was erected for him, and students came from great distances to listen. Even Chu Hsi is said to have admitted that most of the scholars of eastern China were disciples of Lu. The two eminent philosophers met and wrote letters to each other, in an effort to resolve the differences in their ideas, but finally they had to agree to disagree. Lu suffered from recurring illness. On January 3, 1193, he told his family, "I am dying." When they were distressed he told them to remember that, after all, death "is only a natural event." A week later he died.[33]

Perhaps the most basic difference between Chu Hsi and Lu lay in their metaphysics. Chu Hsi, as we have seen, believed that all things are composed of *li*, "principle," and *ch'i*, which is more or less akin to our idea of "substance." But Lu believed that everything that exists is nothing but *li*. Thus Lu is a monist, and certainly monistic thought as such seems to be more like early Chinese thought than does Chu Hsi's dualism. Yet the particular type of monism that Lu taught has much in common with some currents of Indian thought and with Zen Buddhism; and Chu Hsi's pupils attacked it on this ground.

Chu Hsi said that we should seek knowledge by "investigating things," not merely their *li* or principles. Our ultimate goal is to understand the *li*, but, in order to understand this abstraction, we must examine its concrete manifestations. Lu said, however, that since things are so numerous that we cannot investigate them all, what we should do is rather to investigate their *li* or principles. This is relatively easy, since all principles are really one, and one's own mind is one with the one great principle. In fact, he said, "the universe is my mind; my mind is the universe."[34] Thus as Mencius said, "All things are complete within me," and one who truly understands his own mind will understand everything.

The doctrine of the mind was an important point of difference between Lu and Chu Hsi. Chu Hsi said that man's nature is *li* ("principle"), but that the mind is composed of a combination of *li* and *ch'i* ("substance"). This must be so, he believed, because the mind is active and characterized by feelings and emotions, but *li* is pure, without consciousness, and eternally unchanging. Lu, however, like Mencius, was more interested in ethics than in metaphysics, and he says that the nature, mind, and feelings are all the same thing seen from different aspects. Thus, like Mencius, he believes that the process of moral cultivation consists in looking for one's "lost mind," that is, one's true nature, which was originally good.

Lu also resembles Mencius in his doctrine of evil. Chu Hsi had explained evil as arising from differences in men's *ch'i*, their "substance" (this also was like *one* of Mencius' arguments). But Lu said that men's originally good nature was led astray by external things, so that their minds were contaminated by desire.

Lu advocated practical methods for regaining the "lost mind." "For man," he said, "there is nothing prior to knowing himself."[35] One must also establish his own independent character and become master of himself, and he must embody what he has learned in practical moral conduct. For attaining knowledge, Lu recommended the practice of "quiet sitting," meditation, much in the manner of Zen Buddhism. All these techniques, he said, if practiced assiduously, would lead to the sudden realization that one's own mind is one with the totality of all things. This is extremely similar to the statement of one of the Upanishads: "That art Thou." In some ways it is almost identical with the doctrine of sudden enlightenment of

Zen Buddhism. Lu says: "If one plumbs, investigates into, sharpens, and refines himself, a morning will come when he will gain self-enlightenment."[36]

Lu seems also to have been influenced by Zen Buddhism in his comparative neglect of the authority of written texts and in the fact that he himself wrote relatively little. This undoubtedly placed his teachings at a disadvantage, after his death, as compared with those of Chu Hsi, who was a prolific author. The Sung Neo-Confucians in general went through many political struggles, and even Chu Hsi underwent a brief period of political disgrace near the end of his life. But in 1313 his commentaries on a number of the classics received, and from then on retained, official approval as the standard for the government examinations.

This official patronage gave the philosophy of Chu Hsi a tremendous advantage of one sort, but at the same time it probably had a tendency to repel the most vigorous and independent minds from it. In any case Wang Yang-ming, the most outstanding philosopher of the Ming dynasty, in most respects continued and developed the philosophy of Lu Hsiang-shan rather than that of Chu Hsi. He defended Lu against the charge of being a Zen Buddhist and praised his philosophy, in a Preface which he wrote for an edition of Lu's collected writings.[37]

Wang Yang-ming was born in 1472, the scion of a line of distinguished scholars and officials. Although he took the second degree in the examinations at the age of twenty-one, he repeatedly failed the examination for the highest degree, which he did not achieve until he was twenty-eight. In the interim he had studied military tactics, in a period when the borders of the empire were harassed by enemies. He seems to have studied both Taoism and Buddhism, but ended by being a staunch Confucian. He held various governmental posts and, in addition, taught disciples. At thirty-five he had the courage to oppose one of the powerful palace eunuchs, who were the scourge of the Ming dynasty. He was punished by being flogged and sent to a menial post in the southwestern wilds.

It is not very surprising that it was in this lonely exile that Wang experienced enlightenment. At a later time he told his disciples about his intellectual progress in these words:

> Everyone says that in investigating things one should use the method of Chu Hsi, but how can it actually be done? I have tried to do it. Formerly I discussed this with my friend Ch'ien. I asked, "If one has to investigate everything in the world to be a sage or a worthy man, how can anyone nowadays command such great strength?"
>
> I pointed to a bamboo in front of the pavilion, and told him to investigate it. Day and night Ch'ien meticulously investigated the principle of the bamboo. For three days he exhausted his mind, until his mental energy was overtaxed and he became ill. At first I said that this was because his strength was insufficient. I took up the task myself, and investigated the bamboo early and late, but still I could not discover its principle. After seven days I too became ill because of having worn out my mind. So we sighed together and said, "The reason we cannot be sages or worthy men is that we lack the great strength that is needed for the investigation of things."
>
> Later, however, while living among the barbarian tribes for three years, I came to understand that there is no one who can investigate everything in the world. The task of "investigating things" has to do only with investigating one's own body and mind.[38]

Wang's biography describes the enlightenment he experienced while "living among the barbarian tribes" as follows:

> All his followers fell ill. Wang Yang-ming cut wood, drew water, and cooked gruel for them. To keep them from being depressed he sang songs for them. . . . He wondered what method a sage would adopt, if he were to find himself thus exiled and in difficulties. Suddenly in the middle of the night he realized the true meaning of the expression, "investigate things so that knowledge may be extended to the utmost." The revelation was as if someone had spoken to him; without knowing what he was doing he cried out and leaped out of bed. All his followers were frightened [but Wang said], "Now for the first time I understand the teaching of the sage. My nature is in itself sufficient. To search for principles (*li*) in affairs and things was an error." He meditated on the words of the five classics to test this view, and found that they agreed with it completely.[39]

Here Wang was in effect echoing the doctrine of Lu Hsiang-shan, that one should not study things but only their *li*, which is completely contained in one's own mind.

After some four years Wang was restored to official favor and began a steady rise to power. Some of his posts were military ones, and one of his accomplishments was the crushing of a rebellion. At fifty he was made President of the Board of War, and ennobled as an earl. Later he was made viceroy of southern China. All this time he had many disciples and did a great deal of teaching. When Wang died, in 1529, at the age of fifty-seven, there was much criticism of his philosophy as heretical, with the result that its dissemination was forbidden by the emperor. Fifty-five years later, however, his tablet was placed in the Confucian temple.

Wang's philosophy seems to show little fundamental difference from that of his predecessors in the same current of Neo-Confucianism, but his vigorous mind, attractive personality, and active pen did much to organize and propagate it. Probably his most characteristic doctrine (which had at least been suggested earlier by Lu Hsiang-shan) was that of the inseparability of knowledge and practice. He said:

No one who really has knowledge fails to put it into practice. To know and yet not do is in fact not to know. The sages taught men both knowledge and action, precisely because they wished them to return to their true nature. They did not say that it is enough merely to think. The *Great Learning* sets forth the true relationship between knowledge and action when it says, "As in the case of loving beauty," and "As in the case of disliking a bad odor."[40]

Seeing beauty is a matter of knowledge; loving the beautiful is action. And yet, the moment one sees beauty one already loves it; one does not first see it and then form a firm resolve to love it. In the same way, smelling a bad odor pertains to knowledge; disliking it is action. Yet as soon as one smells a bad odor, he already dislikes it. . . . A man whose nose is stopped up may see an ill-smelling object without disliking it, but in this case he does not know that it is ill-smelling. No one can properly be said to understand filial piety and brotherly respect unless he actually practices them. Merely to be able to talk about these virtues does not constitute understanding them.[41]

The influence of Zen Buddhism on Wang's branch of Neo-Confucianism is very obvious, and he was tolerant toward both Buddhism and Taoism. Nevertheless, he assigned both of them a lower place than Confucianism and declared that, instead of trying to solve the world's problems, the Buddhists just ran away from them. Other Chinese scholars went much further in their criticisms. The time was at hand for a major revolt among China's most vigorous thinkers, not only against Buddhism and Taoism but also against Neo-Confucianism itself.

Chapter XI

The Reaction against Neo-Confucianism

BUDDHISM continues important in China to this day, especially among the common people. As an intellectual force it played some part even in connection with the revolution that overthrew the Manchu dynasty. Notwithstanding these facts, it is undoubtedly true that in recent centuries Buddhism has exerted less influence than it formerly did in intellectual circles.

During the last four centuries two new forces have arisen to play major roles in the development of Chinese thought. One of these is the revolt against Neo-Confucianism. The other is the impact of the West. The latter, at first of minor importance, has grown until there are now those who predict that, in the future, Western ideas will displace China's traditional thought almost entirely. The revolt against Neo-Confucianism, however, was a move in quite a different direction. It was in large measure a reaction against the influence of Buddhism, which it sought to counteract by going back to what were conceived to be the true teachings of Confucius and Mencius.

We have seen that in Han times, especially under the Emperor Wu, the attempt was made to warp Confucianism so far from its original nature, as a force for political and social reform, as to make it the handmaiden of monarchical despotism. Although never completely successful, this attempt was continued in most periods henceforward. Sacrifices to Confucius were established by imperial decree in A.D. 59. Interestingly enough, it was the Mongol and Manchu dynasties that particularly outdid themselves in offering elaborate and flattering sacrifices to the Chinese sage. By this means these invaders hoped to win over at least the scholars among their conquered subjects.

The ineradicably democratic spirit of early Confucianism continued to crop up, however, as a ghost that would not be laid, to plague the imperial sponsors of the doctrine. It made so much trouble that the second Manchu emperor found it necessary to have a board of editors prepare an expurgated edition of three of the Confucian classics. This imperially sponsored edition condemned, as false, passages which asserted that a tyrannical ruler has no proper claim to loyalty.[1]

Individual scholars of independent spirit had from time to time criticized the system whereby candidates for office were examined on their knowledge of certain officially approved "Confucian classics" and graded according to the degree to which their answers conformed to the philosophy approved by the state. This kind of criticism naturally increased in periods when large numbers of scholars found themselves at odds with the government. Such a condition became acute during the latter part of the Ming dynasty. We have already noticed that in this period Wang Yang-ming suffered at the hands of one of the powerful eunuchs who dominated the corrupt court. Weakness and disunity under the Ming rulers opened the way for invasion by the Manchus, who founded a new dynasty in 1644.

The Manchus had great difficulty in making their hold on China secure, but they did so by several methods. By military and police measures they suppressed any tendencies toward rebellion. By an extensive and elaborate literary inquisition they sought, with some success, to destroy all literature that they considered dangerous or objectionable.[2] By taking over Confucian orthodoxy, subsidizing scholarship, and becoming (as someone has said) "more Chinese than the Chinese," they tried to win over the scholars, who were the most articulate and influential part of the population. In the case of some of the most intelligent and independent scholars this attempt failed. After the Manchus were in control of the country some scholars fled to the mountains and to the end of their lives refused to take office under the invaders.

The Reaction against Neo-Confucianism

Thus both in late Ming and in early Ch'ing (that is, Manchu dynasty) times, large numbers of scholars stood in more or less avowed opposition to the government. Many of them also stood out against the oppression of the people, and some of them lost their lives for this, in the best Confucian tradition. It was natural that some of them were moved to oppose the kind of Confucian orthodoxy that the government espoused, namely, Neo-Confucianism. Hu Shih has observed that "Neo-Confucianism developed in a united empire of absolute rule and as a political philosophy failed to grasp the democratic spirit of classical Confucianism and tended to strengthen the hand of despotism."[3] It was under the hated dynasty of the Mongols that Chu Hsi's commentaries on several classics had first been made the official standard of correctness for the governmental examinations.

It is probable that the factor of Western influence, then in its infancy, played some part in the reaction against Neo-Confucianism, and in a very curious manner. Shortly before 1600 a few Jesuit missionaries gained access to China. By means of their learning some of them came to occupy posts of considerable importance in the Chinese government. Their first concern was to convert the Chinese to Christianity. For this purpose, as well as because they were intelligent and curious men, they studied Chinese literature and philosophy very thoroughly. As a result, some of them became extraordinarily impressed with the philosophy of Confucius, which they declared to be very similar to Christian morality. At the same time they asserted that the metaphysics of Neo-Confucianism had not been derived from Confucius at all but from Buddhism.

It is known that these Jesuit scholars were at least in indirect contact with some of the Chinese scholars who opposed Neo-Confucianism. The sequence of events is such that it appears possible that the Chinese philosophical movement may have been influenced, in some degree, by this criticism by alien observers. It also appears that the Chinese philosophers took over, from the Jesuits, scientific techniques in such fields as that of linguistics, which played a role of some importance in their movement.

Lest we Occidentals congratulate ourselves too much, however, on the possibility that Europeans may have influenced the course of development of Chinese philosophy, we should note another point that is seldom recognized. The knowledge of Chinese thought and institutions that the Jesuits sent back to Europe in their letters also influenced Europeans like Leibniz, Voltaire, Quesnay, Oliver Goldsmith, and a host of others. We should not exaggerate the role of Chinese thought in the development of such equalitarian ideas as were given concrete form in the French Revolution, but there is no question that it did play a role, if only as a catalyst.[4]

The school of revolutionary thinkers that took its rise at the beginning of the Ch'ing dynasty was known, for reasons we shall consider later, as the school of Han learning. Its eldest representative, who is often considered its founder, was Ku Yen-wu.* He was born in 1613, into a family that had produced many scholars and officials in the Ming period. As a boy he was stubborn and independent, but a good student, and he gradually achieved fame as a scholar. He was much more critical than most scholars of the time and read widely even in such (in China) unacademic fields as economics and military strategy.

The latter subject proved useful when he helped direct the defense of his native city against the invading Manchus, but it was taken while he was absent. His foster-mother, to whom he was indebted and devoted, would not live under Manchu rule; she starved herself to death, expressing the hope that her son would never take office under the Manchus. He fought against them until they were firmly established, and thereafter traveled about working at various enterprises, in which he proved himself to have the gifts of a captain of industry.

---

* Also commonly known by his *hao*, as Ku T'ing-lin.

Business was not his real interest, however, and it has been said that he was raising money in the hope of financing a revolution against the Manchus. He was imprisoned for a brief period, but later the Manchus urged him to take office. He replied, "If you insist, I shall commit suicide." In 1679 he settled down in a small town, to study and teach until his death in 1682.

As a scholar Ku was omnivorous, collecting and collating information through extensive travels and wide reading in all sorts of books. This was an important corrective to the narrowly classical scholarship of the day. Perhaps his greatest contribution was in the study of phonetics, in which he continued and amplified the work of his predecessors; he popularized the use of phonetics as a tool for philological and historical research. He was also a historical geographer of note and a compiler and student of ancient inscriptions on stone and bronze.

As a philosopher he vigorously attacked the Neo-Confucianism of Lu Hsiang-shan and Wang Yang-ming, which he clearly saw to be indebted to Zen Buddhism. He had observed that most of his contemporaries, steeped in Neo-Confucian studies, took little effective action against the evils that corrupted the Ming government and oppressed the people. They were also incapable of withstanding the Manchu invasion. Still worse, from his point of view, many of them readily gave their allegiance and service to the foreign regime. He wrote:

Alas, the scholars of the last century and more have constantly talked of "mind" and "human nature" but have been so confused that they could not explain them. Confucius seldom spoke about "fate" or "benevolence," and his disciple Tzŭ-kung had never heard him talk about "human nature" or "the Way of Heaven." . . .[5] The scholars of today are different from this. They . . . discourse at length about "mind" and "human nature," but neglect Confucius' method of "studying much and remembering it" in order to seek "one principle to connect it."[6] Forgetting that the whole country is afflicted with distress and poverty, they say nothing of this but spend their whole time in expatiating upon the "lofty," the "minute," the "essential," and the "uniform."

It must be, then, that their doctrines are superior to those of Confucius, and their disciples more worthy than Tzŭ-kung . . . as to this, I do not presume to know.

The whole book of *Mencius* repeatedly discusses "mind" and "human nature," but the questions asked by . . . [his disciples] and the answers Mencius gives commonly have to do with practical questions of how to conduct oneself. Thus Confucius seldom spoke about "human nature," "fate," or "Heaven," but present-day scholars constantly discuss them. Confucius and Mencius constantly discussed practical questions of conduct, but present-day scholars seldom mention them. . . .

In my humble opinion the Way of a sage is [in the words of Confucius] to be "widely versed in learning" and "in one's personal conduct to have a sense of moral obligation."[7] "Learning" has to do with everything from one's personal conduct to affairs of state. The "sense of moral obligation" applies to every relationship—those of the son, the subject, the brother, and the friend—and to every problem of social intercourse. The sense of moral obligation is extremely important. One should [as Confucius said] feel no shame at "wearing shabby clothes and eating poor food."[8] But one should feel deeply ashamed if he does nothing to alleviate the poverty of the common people.[9]

Ku Yen-wu blamed the philosophy of Lu Hsiang-shan and Wang Yang-ming for the complacence and subservience to monarchical authority of many of his contemporaries. Yet one among them (whom Ku Yen-wu admired despite the fact that he was an avowed follower of Wang Yang-ming) dared to express ideas so liberal that he was hailed more than two centuries later as an early revolutionary.

This scholar, Huang Tsung-hsi (1610–95), was the son of a Ming dynasty official who dared to defy the corrupt eunuch clique that dominated the court. For this the father was executed when his son was sixteen. Two years later Huang Tsung-hsi went to the capital and exacted vengeance for his father's death by his own hand.[10] These early experiences undoubtedly contributed toward the low esteem in which he held the monarchical institution as it existed in his own day. Nevertheless, after China was invaded by the Manchus, he led troops and held office during the vain attempts to save the Ming dynasty. Once the Manchu dynasty was established he retired to a life of study, writing, and teaching, resisting all attempts to appoint him to office.

A book that Huang wrote in 1662 included an essay called "On Monarchy." Anciently, he said, rulers were exceptional men who were willing to set aside their own welfare and labor for the public good. Such were the sage rulers of antiquity. But later rulers were not so. Huang described them as follows:

They considered themselves to be the dispensers of the benefits and evils of the world. They considered it quite proper that they should take all the benefits to themselves while turning all the evils toward others. They forbade their subjects to act selfishly, but called the great selfishness of the ruler "the public good." At first they felt some shame about this, but as time went on they became quite accustomed to it.

They looked upon the world as their huge private estate, which they handed down to their sons and grandsons to enjoy in perpetuity. . . . Anciently the people were regarded as the hosts, and the ruler as merely a guest; the ruler spent his whole life in working for the welfare of the people. Today, however, the ruler is considered the host while the people are guests on his estate; thus there is not a single spot where the people may enjoy themselves in peace, and all because of the ruler.

Before an aspirant for the throne has won it, he causes great numbers of people to be butchered and families to be torn asunder, all in order to enlarge his property. Concerning this he feels no pity; he says, "I am establishing a patrimony for my descendants." After he has gained the throne, he grinds the very bones of the people with toil and tears families apart, all to provide licentious pleasures for himself. He considers this perfectly proper; he says, "This is my profit on my property."

Certainly, then, the great scourge of the empire is its ruler! If no ruler had ever been set up, then men would be able to act for their own benefit. How can it be supposed that the establishment of the monarchy was intended to bring about such conditions as prevail today?

Anciently the people loved and supported their ruler, looking upon him as a father, considering him to be like Heaven, and in fact he was. Nowadays the people resent and hate their ruler, regarding him as a thieving enemy, calling him a "mere fellow" without any rightful claim to their allegiance, and in fact he is.[11]

In the renewed emphasis on antiquity that characterized this period special attention was paid to Confucius, who was interpreted as having been a practical reformer rather than a man content to deal only with words and ideas. A scholar of the time wrote: "Confucius said: 'The gentleman wishes to be slow to speak, but quick to act.' 'He is vigorous in action, but careful in his speech.' 'A gentleman acts first, and talks about it after he has acted.' 'The gentleman is ashamed to let his words outstrip his actions.' "[12]

The emphasis on practicality was made the basis of a philosophy by Yen Yüan (1635–1704).* As a boy he had to work in the fields, and later supported himself by practicing medicine and by teaching in country schools. When very young he was an ardent student of Taoism. Later he became as deeply immersed in Neo-Confucianism, practicing the meditation it enjoins as the path to enlightenment. In middle life he became completely disillusioned with all such ideas and came to believe that Neo-Confucianism was deeply tinctured with Buddhism and Taoism.

Yen Yüan criticized the doctrine of Chu Hsi which held that all things are made up of two aspects, *li* or principle (which is always perfect) and *ch'i* or substance (which may be far from perfect). Man's nature, Yen said, is one, and can no more be divided into two than the eye can be separated into a virtuous aspect that sees only correct phenomena and a physical aspect that sees incorrect phenomena. He wrote:

The socket, the eyeball, and the lens are the physical substance of the eye. The vision which resides in them, which can see things, is the nature of the eye. Are you going to say that the principle of this vision is to see nothing but correct phenomena, while the socket, eyeball, and lens see incorrect phenomena? I say that both the eye's principle of vision and its physical parts are ordained by Heaven.

There is no point in trying to distinguish between what is the nature ordained by Heaven and what is the physical nature. One ought only to say that Heaven has endowed man with the nature

* Also known by his *hao* as Yen Hsi-chai.

of the eye, which is vision. Since it is able to see, then the eye's nature is good. . . . But whether its sight is keen or blurred, and whether it sees far or only a short distance, depends upon the strength or weakness of its powers.

Yet none of this can be called bad. If the eye sees keenly and far, this is certainly good; but if its vision is blurred and it can see only a short distance, this is still good, although not the best. How can it be called bad? When there are incorrect phenomena which seduce the eye and obscure its vision, then there are evil sights; here for the first time we may apply the term "bad." But is this seduction the fault of the eye's nature? Is it the fault of its physical substance? If we say that it is the fault of its physical substance, we then have to say that the eye's nature can be perfect only if the eye itself is not present![13]

Yen Yüan had nothing but scorn for bookworms. He described scholars as "sitting majestically in their studies, every one of them a frail weakling, laughed at by soldiers and farmers—what sort of behavior is this for a man?"[14] Reading books is useless, he declared, unless one puts what one learns from them into practice. Can one learn to play a musical instrument, he asks, merely by endlessly reading books about it, without ever actually laying one's hands on the instrument? In the same way one has to put into practice what he learns from the classics, if his study is to mean anything.[15]

The sage rulers of antiquity as well as the Duke of Chou and Confucius were, Yen wrote, "all sages who taught the necessity of action. And they themselves all worked practically to bring about the right way in the world. . . . The Han and T'ang dynasties inherited only one or two tenths of this active spirit. But the Chin [A.D. 265–419] and Sung [960–1279] dynasties unthinkingly approved of the Buddhist doctrine of 'the void' and of Lao Tzŭ's 'nonaction.' They also approved the procedure of Chou, Ch'êng, Chu [Hsi], and Shao [all Sung Neo-Confucians], who sat in meditation and worked with nothing but their mouths and pens. To sum it up, none of these acted, men's faculties atrophied, and the way of the sages was lost."[16]

Yen's prescription was practical action to remedy the ills of the world. He said that the Confucian scholars of his own day ought to work at some practical calling like farming or medicine or divination, at the same time that they pursued their studies.[17] "All the world's work that is waiting to be done is the business of us Confucians," he asserted. "If we do not exert ourselves, who will? For an example, look at the career of our Master!"[18]

Confucians in general had long looked down upon the army. Yen Yüan called it "the noblest group of men in the world." He asserted that Confucius had practiced the use of weapons with his disciples, and that in antiquity youths had been taught the honorable business of bearing arms to protect the nation.[19]

Yen was outspoken in his denunciation of the inequalities of wealth and poverty and the concentration of the holding of land in the hands of the few. "All the land in the world," he wrote, "ought to be enjoyed by all the people in the world in common. If the desires of the rich were accorded with, the patrimony of ten thousand persons would be given to one man, to appease his insatiable avarice." Yen's remedy was to go back to the "well field" system which, as we have seen, was advocated by Mencius. If actually put into practice, this would have brought about a redistribution of land.[20]

On the basis of his ideas concerning landholding it might be argued that Yen Yüan was a forerunner of the Chinese Communists. But he also made a vigorous defense of the institution of feudalism as it had existed in ancient China, and declared that endless troubles had resulted from its abandonment. He strongly urged that it be revived.[21] The Chinese Communists, as is well known, consider the "feudal period" in China to have come down to our own century, and regard feudalism as one of their principal adversaries.

It is generally believed that the thought of Yen Yüan influenced that of Tai Chên (1724–77),* the most important philos-

* Also known by his *hao*, as Tai Tung-yüan.

opher of the Ch'ing dynasty. Tai began life so poor that he was able to study only by borrowing books from more well-to-do neighbors.

The quality of his mind may be judged from an incident which, it is related, took place when he was ten years old. His teacher was expounding the classic called the *Great Learning*, when suddenly his small pupil asked, "How do you know that this book contains the words of Confucius, which were recorded by his disciple Tsêng Tzŭ? And how do you know that it contains the ideas of Tsêng Tzŭ, as they were set down by his disciples?" The teacher told him, "That is what Chu Hsi says."

"And when," the little boy asked, "did Chu Hsi live?" "In the Sung dynasty." "And when," the boy went on, "did Confucius and Tsêng Tzŭ live?" "In the Chou dynasty." "And how many years separated the Chou dynasty and the Sung dynasty?" "About two thousand years." "In that case," the child concluded, "how did Chu Hsi know?" The teacher could not answer. He merely shook his head and said, "This is no ordinary child."[22]

It was prophetic of Tai Chên's later interests that his first book, completed when he was twenty, was on mathematics, and that his second was a commentary on a technological section of one of the classics. Before the end of his life he had written or edited about fifty works.

His official career was brilliant even though he repeatedly failed the examination for the highest degree. He became one of the editors of the vast imperial manuscript library that was then being compiled, and the Ch'ien Lung emperor wrote and published a poem in praise of one of his scholarly achievements. When, at the age of fifty-one, Tai failed the highest examination for perhaps the sixth time, the same emperor, by special decree, conferred upon him the degree that he had failed to win. He died two years later.

It may seem surprising that a man so specially honored by a Manchu emperor should have attacked the very philosophical foundations of the dynasty. But it is significant that Tai never passed the examination, which was based upon the very Neo-Confucianism that he deplored.

Tai inherited the thought of his predecessors among the Ch'ing thinkers, but he developed their ideas in a thoroughgoing manner that surpassed them. He refuted the dualism of Chu Hsi as completely as Yen Yüan had done, and went even further. He would have none of the idea that the *li*, the principle of things, is conferred by Heaven. All things, he said, are made up of *ch'i*, substance. This does not mean that they do not have *li*, principles; they do, but these are simply the *manner* in which their substance is arranged and organized, not portions of some cosmic spirit.[23] There is not a body and a soul. "It is because man has a living body that he has a mind."[24]

Although Tai is sometimes called a materialist, he did not disregard what are commonly known as "spiritual" values. He believed (as Mencius did) that the virtues are evolved from the instinctive tendencies that everyone possesses. "All living things," he said, "know enough to hold fast to life and fear death. For this reason they move toward what is advantageous and avoid the harmful. Even though there are differences in intelligence, they are all alike in holding to life and fearing death. The difference between men and animals is not to be found here."

One cannot even say that animals do not have the virtues, in their rudimentary form, just as men do. But the difference is that man can enlarge his virtue to the fullest point and develop his knowledge until it is like that of the gods.

Mencius said, "If anyone sees a little child about to fall into a well, he will immediately feel horror and pity."[25] Since this is so, it is evident that what we call pity and benevolence are not external things which come from outside the mind and heart, but are part of the very essence of the heart itself. Since each individual holds fast to his own life, and fears death for himself, he is therefore alarmed and moved to pity by the child's danger.

If one did not hold to life and fear death for himself, how could this alarm and pity arise? The same thing is true of such virtues as the sense of shame, humility, and the knowledge of right and wrong. If it were possible to get rid of the desire for food and drink and sexual satisfaction, so that one were unaffected by external stimuli and remained in a state of complete quiescence, how would it be possible for the sense of shame, humility, and the knowledge of right and wrong to come into being?

The same is true, Tai insists, of all the other virtues. They do not depend on getting rid of the natural desires and impulses of man; on the contrary, if properly understood and guided, these desires and impulses are the very ground from which virtue arises. The ancient sages, he says, did not make the mistake of supposing that the basis of virtue was to be sought "outside of the natural desires, and the bodies and minds, of men."[26]

When we consider that this was written by a Chinese scholar at the time of the American Revolution, it is remarkably similar to modern Western psychological theory. In its basic assumptions it was probably not much more than a century behind the most daring advances of psychological theory in Europe.[27] It is significant that Tai Chên was deeply interested in such sciences as mathematics and astronomy. Like every other Chinese scholar of his day he had been influenced by some knowledge of Western science; there seems to be no indication, however, that he was influenced by Western psychological theory.

What is remarkable is the fact that much of his psychology was set forth in passages (like the one last quoted above) in his commentary on the book of *Mencius*. A large proportion of his writing was concerned with an effort to get at the genuine teachings of Confucius and Mencius, which he, like other progressive scholars of his time, believed to be identical with the scientific outlook that was rapidly developing. There is no doubt that they exaggerated this. But there is also no doubt that the philosophy of Confucius and Mencius was much more compatible with modern science than was the Neo-Confucianism that had developed under the influence of Indian thought.

Tai's point of view was in many respects that of the scientist. As Hu Shih has pointed out he was skilled in mathematics and astronomy, and deeply impressed by the fact that the heavenly bodies follow regular courses that can be calculated and plotted by research.[28] In the same way, he believed, one should learn about the world by study, investigation, and analysis.

This essentially empirical view (which was shared by some other scholars of this period) had played little part in Chinese thought for thousands of years. Confucius had emphasized the role of experience and observation as means by which the individual could attain to a knowledge of the true and the good. But Mencius, although he emphasized the importance of the individual, talked at least part of the time as if knowledge were innate. Mencius also exalted the authority of the sages. As Confucianism developed, less and less possibility was left for the individual to contribute in any basic way to what was known. He might comment on the classics, but he must not differ from them.

In Neo-Confucianism a new standard of static authority was injected—the cosmic *li* or principle. This *li* was considered to be absolute truth, "without birth and indestructible," permanent and forever unchanging. Once the Neo-Confucians had established the proposition that their philosophy conformed to the cosmic *li*, then it was obviously foolish to think of disagreeing with it. The emperor and all others in superior positions argued that their wishes and decisions were supported by the *li*, the cosmic principle of right, from which there was no appeal.

Tai Chên made a frontal attack on the whole concept. He wrote:

> This word *li* does not occur often in the six classics, in the words of Confucius and Mencius, nor in the various records and collected writings. Yet nowadays even the most stupid and violent of men, when rendering a decision or upbraiding someone who has become the object of their anger, never fail to justify themselves by shouting the word "*li*."
> The reason for this is that since the Sung dynasty there has grown up the habit of regarding *li* as if it were a veritable object, received from Heaven and present in the mind. The result is that those who are able to do so regard their mere opinions as being *li*.

Thus those who are forceful, and possess the advantages of influence and position and glib tongues, are found to have the *li* on their side, while the weak and timorous, who are unable to debate, are defeated by this same *li*. Alas! . . .[29]

The superior commands the inferior in the name of *li*, and the elder and the aristocrat use the same catchword in laying demands upon the junior and the plebeian. Even though they are wrong, they insist that they are correct. But if the inferior, the junior, or the plebeian tries to remonstrate, arguing that the *li* is on his side, then even though he may be right he is condemned as being insubordinate. . . .

When a man is condemned by the law, there are still those who will feel compassion for him. But when he is condemned by *li* [the cosmic principle of abstract justice itself], who can feel any pity for him? . . . Where in the six classics or in the books of Confucius or Mencius is it stated that *li* is such an external object, existing apart from men's feelings and desires, and designed sternly to repress them?[30]

Like Mencius and like modern psychiatrists, Tai Chên believed that men's desires should not be repressed, but socialized. He wrote:

The Confucian gentleman simply tries to bring human desires into accord with the right way. It is futile to try to control a river simply by blocking its passage. If you obstruct it on the east, it will flow out on the west; or, worse, it will break your dam and create an ungovernable flood. Similarly, if one tries to control himself or to govern others simply by repressing the human desires, he may succeed in quieting them temporarily, but in the end the desires will inevitably outwit all attempts to restrain them. This is not what the Confucian gentleman does. Instead, he concentrates his attention upon the right way, and merely seeks to cause men not to do those things that do not accord with it.[31]

For Tai Chên as for Confucius and Mencius, the Way was a way of human co-operation for the good of all. "The benevolent man," Tai said, "wishing to live his own life fully, helps other men to live their lives to the full."[32] "Before one takes any action with regard to another person, he should quietly ask himself, 'Would I be willing to have that done to me?' Before one charges another person with a duty, he should quietly ask himself, 'Would I be able to fulfil it?' "[33]

If this same spirit were applied to government, it would of course make despotism impossible. Tai wrote: "Alas! The men of the present day do not think. The way of the sages was to make it possible for everyone in the world to express his feelings and fulfil his desires. As a result, the world was well governed." But later Confucians, he lamented, had made of their philosophy a veritable strait jacket, to bind and destroy the human spirit.[34]

Tai Chên served, and was signally favored by, the Ch'ien Lung emperor. This emperor was exceedingly strict in his efforts to quell any tendencies toward sedition, and had many books condemned to destruction on this ground. One wonders if he ever read any of Tai Chên's essays attacking the philosophical foundations of despotism.

If he did, they probably did not alarm him, and there was little cause for alarm. However independent exceptional scholars might be, the great mass of intellectuals continued to think the kind of orthodox thoughts that would enable them to pass through the examination system—which Tai Chên never succeeded in doing. When the problems of the world became too difficult, most of them turned to the abstractions of Neo-Confucianism for "the consolations of philosophy."

Paradoxically, the extremely critical temper of Ch'ing dynasty scholarship had the effect of turning many of the keenest minds away from the consideration of political, social, and economic problems, toward criticism of a narrower scope.

From the beginning of the dynasty there had been a strong and growing movement directed toward the critical study of early commentaries and ancient texts, which would provide a basis of authority older and therefore more authoritative than the works of the Neo-Confucians. As we saw earlier, Ku Yen-wu contributed greatly to the study of phonetics. Building on the foundations that had been laid by a late Ming scholar, Ku succeeded in establishing the ancient pronunciations, which had long been unknown, of a large number of characters. This was only one of the tools that Ch'ing scholars used in their unparalleled activity in criticizing the ancient literature, exposing forgeries, solving old problems, and even in some cases reconstituting texts that had long been lost.

The earliest commentaries on the classics were those of the Han dynasty. It was reasoned that since the Han commentators had lived closest to the times in which the classics had been written, they should have understood them best. Thus the Han commentaries were considered to be the most reliable. For this reason this branch of Ch'ing scholarship is known as the "school of Han learning."

The men of this school were scornful of literary elegance and metaphysical speculation. They emphasized inductive research. Textual criticism was by no means new in China, but the scholars of the Ch'ing dynasty raised it to a new point of excellence. Charles S. Gardner has written that "the Chinese are not a whit behind Western scholarship in the exacting domain of textual or preparatory criticism, that discipline which is concerned with the authentication, establishment, and meaning of texts, but not with their historical appraisal and utilization."[35]

The Ch'ing scholars used philology, textual and (to a lesser degree) historical criticism, and epigraphy, and pushed their researches into the political, social, and economic realms, as well as investigating history and the classics. The men of the school of Han learning as such were primarily concerned, however, to use these various means to discredit the writings of the Neo-Confucians and the materials upon which their studies were based, and to investigate the works of Han date which they believed more authentic.

Tai Chên inherited the techniques of this school and used them to add important works to the literature of criticism. But for him this was not enough. As Fang Chao-ying has pointed out, Tai Chên "had the conviction that these studies were not ends in themselves but must be used to develop a new philosophy whose aim should be the betterment of society. For him, the supreme use of the Classics is the truth they convey; and to display these truths he was as ready to go beyond 'Han Learning' as his predecessors had gone beyond 'Sung Learning.' "[36]

In this Tai Chên was almost unique. His ideas were not well understood, even in his own day, and his importance in the history of Chinese thought has only recently been recognized. Most of the men of the school of Han learning succumbed to the seductions of the study, so that their contributions, though great, were those of specialists, who know "more and more about less and less."

Chapter XII

The Influence of the West

IN THE hundred years that elapsed between the middle of the nineteenth and the middle of the twentieth century, China changed more profoundly than in the previous two thousand years. The transformation has affected, in varying degrees, political institutions, the structure of society, and economic life. Inevitably, the pattern of Chinese thinking has been altered at the same time.

These changes, and the causes that produced them, are so many and complex that it would be impossible for anyone to analyze them completely. Yet there is one fundamental fact that has been more important than any other, and that goes far toward providing a key to the whole situation.

The Chinese had long considered themselves the most cultured, the most important, and indeed the only really important people on the face of the earth. They believed all other peoples to be "barbarians," who ought properly to acknowledge the sovereignty of the Chinese emperor. They had had little contact with the outside world, except for neighboring countries that freely acknowledged their cultural superiority. For this reason they assumed that the rest of the world accepted them at their own valuation. When the British Empire sent ambassadors to negotiate with the Chinese court, most Chinese believed that they had come to bring tribute and pledge allegiance to the Chinese emperor. Suddenly, and cataclysmically, all this was changed.

The expanding nations of the West, seeking trade and empire, began knocking at China's doors as early as the sixteenth century. They were held at bay until China was defeated in war by Britain in 1842. From that time onward it became increasingly clear that China could not win a trial of strength with the Occidental powers, and she was compelled to yield point after point.

Her customs service and her post office were to a large extent manned and controlled by Westerners. China was compelled to permit the ships of Western nations to navigate freely in her waters, and even to demolish some of her coastal defenses. Western nations stationed troops at a number of points in China on a permanent basis. Pieces of territory in various parts of the country were taken over as concessions by Western powers. Some nations staked out whole areas of China as "spheres of interest." Only rivalries between the Western powers prevented them from annexing some of these territories as colonies, and it was openly predicted that China would be "carved up like a melon."

This loss of power was bad enough, but China's loss of prestige may have bothered thinking Chinese even more. The Chinese had always considered their culture supreme, and in the seventeenth and eighteenth centuries many Europeans had agreed with them. But after her weakness stood revealed, most Westerners came to regard China as a backward and perhaps even a primitive nation. If the Chinese could have defeated the foreigners and thrown them out, they could have dismissed their scorn as mere "barbarian ignorance." But when they were compelled to accept the dictation of men who looked down upon almost everything they held sacred, something had to be done.

What could be done? This problem has usurped most of the energy of thinking Chinese during the past century. It is not to be wondered at that they have contributed relatively little that is new in the realm of basic philosophical theory. A man whose house is on fire does not sit down in the midst of the flames and compose a treatise on logic.

Chinese have attempted to meet the challenge of the West in

three ways. Some have insisted that China's traditional patterns of life and thought are superior to all others, and that the Chinese have found themselves in difficulty not because they have been too conservative but because they have not lived up to the traditional ideals; if they did so, China would be so strong that her troubles would vanish. Others have taken a more moderate view; while they believed that Chinese culture provided the soundest basis for China's development, they wished to modify it to meet the conditions of the modern world, and to take over such Western techniques as appeared to be advantageous. A third group has insisted that China's entire traditional pattern of political, social, and economic organization is unsuited to the world of today, and that the whole manner of life and thought must be revolutionized.

Most of the conservatives were men trained in the age-old classical manner, knowing little of the outside world. But some of those who had learned to know the West well, and had gone through a period of admiration for its culture, became disillusioned. An interesting example is Yen Fu (1854–1921). After being educated at the University of Edinburgh, he became a pioneer in translating Western philosophical works into Chinese. His translations of books by T. H. Huxley, John Stuart Mill, Herbert Spencer, Adam Smith, and others played an important part in introducing Occidental thought to China. Yet after the first World War he came to think that China's was, after all, the better way. He wrote:

Western culture, after this European War, has been corrupted utterly. . . . Formerly, when I heard our scholars of the old school say that there would come a day when the teachings of Confucius would be practiced by all mankind, I thought they were talking nonsense. But now I find that some of the most enlightened men in Europe and America seem to be coming gradually to a like opinion. . . . It seems to me that in three centuries of progress the peoples of the West have achieved four principles: to be selfish, to kill others, to have little integrity, and to feel little shame. How different are the principles of Confucius and Mencius, as broad and deep as Heaven and Earth, designed to benefit all men everywhere.[1]

Confucian principles are undoubtedly a noble reply to gun-fire, but they are not an effective one. It was widely realized that, however much the Chinese might dislike the Westerners and all their works, they would have to learn some Western techniques if they were to defend themselves. The use of fire-arms was such an obvious example that the Chinese had had cannon cast for them by some of the Jesuit missionaries in the seventeenth century. The merits of Occidental mathematics and natural science were also recognized from an early date.

For a time during the nineteenth century it was believed that the power of the Westerners depended upon a few easily dis-covered secrets, such as mathematics, natural science, military and naval science, and the use of machinery. It was reasoned that if the Chinese could only add a command of these tech-niques to their own superior culture, they could quickly dem-onstrate their supremacy. Western scientific works were trans-lated, a few Chinese went abroad to study, attempts were made to develop an army and navy on the Western model, and a few arsenals, shipyards, and factories were erected. Yet the re-sults were disappointing.

Chinese of discernment, especially among those who traveled abroad, came to realize that it was not so simple. The real secret of the power of Western nations, they said, lay rather in the solidarity between their governments and their people. This was based, some of them believed, upon general education, political justice, equitable distribution of economic goods, and enlightened social institutions. Increasingly it was urged that if China were to withstand the West she would have to modify her political, social, and economic institutions.

Undoubtedly this was true. However much one may admire China's traditional ways of life and thought, they were not de-signed to withstand the aggressive pressure of the West. They were closely linked with the traditional structure of Chinese society. At its head was the emperor. Its base was the great mass of the common people, nearly all of whom were farmers. Between them, acting as mediators and seeing that both emperor and people performed their duties as prescribed by custom, were the scholar-officials, versed in the classics and schooled in the Confucian virtues.

The individual's strongest loyalty was to his family, which performed many functions that with us are performed by the state. Other bodies, such as the village or perhaps a guild, might be important to him. But the state was very remote from the ordinary Chinese. In normal times the state did not intervene in the life of the people, but acted more like a referee between groups that might come into conflict. The hand of custom was strong, upon everyone from the emperor down, but in many respects old China was a laissez-faire state.

This was a structure, but it was scarcely an organization. An organization worthy of the name should be tightly knit, yet flexible, able to function in a disciplined manner under varying circumstances. The Chinese empire did not (in the nineteenth and twentieth centuries, at any rate) have these characteristics. The emperor was in theory a despot, yet the President of the United States is able to command a degree of obedience to his orders that the emperor of China might sometimes have envied. High officials and generals seldom defied the emperor, but they often failed to carry out his instructions, explaining that they were unable to do so for reasons that were often flimsy. They might be punished if they were sufficiently lacking in prestige—but in that case they usually obeyed the orders.

In an organization power does not depend primarily upon the individual but upon the position he holds. In a disciplined army privates obey sergeants, and colonels obey generals. In a factory the laborer obeys the foreman, and the vice-president obeys the president. In China, however, much depended upon the individual, his friendships, his family connections, his prestige. An officer of the government or of a company could not be discharged, no matter how inefficient he might be, if he were sufficiently well connected.

The pattern of human relationships was much more complex than in the West. We tend to dehumanize people, make them cogs in machines, move them about like pieces on a checkerboard. If they perform their jobs to the satisfaction of their superiors, well and good; if not, they are discharged. In China a whole series of relationships had to be taken into account, including customary rights and privileges. If the law of the land and the customs of a guild came into conflict, the courts would sometimes rule in favor of the guild. Even the prices of commodities were negotiated in each instance between buyer and seller, so that a man with a winning personality and the gift of bargaining could buy much more cheaply than a less talented competitor.

This was a much more "human" society than ours, and a much less efficient one. When well-disciplined Western armies fought against Chinese armies in which the officers executed such orders as pleased them, the Westerners always won. Furthermore, the manufacture of warships and artillery and the myriad supplies needed for modern war demands industrial power. And industrial power cannot be achieved without tight and even ruthless organization.

More and more Chinese came to realize that it would be impossible to continue to enjoy their traditional manner of life, and at the same time to achieve the goal of expelling the foreigner and winning China's independence. Inevitably, China must to some extent "Westernize."

It was natural that the pattern looked to was, in the first instance, predominantly that of the Western democracies. For any people contemplating revolution, either political or social, the French and American revolutions supplied the most prominent precedents. And China's ancient philosophy included, as men like Sun Yat-sen were fond of pointing out, not a few ideas that were remarkably akin to the principles of Western democracy.[2]

The Western democracies were represented in China by a large number of Christian missionaries, many of whom not only preached the gospel but also rendered service as teachers or physicians. It would be hard to overestimate their role in winning acceptance for Western culture.

"Science and democracy" were believed to light the road that would inevitably lead to a new day. Britain was admired for her political institutions and her economic and military strength. A revolutionary society organized by Sun Yat-sen in 1905 took as its goal "liberty, equality, fraternity."[3] In 1912 when the Republic of China was established, Sun declared in accepting the office of president that the Chinese people were "continuing the historic struggle of the French and American peoples for republican institutions."[4]

In the general intoxication with "science and democracy" most of the reformers had little to say, or at least little good, of China's traditional culture. China's own philosophy was not forgotten, but it was little emphasized. Attempts to revive a strong interest in Buddhist thought have attracted only a limited group. Taoism and Moism have been studied, but rather as a matter of scholarly research than of actual philosophical movements.

Although Hu Shih and a few other intellectual leaders have acknowledged "the democratic spirit of classical Confucianism,"[5] there has been little attempt to use it as the basis of a modern democratic philosophy. Confucianism has at last been discredited by too many bad associations. Two thousand years ago emperors began to use it (in distorted form) as a cloak for despotism. During the past century conservatives who tried to block all change rallied most frequently under the banner of Confucianism. After the Chinese Republic fell apart in civil war, some of the most notorious warlords posed as particularly pious Confucians. When the Japanese occupied much of China, between 1931 and 1945, they tried to revive the cult of Confucius to make their regime more palatable to the Chinese. It would be hard for any philosophy to rise superior to such misfortunes.

Confucianism continues deeply to influence every Chinese,

whether he likes it or not, for it is an essential ingredient of the culture that has made him what he is. But it is undoubtedly true, as Chan Wing-tsit has written, that Chinese thinkers in general "agree that Western philosophy is that of the future, in contradistinction to that of Confucianism, which most of them regard as the philosophy of the past."[6]

From 1917 onward China's intellectuals have been deeply influenced by a movement known both as the "New Tide" and as the "Chinese Renaissance." Among those who launched it the scholar best known to the West is Hu Shih, a student of John Dewey and an advocate of pragmatism. It began with the daring proposal that Chinese books and articles should be written in the language of speech.

From time immemorial almost all serious writing in China had been done in a literary style that differed from speech, to some extent, both in grammar and in vocabulary. It was also customary to write literary Chinese in a rather stilted manner and to make many obscure references to the classical literature, so that only scholars could read it and even they sometimes had their difficulties. The result was that writers often paid much more attention to writing in an impressive style than to expressing their ideas effectively. Against all this Hu Shih and the many who sided with him declared war; they wanted Chinese written as it was spoken, and as clearly and effectively as possible. The battle raged hotly for a time, but the rebels won most of their objectives. Today even those who continue to write in the literary form commonly write simply and clearly.

This movement was not literary alone. It became a center around which many of those who were fighting for new ideas ranged themselves in battle array. It was not truly a "renaissance" in the sense that most of its adherents derived their principal inspiration from a reinterpretation of China's own cultural heritage. Nevertheless, such a reinterpretation was an important part of the movement.

In the beginning it was largely iconoclastic; one of its chief standard-bearers even changed his name to the Chinese equivalent of "Mr. Doubter of Antiquity." It rapidly passed to the constructive aspect and utilized both the critical results of previous Chinese scholarship and the methods of modern science to evaluate the literature of the past and the discoveries of archeological excavations. As a result, Chinese scholars have learned more during the twentieth century, about the true nature of their history and traditions, than in any previous period.

For two thousand years Chinese had been studying the classics, and for much of that time a knowledge of the classics had provided the surest means to political preferment, social prestige, and even financial prosperity. When the official examinations for office were abolished in 1905, this tremendous stimulus to classical study was removed. When, after 1920, the "New Tide" movement caused the textbooks in elementary and secondary schools to be written in the colloquial rather than the literary language, this did not only mean that many educated Chinese would henceforth have considerable difficulty in reading the classics. It also meant that many of them would find a large proportion of all of China's traditional literature so hard to understand that they would not bother to read it. This was no slight break with the past. It tended to create an ideological vacuum.

Although the reformers in general denounced conservatism, not all of them by any means desired to scrap China's cultural tradition. Sun Yat-sen, who did more than any other man to abolish the empire, retained distinctively Chinese features in the constitution he proposed for the Republic. He asserted: "What we need to learn from Europe is science, not political philosophy. As for the true principles of political philosophy, the Europeans need to learn them from China."[7]

Under more favorable circumstances, it is altogether possible that China might gradually have developed into a nation possessing many of the characteristics of Western democracy, yet retaining much of the essence of her traditional culture. Democracy is a system of compromises, and the "middle way" of compromise is age-old in China. Democracy values freedom and the individual, and denies unlimited authority to the state; so does Confucianism. The entire humanistic and liberal background out of which Western democracy grew has much in common with the best traditions of Chinese thought.

Democracy is a growth, however; it is never achieved overnight. To develop into a fully democratic state China needed time, which history did not grant. In the years between the revolution of 1912 and the success of the Nationalist party in 1927, civil war and disunity were more or less constant. Even after that there was fighting with the Communists and others, and the so-called "Manchurian incident" of 1931 brought new troubles. After 1937 China was continuously involved in war with Japan until the end of the second World War. Under such conditions it would have been difficult for full democracy to be developed in any country.

China's intellectual tradition, comprising at least three thousand years of gradual evolution, is one of the oldest in the world. That tradition appears to have come, if not to an end, at least to its most abrupt turning point, with the ascendancy of the Chinese Communists in 1949. Since the Chinese Communist party was organized only in 1921, its rapid success is quite remarkable.

It is often argued that this success was primarily the result of a revolutionary upsurge by China's masses, reacting against poverty and economic exploitation. This accords with the Marxist dogma that the causes of social and political change are to be found solely in economic conditions. Like much of Marxist doctrine this explanation oversimplifies, and neglects an important part of the facts.

The small urban laboring class, which according to Communist principle should have led the revolution,[8] dismayed the Chinese Communists by showing, on the whole, very little inclination toward Communism.[9] Many of the peasants, however, have supported the Communists with enthusiasm, and they have supplied a large proportion of the men of the Chinese Communist armies. For them, economic motives have been very important. Programs for the reduction of rents and for the confiscation and redistribution of farm lands quite naturally made a great appeal.

The leadership and the initiative in the Chinese Communist revolution have not come, however, primarily from the peasants, but from the intellectuals.[10] Not all of China's intellectuals became Communist, by any means. Nevertheless it is clear that a large proportion of the students, professors, and other intellectuals favored the Communists even before they controlled the country.

Robert C. North wrote in 1951: "Although Chinese Communists hail their party as the vanguard of the proletariat, no Politburo member is known to have come from a working-class family. On the contrary, four admit wealthy landlord antecedents, one came from a line of small landlord-officials, four class their parents as well-to-do landlords, and two emerged from the lesser peasantry. The social origins of two are uncertain. The educational level of these men is generally high. Nine have attended advanced institutions."[11] It is doubtful that such men became Communists solely in the hope of personal economic gain. While the economic motive may have been present, it can hardly be the whole story.

Since intellectuals played such a vital role in the success of Communism in China, it is important to ask why so many of them joined the Communist cause. Part of the reason was undoubtedly economic; the plight of the intellectual class was desperate. But another and an important part of the reason lay in dissatisfactions with the Western democracies that were already present, and were easily magnified by Communist propaganda.

Confucians, as far back as Confucius and Mencius and continuing over the centuries, have denounced the economic exploitation of the masses.[12] From time immemorial both the Chinese people and their government have looked with distrust upon the concentration of economic wealth and power in private hands. In the twentieth century China's political leaders—even those who looked most to the West—have in general considered private ownership of large enterprises an evil, and have been determined that their control should rest with the state. On this point the pronouncements of Sun Yat-sen, Chiang Kai-shek, and Mao Tsê-tung show remarkable similarities.[13]

Most Chinese had little opportunity to see the advantages of free enterprise and economic competition. In such factories as existed in China working conditions were often very bad indeed. Western businessmen, operating in China under privileged extraterritorial status, were frequently arrogant, cynical, and predatory. These things made it easy for the Communists to represent that capitalism, as practiced in the Western democracies, is nothing but a system of oppressive economic exploitation.

Moreover, a century of invasion of China's territory and independence had left scars that could not quickly heal, even after concessions were returned and special privileges for foreigners in China were abolished. How, many Chinese asked, could nations that had been guilty of such injustice, and practiced the barbarity of two world wars, have a culture that offered the perfect pattern for mankind?

The Communists promised that China's wrongs should be avenged by a world crusade, waged on behalf of oppressed men everywhere, which should wipe the "imperialist" governments off the face of the earth.

Nevertheless, China might have been able to forgive the Western nations their injuries, but she could not forgive their charity. The proud can bear abuse far more easily than charity, and the Chinese are one of the proudest of peoples. For many years the peoples of the West, and especially of the United

States, have been sending to China missionaries, doctors, and teachers, and money for schools, hospitals, famine relief, and general assistance to the government and the people. They have done these things in a spirit of the purest altruism, accompanied by a complacent assurance of their own superiority that could only be infuriating to any normal human being on the receiving end.

All this might have been bearable if there had been any adequate appreciation of the fact that China had, in her culture, something from which the West might learn and by which it might profit, as a *quid pro quo*. But there was little of this. Even some of the most "pro-Chinese" Westerners constantly told the Chinese, like adults speaking to children, that they must "modernize," that is, that they must abandon their traditional ways in government, in law, in religion, and in social and economic practices, and copy ours. Then and only then, they were told, could they be received as partners into the family of nations.

The fact that many Chinese were themselves quite as critical of China's ways did not make this faultfinding by outsiders more palatable. Few of us will accept, from foreigners, the same criticisms of our country that we ourselves make quite readily. No self-respecting people could have been expected to receive, with gratitude, such a combination of charity and disparagement.

The Chinese Communists' "hate America" campaign was a logical result. The Communists interpret every gift, and every generous and helpful act directed toward the Chinese, as part of a gigantic imperialist plot. Schools and hospitals financed by the West are explained as tentacles of the vast octopus of "cultural imperialism," designed to draw the Chinese into the maw of capitalist and imperialist exploitation. Thus, by one ingenious stroke, the Chinese are absolved of any debt of gratitude, and their self-respect is restored and made whole. It is no wonder that many intellectuals accepted this explanation with enthusiasm.

In seeking to annex China to the Soviet sphere, the Russians appear to have taken considerable care not to offend the Chinese by assuming a posture of superiority. They have, it is true, strongly condemned China's traditional pattern of political and economic organization. But they have attributed it wholly to what they call China's "feudal ruling class," which used it, they assert, to oppress the people.

The Russians have not asked the Chinese to discard their own culture and replace it with that of Russia. Instead, they have invited the Chinese to join with the Russian and other peoples in adopting what is claimed to be a new order of economic, social, and political justice, to be founded on the premise of complete equality among all nationalities and races. Such a note, attuned not only to China's recent struggles but also to the ancient humanitarian and cosmopolitan doctrines of Confucianism, could not fail to find a response in Chinese hearts.

Toward the end of his career Sun Yat-sen was deeply impressed by the fact that, among the Western powers, only Soviet Russia represented itself as being ready to co-operate with China on a basis of full equality. In his immensely popular *Three Principles of the People*, Sun said that Russia "aims to curb the strong, support the weak, and promote justice. . . . It aims to destroy imperialism and capitalism throughout the world." And the Chinese would take their stand, he promised, beside the Soviet Union, to "use the strength of our four hundred millions to fight against injustice for all mankind; this is our Heaven-appointed task."[14]

Soviet Russia did not depend upon propaganda alone to win China to its cause. Numerous Russians were educated in the Chinese language, history, and culture, and prepared to operate in China with trained effectiveness. Many Chinese were invited to Russia and schooled in Communist doctrine and tactics at the expense of the Soviet government; it is believed that at least

eight of the thirteen members who made up the Chinese Politburo had studied in Russia.[15] Under the leadership of such men
Chinese Communists were organized into a network of tightly
disciplined cells, having as their objective the creation of a Communist China, and devoted to the overthrow of any other form
of government. Against such carefully planned operations the
almost careless gift of millions by the government of the United
States could accomplish little.

To those who believe that Soviet Russia is one of the greatest
imperialist powers the world has ever known, and that the men
in the Kremlin are bent upon the enslavement of the human
race, it may seem that those Chinese intellectuals who saw in
Communism their only hope for national independence and personal liberty were excessively naïve. It should be remembered,
however, that they had little access to any dispassionate appraisal of Communist theory and practice. The Nationalist
party and the Chinese Communists were bitter enemies; each
side praised itself and damned the other.

Another circumstance that aided the Communists was the
rather general disillusionment, in China, with democracy. After
the establishment of the Chinese Republic, many Chinese expected that the mere institution of democratic forms would
bring some marvelous change. They failed completely to realize that only a process of careful education could be expected
to make democracy work in China. After little more than a
decade of purely nominal "democracy," Sun Yat-sen, the
"father of the Chinese Republic," declared himself disgusted
with representative government and asserted that it could only
lead to corruption.[16]

During and after the second World War, the Nationalist government of Chiang Kai-shek was faced by problems that no
government could have solved with complete success. Its most
ardent defenders do not contend that it always made the wisest
choice. Its most bitter critics—and these came to include many
of the intellectuals—condemned it as hopelessly inefficient and

corrupt. When the Nationalists took police measures which they claimed were necessary to combat Communism, their critics denounced the Nationalist regime as a ruthlessly repressive police state. Since the Nationalists owed much of their power to the support of the Western democracies, and especially of the United States, this situation was utilized for very effective anti-Western propaganda by the Communists.

After the second World War a vast number of China's students and intellectuals were bent on the quest for a way out of China's desperate position. They were ready to throw themselves, with idealistic devotion, into any movement that seemed to promise the restoration of national self-respect, economic sufficiency, and individual dignity.

Many of them looked with favor upon Western democracy. But it was far from clear that it could be made to work, in China, with sufficient speed to solve the problems that would not wait. How could one go about making it work? It was difficult even to find a definition of democracy upon which Occidentals would agree. And democracy had no program for a country like China. Indeed, the Western democracies had never given much real thought to China's problems.

Soviet Russia had. In the Chinese Communist party a corps of Chinese, tested by time and hardened by battle, stood ready not only to propose a program but to undertake to make it work. They were not uncertain. They had precise definitions, catechisms, and schedules of operation. They not only knew what to do themselves, but were prepared to assign everyone else to his role in the common task. The part Communism proposed for the intellectuals was an attractive one. As Benjamin Schwartz has written, "The role it offered to the intelligentsia was a spectacular role of leadership in an atmosphere supercharged with the promise of imminent redemption. It called upon the intelligentsia to agitate and to organize and then to lead the organizations thus formed."[17]

To be sure, Communism required the individual to merge his

will in that of the party, but by this act of almost religious devotion he would come to participate in what was hailed as the most gallant community the world had ever known. He would have to submit to iron discipline, to work unceasingly, he might lose his life—but how gloriously! This appeal was far more akin to the sermons of Confucius to his disciples, urging them to give up everything to combat the oppression of the people, to work and if necessary to die for the Way, than were any of the sober preachments of Western democracy. It is not very remarkable that it won over enough of the intellectuals to throw the control of China into Communist hands.

For a century thinking Chinese have felt their country to be at a disadvantage, and some of them have even been ready to admit its culture to be inferior to that of the West. With the advent of Chinese Communism this is changed. For many of them believe that the Communist party "represents the most brilliant and progressive side of contemporary human society," and that "the Chinese Communist Party is one of the best Communist Parties in the world."[18]

The West has sent the Chinese missionaries to Christianize them, teachers to educate them, and money to alleviate their distress. But now the Chinese Communists propose to turn the tables. For it is the reactionary capitalist world above all, says Mao Tsê-tung, that constitutes a "world of darkness"; the Communists, he says, will overturn it and transform it "into a world of light that never existed before."[19] To do this, much patience will be required. Nevertheless, one of Mao's lieutenants declares, even the least promising members of the human race "can in the long course of struggle be . . . converted into highly civilized Communists."[20]

In the past, Western nations have repeatedly used force against China. At the cannon's mouth China has been compelled to sign treaties, permit trade, and admit foreigners she did not want to her borders. Here again, it is promised, the roles will be reversed. In the future it will be the Chinese Communists who will, as a part of the world crusade of Communism, use force against all those, throughout the world, who object to being "remolded" into Communists. Mao Tsê-tung says that "they will have to go through a stage of compulsion before they enter into a stage of remolding of their own accord."[21]

Finally, the nations of the West have long regarded China with thinly veiled contempt. Unable even to keep her own house in order, she was regarded as a negligible quantity in world affairs. Occidentals, ignorant of China's history, have dismissed her with the dictum that "the Chinese can't fight." That myth has been exploded on the battle fields of Korea. And speculation over what the Chinese Communists will do next keeps the lights burning late in every major capital of the world. China is no longer negligible.

Even Chinese who are strongly anti-Communist cannot avoid being gratified that their country again wields an influence, in world affairs, such as it has not enjoyed in many, many years. Many Chinese would prefer that this had not come about under Communist auspices, but whatever the auspices they find it hard not to applaud the result. This factor cannot be overlooked if we would understand why the Chinese Communists have won so large a degree of acceptance in so short a time.

What has been the effect of the victory of the Chinese Communists upon the thinking of the Chinese people? It is too early to answer this question with any precision, but some significant facts are quite clear.

If one examines such pronouncements of Mao Tsê-tung as *The New Democracy* and *On People's Democratic Dictatorship*, there is little to indicate that they were written by a Chinese. The framework of thought is Marxist; the very rare illustrations relating to Chinese culture seem almost self-consciously added, to keep the writings from seeming too "foreign." Considerable portions of these works read like paraphrases into Chinese of standard Communist tracts.

Naturally the Chinese people in general have not moved so rapidly, in their absorption of Communist doctrine, as has Mao Tsê-tung. Yet they have moved with a speed that would be quite astounding to anyone who did not know what has been going on in China during recent years. All over Communist China "re-education" is the watchword. Many persons spend hours every day, and many millions spend some time daily, in studying the works of Marx, Engels, Lenin, Stalin, and Mao Tsê-tung. Study groups are conducted by banks, factories, labor unions, and villages. Special schools give indoctrination courses of varying duration. Individuals considered politically unreliable are subjected to intensive indoctrination. It is probable that never before in human history has the attempt been made, on so large a scale, to change the whole pattern of thought of an entire people so quickly.

It is impossible to know to what extent their pattern of thought has actually been changed. There is evidence, however, that in various specific ways changes have been brought about that cannot be dismissed as superficial. A striking example has to do with the attitude of children toward their parents.

We have seen that the importance of the family in China goes back to a time before our knowledge of Chinese history begins. Three thousand years ago the principle was already established that a child's first loyalty was due its parents; this principle persisted to our own day. In traditional China it was unthinkable that a child should give evidence against his or her parents; to do so was in fact a legal offense.

An important technique of Chinese Communist propaganda is the "mass trial," a public spectacle in which one or more persons charged with being "enemies of the people" are denounced by a succession of accusers. In some of these trials the high point of drama has been reached, it is reported, when a child of the accused demonstrates loyalty to Communism by denouncing his or her parent. Undoubtedly, there are many Chinese who still disapprove such conduct. Yet we may be sure that the party leaders who arrange these trials do not believe that the general reaction to denunciations of this sort will be entirely negative. Nothing could better demonstrate the success which the Communists have had in changing some fundamental attitudes of the Chinese people. Still greater changes will undoubtedly result from the profound modification of the structure of the family and society by the institution of "communes."

Certain traditional attitudes have been in the Communists' favor. George E. Taylor goes so far as to say that the Chinese Communists "stem from the traditional Chinese bureaucratic ruling class" and that the Chinese Communist party represents "the bureaucracy, with all its tradition of political, social and economic monopoly."[22] This is perhaps to put the case too strongly. But there is no doubt that the long tradition of rule by a Confucian elite makes it easier for the Chinese people to accept, as reasonable, the continued dominance of the Communist elite.

Confucius himself was one of the most uncompromising opponents of dogmatism that ever lived. It is an ironic paradox, therefore, that the "immutable *li* (principle)" of Neo-Confucian orthodoxy provided a precedent that makes it less difficult for the Chinese to subscribe to what the Communists call "the universal truth of Marxism-Leninism."

Notwithstanding all this, the men who played the largest role in founding the Chinese Communist party were outspokenly hostile toward the Chinese tradition.[23] Such hostility continues to characterize the attitude of many Chinese Communists. Robert Payne states that the thinking of Mao Tsê-tung has been strongly influenced by Confucianism, but he also quotes Mao as having said, "I hated Confucius from the age of eight."[24] In *The New Democracy* Mao wrote that "emphasis on the honoring of Confucius and the reading of the classics, and advocacy of the old rules of propriety (*li*) and education and philosophy" are part of China's "semi-feudal culture" which must be overthrown. "The struggle between the old and new cultures," he wrote, "is to the death."[25]

This does not mean, however, that Mao and the Communists are trying to impose on China a cultural pattern that is wholly Marxist or Russian. Mao has explicitly disavowed this, saying: "In the past China has suffered greatly by accepting foreign ideas simply because they were foreign. Chinese Communists should remember this in applying Marxism in China. We must effect a genuine synthesis between the universal truth of Marxism and the concrete practice of the Chinese revolution. Only after we have found our own national form of Marxism will it prove useful."[26]

In developing her new culture Communist China will, Mao has said, accept some materials "even from the culture that existed in capitalist countries during the period of the Enlightenment." But everything will be subjected to a careful process of discrimination. Mao proposes to apply the same scrutiny to China's own traditional culture.

China's culture should have its own form, the national form. . . . The long feudal period* in China's history created the brilliant culture of previous ages. To make clear the process by which this traditional culture developed, to discard its feudal residue, and to absorb its democratic essence, are necessary steps for developing our new national culture and heightening our national self-confidence. This assimilation, however, must never be uncritical. We must carefully discriminate between those completely rotten aspects of the old culture that were linked with the feudal ruling class, and the excellent popular culture, which was more or less democratic and revolutionary in character.[27]

China's entire intellectual tradition is intimately linked with what the Communists call the "feudal ruling class." If the Chinese were to apply this criterion for selection literally, they would have to abandon their philosophical heritage in its entirety.

---

* The Chinese Communists consider China to have been "feudal" (or, during the last hundred years, "semi-feudal") until they themselves came to power. Most historians consider feudalism in China to have come to an end before the beginning of the Christian Era, although there was some recrudescence of feudal phenomena in certain later periods. Obviously, this difference arises partially out of different definitions of "feudalism."

The Chinese Communists are much too intelligent to attempt to abandon China's cultural tradition. They are in fact making a great deal of use of it. Since the Chinese love the theater, the Communists find it a most effective vehicle for their propaganda. They are not only writing new plays but also revising and "reforming" some of the old favorites to make them serve this purpose.[28] It has been reported that some of the ancient literature is being re-edited. Even the results of archeological excavations are being reinterpreted in terms of the light they are believed to throw on the "class struggle" in the second millennium B.C.

There has been much speculation as to whether the Marxists will be able to Communize the Chinese, or whether the Chinese will Sinicize Communism. There are many indications that, if China remains Communist, both of these processes will operate.

Liu Shao-ch'i, a vice-chairman of the Peking government, is considered the principal theoretician, after Mao Tsê-tung, of the Chinese Communist party. In his long and important treatise on *How To Be a Good Communist,* Liu quotes repeatedly from Marx, Lenin, Stalin, and other Communist authorities. He faithfully accords with the basic philosophy of Communism, which at some points conflicts sharply with China's traditional attitudes.

Nevertheless this is not merely a Communist, but a *Chinese* Communist work. Liu says that the Chinese Communist party "is one of the best Communist Parties in the world," being "powerfully armed with Marxist-Leninist theory, and the heir of all the splendid traditions of the many progressive men of thought and action who have illumined the pages of Chinese history."[29]

Liu quotes from Confucius, Mencius, and other Chinese philosophers of the past. He does not condemn them but, instead, borrows their authority to bolster Communist arguments. The pouring of the new wine of Communist dogma into the old bottles of the Chinese form is especially clear in this passage: "There are those who say that it is not possible, by means of study and self-cultivation, to attain to the qualities of such revolutionary geniuses as Marx, Engels, Lenin and Stalin. . . . They consider Marx, Engels, Lenin and Stalin to have been mysterious beings from birth. Is this correct? I think not."[30] This is quite like the discussion, in Mencius' day, of the problem of whether the sage emperors Yao and Shun were spiritual beings, possessing qualities to which ordinary men might not aspire.[31] Liu Shao-ch'i makes it clear that he has precisely this discussion in mind, for in support of his view he writes, "Mencius said, 'Any man can become a Yao or a Shun.' "[32]

In this work Liu does not reject China's traditional philosophy; instead, he denounces those who have failed to live up to it. He criticizes those who have pretended to honor the teachings of Confucius but in fact have only sought to use them to oppress the people and to further their own careers. "Of course," he writes, "we Communist Party members cannot adopt such an attitude in studying the principles of Marx and Lenin, and the excellent and useful teachings bequeathed to us by the ancient sages of our nation. As we speak, so we must act. We are honest and pure; we cannot deceive ourselves, the people, or the men of old."[33]

There would seem to be little doubt that, as time goes on, a great many elements of China's tradition that have been called "feudal" and "reactionary" will gradually find their way back into good standing. What is to happen to Confucius is not yet clear. Many Chinese of this century, and many Communists, have damned him as the chief foe of progress. Others, however, have felt differently. A book that is interesting in this connection was written in 1945 by Kuo Mo-jo, later vice-premier of the Peking government. In this work Kuo depicted Confucius not only as a champion of the rights of the common people but also as a fomenter of armed rebellion.[34] Thus it is by no means impossible that the idol of old China may come to be hailed as a forerunner, in the revolutionary tradition, of Marx, Lenin, Stalin, and Mao Tsê-tung, a hero of the new China.

Chapter XIII

In Retrospect

No one will ever again think exactly as did Confucius, or Chuang Tzŭ, or Chu Hsi, or even as the Chinese of 1900 did.* Neither, for that matter, can anyone living today agree with all of the ideas of Plato. Yet Plato's dialogues continue to be important, and have much to say that is helpful and useful in our modern world. So does much of Chinese philosophy.

When anti-Christian Chinese charged that missionaries gouged out the eyes of Chinese children, we could smile and shrug our shoulders. But when Yen Fu writes that Western progress has culminated in four achievements, "to be selfish, to kill others, to have no integrity and little sense of shame," there is a certain bite in his words. Not because we agree that he is right. Not only our Christian principles but a great host of self-sacrificing actions attest that he is wrong. And yet, when we look about us, we cannot escape the uneasy feeling that our principles do not always find complete fulfilment in our lives. Perhaps a little of the difficulty may lie in our philosophy.

Chinese, who look upon our culture with the surgical eye of the outsider, find it to be characterized especially by the spirit of aggressiveness and competition. Undoubtedly, these are qualities that ought to be included, in moderation, in the makeup of every nation and every individual. But when they are excessive they lead to quarrelsomeness in individuals and saber-rattling by nations.

* H. Arthur Steiner wrote in 1951: "The two years of shock treatment [the Chinese Communists] have administered to the traditional institutions of Chinese society have rendered virtually impossible a reconstitution of the pre-1949 forms of Chinese life" (*Annals of the American Academy of Political and Social Sciences*, 277.vii).

The aggressive and competitive tendency shows itself in one of the virtues of which we are most proud, our spirit of expansionism. Individuals and businesses must make more money this year than last year. Nations must "export or die," find new markets, and constantly widen their territories or at least their spheres of influence. Sooner or later expanding empires (both personal and national) must meet, and something must give. The result is conflict, which we deplore more often than we analyze its cause.

"Contentment" is a word that is not often heard in the modern West. Technically it is listed among the virtues, but in reality we seem to consider it a sin so dark that we are reluctant to pronounce its guilty name. There is some basis for this; in excess it becomes laziness and irresponsibility. Yet most psychiatrists, whose business it is to patch up the wreckage on the speedway of modern living, would probably agree that a reasonable dose of contentment would be excellent medicine for most of us.

Most Chinese philosophers have preached the virtue of contentment, and most Chinese have practiced it to a remarkable degree. Like other human beings, they have sometimes been guilty of greed and lust and overweening ambition. But most of them have shown an unusual talent for happiness, even in the midst of poverty and suffering. They have been able to find joy in things that many of us overlook: the interesting and humorous things that happen to people around one, the dramatic unfolding of the life of one's family, a bird, a flower, or even the singing of a cricket. Realizing that tomorrow never comes, they have enjoyed living today. They have indulged in competition with each other much less than we do, but that does not mean that they have lived in a state of stagnation. There has always been the goal of excelling one's own previous achievements, and an emphasis upon improving quality rather than increasing quantity.

It will probably be said that this idealizes the traditional

Chinese way of life; perhaps it does. Contentment has been denounced as the besetting vice of the Chinese people, which has made it impossible for them to progress and to compete in the modern world; perhaps it has. But if it has, it is not because contentment is bad in itself but because it has been carried to an extreme, and not governed by that sense of moderation and balance that has lain at the very heart of China's traditional philosophy.

Balance, poise, is the hallmark of the Chinese who has been reared in the tradition of his nation's culture. This is true whether he is a scholar who studied the classics in the traditional manner, or a farmer or coolie who grew to manhood in a part of China untouched by the storms of "Westernization." It shows itself in a quiet assurance that has none of the assertiveness that goes with what we call "pride," and an affability that is quite imperturbable. It is an enviable quality.

Where does it come from? Not just from moral maxims; this is not merely a way of thought but a way of life. And that way of life comes in part from the practice of *li*, which Confucius taught twenty-five hundred years ago and the Chinese have continued to cultivate to our own century.

Li is (in part) ceremony. Most of us in the modern West have little use for ceremony: we think it is mostly foolishness. Undoubtedly it can be overdone, as Confucius himself recognized. But ceremony of a common-sense variety is simply a means of imparting rhythm to life. When we play tennis or golf we recognize that rhythm is essential, but we live most of our lives at a jerky pace. The result is to injure our digestions, our nervous systems, and even our productivity. The traditional Chinese habit is to live in a more ordered way.

Of course, ceremony sometimes involves inconvenience. I used to wonder why it was that in imperial China court was always held at dawn—a horrible hour to get people out of bed. And I thought it still stranger that, even in the time of Confucius, when matters of the gravest importance were to be discussed, those taking part in the conference were supposed to sit up the whole night before; this seemed nothing but a primitive religious ritual. Then I had the opportunity to attend a sacrifice at the temple of Confucius in Peking.

It was held at dawn, and I had to get out of my bed at two A.M.—how willingly you can imagine. For most of the long ride to the temple I felt very sorry for myself. Gradually, however, the impressiveness of the situation and the magnificence of my surroundings took me out of myself. The sky was a deep, luminous blue that was quite unbelievable. The temples and the pine trees had indeed passed before my eyes on other occasions, but my senses were so sharpened by the dawn that I now realized that I had never before really seen, much less appreciated them. After many years I can still see the details of that ceremony much more clearly than I see the room about me. And I now understand why the Chinese held court at dawn. If it had been my business to deliberate upon affairs of state, I would have done a far better job of it that morning than I could ever do over a luncheon table, or drowsing in midafternoon.

It is not necessary, however, to get up in the middle of the night in order to profit by the Chinese idea that one should approach each task in the proper frame of mind for it. I was taught that during the second World War, while working in a government office in Washington, D.C. In another office in the same building was a Chinese scholar, a young man educated in the classical tradition who has an excellent knowledge of Chinese painting. To relieve the tedium of my work I was doing some studying in the evenings, and had encountered problems relating to Chinese art that were over my head. I therefore asked my Chinese friend if he would come to my apartment one evening and give me some help. He kindly agreed. Since we were working in the same building, I suggested that we meet when our work was over, go to a restaurant for dinner, and then go on to my place.

"No," he said, "I thank you, but I think that would not be

the best plan. We are going to discuss art. Let us go our separate ways, and have our dinners quietly. Then when I come to your house you can give me a cup of tea, and we can approach our discussion with our minds properly prepared for it."

He was quite right.

Chinese philosophy does not provide the answer to every problem confronting modern man. Neither, for that matter, does any philosophy that has yet been devised. But the Chinese have seen some things—and some things that we have missed—with particular clarity, and the things they have said about them are often helpful. If this brief introduction has made the reader want to learn more about Chinese thought, it will have served its purpose. A list of suggested works for further reading is appended.

Suggestions for Further Reading

The following works are grouped by topics which correspond roughly, but not precisely, to the chapters of this book. Sources are cited first, followed by secondary works.

GENERAL WORKS

Fung Yu-lan, *A History of Chinese Philosophy*. 2 vols. Translated by Derk Bodde. Princeton, 1952 and 1953.

E. R. Hughes, *Chinese Philosophy in Classical Times*. London and New York, 1942.

Fung Yu-lan, *The Spirit of Chinese Philosophy*. Translated by E. R. Hughes. London, 1947.

Fung Yu-lan, *A Short History of Chinese Philosophy*. Edited by Derk Bodde. New York, 1948.

Studies in Chinese Thought. Edited by Arthur F. Wright. Chicago, 1953.

Chinese Thought and Institutions. Edited by John K. Fairbank. Chicago, 1957.

CONFUCIUS

The Confucian Analects. Translated by James Legge, in "The Chinese Classics," I (2d ed.; Oxford, 1893), 137–354.

The Analects of Confucius. Translated by Arthur Waley. London, 1938.

H. G. Creel, *Confucius, the Man and the Myth*. New York, 1949; London, 1951.

MO TZŬ

The Ethical and Political Works of Motse. Translated by Y. P. Mei. London, 1929.

Y. P. Mei, *Motse, the Neglected Rival of Confucius*. London, 1934.

MENCIUS

The Works of Mencius. Translated by James Legge, in "The Chinese Classics," Vol. II (2d ed.; Oxford, 1895).

Arthur Waley, *Three Ways of Thought in Ancient China*, pp. 115–95. London, 1939.

I. A. Richards, *Mencius on the Mind*. London, 1932.

TAOISM

Arthur Waley, *The Way and Its Power*. London, 1934. This volume includes both a study of Taoism and, on pp. 141–243, a translation of the *Tao Tê Ching*.

The Tâo Teh King. (Tao Tê Ching). Translated by JAMES LEGGE, in "Sacred Books of the East," XXXIX (London, 1891), 47–124.

The Writings of Kwang-zze (Chuang Tzŭ). Translated by JAMES LEGGE, in "Sacred Books of the East," XXXIX (London, 1891), 164–392, and XL (London, 1891), 1–232.

ARTHUR WALEY, *Three Ways of Thought in Ancient China,* pp. 17–112. London, 1939.

HSÜN TZŬ

The Works of Hsüntze. Translated by HOMER H. DUBS. London, 1928.

"Hsün-tzŭ on the Rectification of Names," translated by J. J. L. DUYVENDAK, in *T'oung Pao,* XXIII (Leiden, 1924), 221–54.

HOMER H. DUBS, *Hsüntze, the Moulder of Ancient Confucianism.* London, 1927.

LEGALISM

The Book of Lord Shang. Translated by J. J. L. DUYVENDAK. London, 1928.

The Complete Works of Han Fei Tzŭ, Vol. I. Translated by W. K. LIAO. London, 1939.

ARTHUR WALEY, *Three Ways of Thought in Ancient China,* pp. 199–255. London, 1939.

DERK BODDE, *China's First Unifier; a Study of the Ch'in Dynasty as Seen in the Life of Li Ssŭ.* Leiden, 1938.

HAN DYNASTY THOUGHT

HU SHIH, "The Establishment of Confucianism as a State Religion during the Han Dynasty," *Journal of the North China Branch of the Royal Asiatic Society,* LX (Shanghai, 1929), 20–41.

BUDDHISM

CLARENCE H. HAMILTON, *Buddhism, a Religion of Infinite Compassion: Selections from Buddhist Literature.* New York, 1952.

CHARLES ELIOT, *Hinduism and Buddhism, an Historical Sketch.* London, 1921.

HU SHIH, "Development of Zen Buddhism in China," *Chinese Social and Political Science Review,* XV (Peiping, 1932), 475–505.

NEO-CONFUCIANISM

The Philosophy of Human Nature by Chu Hsi. Translated by J. PERCY BRUCE. London, 1922.

The Philosophy of Wang Yang-ming. Translated by FREDERICK GOODRICH HENKE. London and Chicago, 1916.

Suggestions for Further Reading

J. Percy Bruce, *Chu Hsi and His Masters, an Introduction to Chu Hsi and the Sung School of Chinese Philosophy.* London, 1923.

Siu-chi Huang, *Lu Hsiang-shan, a Twelfth Century Chinese Idealist Philosopher.* New Haven, 1944.

THE REACTION AGAINST NEO-CONFUCIANISM

Mansfield Freeman, "The Ch'ing Dynasty Criticism of Sung Politico-Philosophy," *Journal of the North China Branch of the Royal Asiatic Society,* LIX (Shanghai, 1928), 78–110.

Mansfield Freeman, "The Philosophy of Tai Tung-yüan," *Journal of the North China Branch of the Royal Asiatic Society,* LXIV (Shanghai, 1933), 50–71.

Chan Wing-tsit, "Neo-Confucianism." In H. F. MacNair (ed.), *China,* pp. 254–65. Berkeley and Los Angeles, 1946.

THE INFLUENCE OF THE WEST

Chan Wing-tsit, "Trends in Contemporary Philosophy." In H. F. MacNair (ed.), *China,* pp. 312–30. Berkeley and Los Angeles, 1946.

Hu Shih, *The Chinese Renaissance.* Chicago, 1934.

SUN YAT-SEN

Sun Yat-sen, *San Min Chu I, The Three Principles of the People.* Translated by Frank W. Price. Shanghai, 1927.

Paul M. A. Linebarger, *The Political Doctrines of Sun Yat-sen.* Baltimore, 1937.

CHINESE COMMUNISM

Mao Tsê-tung, *On People's Democratic Dictatorship.* Translated in Otto van der Sprenkel (ed.), *New China: Three Views,* pp. 180–97. London, 1950.

Mao Tsê-tung, *China's New Democracy.* Translator unnamed. New York, 1945.

Liu Shao-ch'i, *How To Be a Good Communist.* Translator unnamed. Peking, 1951.

Documentary History of Chinese Communism. Edited by Conrad Brandt and Others. Cambridge, Mass., 1952.

Annals of the American Academy of Political and Social Science, Vol. 277 (Philadelphia, 1951), *Report on China,* edited by H. Arthur Steiner.

New China: Three Views. Edited by Otto B. van der Sprenkel. London, 1950.

Benjamin I. Schwartz, *Chinese Communism and the Rise of Mao.* Cambridge, Mass., 1951.

Bibliography

AMERICAN CONSULATE GENERAL, HONGKONG. "Survey of China Mainland Press." Mimeographed releases, individually numbered and dated.

BALÁZS, ÉTIENNE. "La Crise sociale et la philosophie à la fin des Han," *T'oung Pao*, XXXIX (Leiden, 1950), 83–131.

CHAVANNES, ÉDOUARD (trans.). *Les Mémoires historiques de Se-ma Ts'ien.* 5 vols. Paris, 1895–1905.

CHIANG KAI-SHEK. *China's Destiny.* Authorized translation by WANG CHUNG-HUI. New York, 1947.

CHIANG WEI-CH'IAO 蔣維喬. *Chin San Pai Nien Chung Kuo Chê Hsüeh Shih* 近三百年中國哲學史. 1932; 3d ed., Shanghai, 1936.

CHU HSI 朱熹. *Chu Tzŭ Yü Lei Ta Ch'üan* 朱子語類大全.

———. *Ssŭ Shu Chi Chu* 四書集注. *Ssŭ Pu Pei Yao* ed.

Chuang Tzŭ 莊子. Also known as the Nan Hua Chên Ching 南華真經. *Ssŭ Pu Ts'ung K'an* ed.

CREEL, H. G. *Confucius, the Man and the Myth.* New York, 1949; London, 1951.

———. *Studies in Early Chinese Culture, First Series.* Baltimore, 1937.

CREEL, LORRAINE. "The Concept of Social Order in Early Confucianism." Unpublished Ph.D. dissertation, University of Chicago, 1943.

DUBS, HOMER H. "The Failure of the Chinese To Produce Philosophical Systems," *T'oung Pao*, XXVI (Leiden, 1929), 98–109.

—— (trans.). *The History of the Former Han Dynasty.* By PAN KU. Vols. I and II. Baltimore, 1938 and 1944.

—— (trans.). *The Works of Hsüntze.* London, 1928.

DUYVENDAK, J. J. L. (trans.). *The Book of Lord Shang.* London, 1928.

———. "Hsün-tzŭ on the Rectification of Names," *T'oung Pao*, XXIII (Leiden, 1924), 221–54.

ELIOT, CHARLES. *Hinduism and Buddhism, an Historical Sketch.* 3 vols. London, 1921.

Encyclopaedia of the Social Sciences. Edited by EDWIN R. A. SELIG-MAN and ALVIN JOHNSON. 15 vols. 1930–35; reprinted, New York, 1937.

ESCARRA, JEAN. *Le Droit chinois*. Peking and Paris, 1936.

FINER, HERMAN. *The Future of Government*. London, 1946.

FORSTER, E. M. *Two Cheers for Democracy*. New York: Harcourt, Brace & Co., 1951.

FREEMAN, MANSFIELD. "The Ch'ing Dynasty Criticism of Sung Po-litico-Philosophy," *Journal of the North China Branch of the Royal Asiatic Society*, LIX (Shanghai, 1928), 78–110.

——. "The Philosophy of Tai Tung-yüan," *Journal of the North China Branch of the Royal Asiatic Society*, LXIV (Shanghai, 1933), 50–71.

FUNG YU-LAN 馮友蘭. *Chung Kuo Chê Hsüeh Shih* 中國哲學史. 2 vols. 1934; 7th ed., Chungking, 1946.

——. "The Philosophy of Chu Hsi," translated by DERK BODDE (from *Chung Kuo Chê Hsüeh Shih*, II.896–927), *Harvard Journal of Asiatic Studies*, VII (Cambridge, 1942), 1–51.

——. *A Short History of Chinese Philosophy*. Edited by DERK BODDE. New York, 1948.

GARDNER, CHARLES S. *Chinese Traditional Historiography*. Cambridge, 1938.

GERTH, H. H., and C. WRIGHT MILLS (trans. and ed.). *From Max Weber: Essays in Sociology*. New York, 1946.

GIBBON, EDWARD. *The History of the Decline and Fall of the Roman Empire*. 3 vols. 1776–88; reprinted New York, 1946.

GOODRICH, LUTHER CARRINGTON. *The Literary Inquisition of Ch'ien-lung*. Baltimore, 1935.

HAMILTON, CLARENCE H. "Hsüan Chuang and the Wei Shih Philosophy," *Journal of the American Oriental Society*, LI (New Haven, 1931), 291–308.

HAN YÜ 韓愈. *Chu Wên Kung Chiao Han Ch'ang-li Hsien Shêng Chi* 朱文公校韓昌黎先生集. *Ssŭ Pu Ts'ung K'an* ed.

HAYAKAWA, S. I. "What Is Meant by Aristotelian Structure of Language," *Etc.: A Review of General Semantics*, V (Blooming-ton, Ill., 1947–48), 225–30.

HENKE, FREDERICK GOODRICH. *The Philosophy of Wang Yang-ming*. London and Chicago, 1916.

Hodous, Lewis. *Buddhism and Buddhists in China*. New York, 1924.

Howe, Mark De Wolfe (ed.). *Holmes-Pollock Letters, the Correspondence of Mr. Justice Holmes and Sir Frederick Pollock, 1874–1932*. 2 vols. Cambridge, 1941.

Hu Shih 胡適. *Chung Kuo Chê Hsüeh Shih Ta Kang* 中國哲學史大綱. Chüan Shang, 15th ed. Shanghai, 1930.

——. "Confucianism." In *Encyclopaedia of the Social Sciences*, IV, 198–201. New York, 1937.

——. "Development of Zen Buddhism in China," *Chinese Social and Political Science Review*, XV (Peiping, 1931–32), 475–505.

——. "The Establishment of Confucianism as a State Religion during the Han Dynasty," *Journal of the North China Branch of the Royal Asiatic Society*, LX (Shanghai, 1929), 20–41.

——. *Tai Tung-yüan Ti Chê Hsüeh* 戴東原的哲學. Shanghai, 1927.

Huai Nan Tzŭ 淮南子. Ssŭ Pu Ts'ung K'an ed.

Huan K'uan 桓寬. *Discourses on Salt and Iron*. Translated by Esson M. Gale. Leiden, 1931.

——, *Yen T'ieh Lun* 鹽鐵論. Ssŭ Pu Ts'ung K'an ed.

Huang Hui 黃暉. *Lun Hêng Chiao Shih* 論衡校釋. Shanghai, 1939.

Huang Siu-chi. *Lu Hsiang-shan*. New Haven, 1944.

Huang Tsung-hsi 黃宗羲. *Ming I Tai Fang Lu* 明夷待訪錄. Ssŭ Pu Pei Yao ed.

Hughes, E. R. *Chinese Philosophy in Classical Times*. London, 1942.

Hummel, A. W. (ed.). *Eminent Chinese of the Ch'ing Period*. 2 vols. Washington, 1943–44.

Ku Yen-wu 顧炎武. *T'ing-lin Hsien Shêng I Shu Hui Chi* 亭林先生遺書彙輯. Wu-hsien, 1888.

Kung-Sun Lung Tzŭ 公孫龍子. Ssŭ Pu Ts'ung K'an ed.

Kuo Mo-jo 郭沫若. *Liang Chou Chin Wên Tz'ŭ Ta Hsi K'ao Shih* 兩周金文辭大系考釋. Tokyo, 1935.

——. *Shih P'i P'an Shu* 十批判書. Chungking, 1945.

Lao Tzŭ 老子. The book is also called the *Tao Tê Ching* 道德經. Its chapters seem to be numbered identically in all texts and translations.

Legge, James (trans.). *The Ch'un Ts'ew, with the Tso Chuen.* ("The Chinese Classics," Vol. V.) London, 1872.

—— (trans.). *The Great Learning.* ("The Chinese Classics," I, 355–81.) 2d ed. Oxford, 1893.

—— (trans.). *The Lî Kî.* ("Sacred Books of the East," Vols. XXVII and XXVIII.) 2d impression. London, 1926.

—— (trans.). *The She King.* ("The Chinese Classics," Vol. IV.) London, 1871.

—— (trans.). *The Shoo King.* ("The Chinese Classics," Vol. III.) London, 1865.

—— (trans.). *The Writings of Kwang-zze.* ("Sacred Books of the East," XXXIX, 125–392 and XL, 1–232.) 1891; reprinted, London, 1927.

—— (trans.). *The Yî King.* ("Sacred Books of the East," Vol. XVI.) 2d ed. Oxford, 1899.

Lieh Tzŭ 列子. Also known as the *Ch'ung Hsü Chih Tê Chên Ching* 沖虛至德真經. *Ssŭ Pu Ts'ung K'an* ed.

Lin T'ung-chi, "The Taoist in Every Chinese," *T'ien Hsia Monthly*, XI (Shanghai, 1940), 211–25.

Liu Shao-ch'i. *How To Be a Good Communist.* Peking, 1951.

Lu Hsiang-shan 陸象山. *Hsiang-shan Hsien Shêng Ch'üan Chi* 象山先生全集. *Ssŭ Pu Ts'ung K'an* ed.

Lü Shih Ch'un Ch'iu 呂氏春秋. *Ssŭ Pu Ts'ung K'an* ed.

MacNair, Harley Farnsworth (ed.). *China.* Berkeley and Los Angeles, 1946.

Mao Tsê-tung 毛澤東. *China's New Democracy.* With an Introduction by Earl Browder. Translator not named. New York, 1945.

MAO TSÊ-TUNG. *Lun Jên Min Min Chu Chuan Chêng* 論人民民主專政. 4th ed. 1949.

———. *On Practice*. Translator not named. Peking, 1951.

MASPERO, HENRI. *Le Taoïsme*. Paris, 1950.

MEI YI-PAO (trans.). *The Ethical and Political Works of Motse*. London, 1929.

NORTH, ROBERT C. "The Chinese Communist Elite," *Annals of the American Academy of Political and Social Science*, 277 (Philadelphia, September, 1951), 67–75.

PAYNE, ROBERT. *Mao Tse-tung, Ruler of Red China*. New York, 1950.

PLATO. *Cratylus*. In *The Dialogues of Plato*, I, 173–229. Translated by BENJAMIN JOWETT. 2 vols. 1892; reprinted, New York, 1937. Pagination given as in Stephens.

———. *Laws*. In *The Dialogues of Plato*, II, 407–703.

———. *Phaedo*. In *The Dialogues of Plato*, I, 173–229.

———. *The Republic*. In *The Dialogues of Plato*, I, 591–879.

REICHELT, KARL LUDWIG. *Truth and Tradition in Chinese Buddhism*. Translated by KATHRINA VAN WAGENEN BUGGE. Shanghai, 1927.

REICHWEIN, ADOLF. *China and Europe: Intellectual and Artistic Contacts in the Eighteenth Century*. Translated by J. C. POWELL. New York, 1925.

RICHARDS, I. A. *Mencius on the Mind: Experiments in Multiple Definition*. London, 1932.

SCHWARTZ, BENJAMIN I. *Chinese Communism and the Rise of Mao*. Cambridge, 1951.

Shih San Ching Chu Su 十三經注疏. Nanchang, 1815.

SHRYOCK, JOHN K. *The Origin and Development of the State Cult of Confucius*. New York and London, 1932.

SOOTHILL, W. E. *The Lotus of the Wonderful Law*. Oxford, 1930.

SUN I-JANG 孫詒讓. *Mo Tzǔ Hsien Ku* 墨子閒詁. 1895.

SUN YAT-SEN. *Chung-shan Ts'ung Shu* 中山叢書. 4 vols. 3d ed. Shanghai, 1927.

———. *San Min Chu I, The Three Principles of the People*. Translated by FRANK W. PRICE. 4th impression. Shanghai, 1929.

TAI CHÊN 戴震. *Mêng Tzǔ Tzǔ I Su Chêng* 孟子字義疏證. Chengtu, 1924.

———. *Tai Tung-yüan Chi* 戴東原集. *Ssŭ Pu Ts'ung K'an* ed.

———. *Yüan Shan* 原善. In Hu Shih, *Tai Tung-yüan Ti Chê Hsüeh* 戴東原的哲學, *Fu Lu* 1–35.

Takigawa Kametaro. *Shih Chi Hui Chu K'ao Chêng* 史記會注考證. 10 vols. Tokyo, 1932–34.

Taylor, George E. "The Hegemony of the Chinese Communists, 1945–1950," *Annals of the American Academy of Political and Social Science*, 277 (Philadelphia, September, 1951), 13–21.

Tuan Yü-ts'ai 段玉裁. *Tai Tung-yüan Hsien Shêng Nien P'u* 戴東原先生年譜. In Tai Chên, *Tai Tung-yüan Chi. Ssŭ Pu Ts'ung K'an* ed.

Tung Chung-shu 董仲舒. *Ch'un Ch'iu Fan Lu* 春秋繁露. *Ssŭ Pu Ts'ung K'an* ed.

van der Sprenkel, Otto B. (ed.). *New China: Three Views*. By Otto van der Sprenkel, Robert Guillain, and Michael Lindsay. London, 1950.

Wang Ch'ung 王充. *Lun Hêng* 論衡. *Ssŭ Pu Ts'ung K'an* ed.

Wang Hsien-ch'ien 王先謙. *Ch'ien Han Shu Pu Chu* 前漢書補註. Changsha, 1900.

———. *Hsün Tzŭ Chi Chieh* 荀子集解. 1891.

Wang Hsien-shên 王先慎. *Han Fei Tzŭ Chi Chieh* 韓非子集解. 1896.

Wang Yang-ming 王陽明. *Wang Wên-ch'êng Kung Ch'üan Shu* 王文成公全書. *Ssŭ Pu Ts'ung K'an* ed.

Williamson, H. R. *Wang An Shih*. 2 vols. London, 1935–37.

Yen Li Ts'ung Shu 顏李叢書. Works of Yen Yüan 顏元 and Li Kung 李塨. Peking, 1923.

References

CHAPTER I

The Chinese View

1. Legge, *The Writings of Kwang-zze*, I.319–20.
2. Forster, *Two Cheers for Democracy* (New York: Harcourt, Brace & Co., 1951), pp. 90–91.
3. Gibbon, *The History of the Decline and Fall of the Roman Empire*, I.303.

CHAPTER II

Before Confucius

1. Legge, *The She King*, p. 468.
2. Kuo Mo-jo, *Liang Chou Chin Wên Tz'ŭ Ta Hsi K'ao Shih*, p. 133a.
3. Legge, *The She King*, p. 458.
4. Legge, *The Shoo King*, p. 623.
5. Legge, *The She King*, p. 257.
6. *Ibid.*, p. 564.
7. *Ibid.*, p. 320.
8. Legge, *The Shoo King*, p. 506.
9. *Ibid.*, pp. 396–97.
10. *Ibid.*, p. 389.
11. *Ibid.*, p. 415.
12. Creel, *Studies in Early Chinese Culture*, pp. 52–53.
13. Legge, *The Shoo King*, pp. 495–502.
14. Legge, *The She King*, pp. 250–52.
15. *Ibid.*, p. 337.
16. Legge, *The Shoo King*, pp. 392–93.
17. Legge, *The Ch'un Ts'ew, with the Tso Chuen*, p. 619.

CHAPTER III

Confucius and the Struggle for Human Happiness

1. See Creel, *Confucius, the Man and the Myth*, pp. 7–11, 291–94.
2. *Analects* 9.6.3.
3. *Ibid.* 17.22.
4. *Mencius* 2(1)2.7.

5. *Analects* 13.30; see also 13.29.

6. *Ibid.* 15.38.

7. *Ibid.* 7.7.

8. *Ibid.* 9.26.

9. *Ibid.* 7.8.

10. *Ibid.* 12.2.

11. *Ibid.* 3.4.

12. *Ibid.* 6.25; see also 4.5.

13. *Ibid.* 4.8.

14. *Ibid.* 15.28.

15. Han Yü, *Chu Wên Kung Chiao Han Ch'ang-li Hsien Shêng Chi* 11.1*a*–3*b*.

16. *Analects* 11.23.3; see also 14.17–18.

17. *Ibid.* 14.13.2, 19.1.

18. *Ibid.* 14.23.

19. *Ibid.* 5.12.

20. *Ibid.* 11.11.

21. *Ibid.* 9.5.

22. *Ibid.* 14.37.

23. *Mencius* 1(1)4.6.

24. *Analects* 6.1.1.

25. *Ibid.* 2.18.

26. *Ibid.* 15.30.

27. *Ibid.* 7.27. Concerning this translation, see Creel, *Confucius, the Man and the Myth*, p. 311, n. 24.

28. Gerth and Mills, *From Max Weber*, p. 293.

29. *Analects* 13.16.

30. *Ibid.* 15.23.

31. *Ibid.* 6.28.

32. *Ibid.* 2.3.

33. *Ibid.* 14.8.

34. *Ibid.* 14.23.

35. *Ibid.* 13.15.

36. *Ibid.* 12.18.

37. *Ibid.* 11.16.

38. *Ibid.* 7.34.

39. *Ibid.* 9.11.

40. Reichwein, *China and Europe*, p. 77.

41. *Analects* 12.22.1.

42. *Ibid.* 15.15.

CHAPTER IV

Mo Tzŭ and the Quest for Peace and Order

1. Hu Shih, *Chung Kuo Chê Hsüeh Shih Ta Kang*, Chüan Shang, p. 151.
2. Mei Yi-pao, *The Ethical and Political Works of Motse*, p. 223.
3. *Ibid.*, p. 89.
4. *Ibid.*, pp. 30–31.
5. *Ibid.*, pp. 49–50.
6. *Ibid.*, pp. 46, 53, 85.
7. Sun I-jang, *Mo Tzŭ Hsien Ku* 12.11*b*. This passage is translated differently in Mei Yi-pao, *The Ethical and Political Works of Motse*, p. 233.
8. Legge, *The Shoo King*, p. 386.
9. Legge, *The She King*, p. 509.
10. Mei Yi-pao, *The Ethical and Political Works of Motse*, p. 249.
11. *Ibid.*, p. 224.
12. *Ibid.*, p. 233.
13. *Ibid.*, p. 234.
14. *Ibid.*, p. 125.
15. *Analects* 3.4, 11.10.
16. Legge, *The Ch'un Ts'ew, with the Tso Chuen*, p. 328.
17. Mei Yi-pao, *The Ethical and Political Works of Motse*, p. 114.
18. *Ibid.*, p. 244.
19. *Ibid.*, pp. 104–6.
20. *Ibid.*, pp. 220–21
21. *Ibid.*, p. 259.
22. *Ibid.*, pp. 79–80.
23. Sun I-jang, *Mo Tzŭ Hsien Ku* 12.3*b*; Mei Yi-pao, *The Ethical and Political Works of Motse*, p. 224.
24. Mei Yi-pao, *The Ethical and Political Works of Motse*, pp. 91–92.
25. *Ibid.*, p. 90.
26. *Ibid.*, p. 89.
27. *Ibid.*, pp. 126–29.
28. *Ibid.*, p. 180.
29. Legge, *Li Ki*, II.127.
30. Mei Yi-pao, *The Ethical and Political Works of Motse*, p. 224.
31. *Ibid.*, pp. 56–57.
32. Quoted in Finer, *The Future of Government*, p. 19.

33. Mei Yi-pao, *The Ethical and Political Works of Motse*, pp. 62–64.

34. *Ibid.*, p. 237.

35. *Ibid.*, p. 139.

36. *Ibid.*, p. 165.

37. *Ibid.*, pp. 251–52.

38. *Ibid.*, pp. 238–39.

39. *Ibid.*, p. 252.

40. *Ibid.*, p. 214.

41. *Ibid.*, p. 254.

42. *Huai Nan Tzŭ* 20.10*a*.

43. *Lü Shih Ch'un Ch'iu* 1.12.

44. *Ibid.* 19.9.

45. *Kung-Sun Lung Tzŭ* 3*b*–5*b*; this whole discourse is translated in Hughes, *Chinese Philosophy in Classical Times*, pp. 122–25.

46. Sun I-jang, *Mo Tzŭ Hsien Ku* 11.11.

47. *Ibid.* 10.5*a*, 44*a*.

48. *Chuang Tzŭ* 10.42*b*.

49. Takigawa Kametaro, *Shih Chi Hui Chu K'ao Chêng* 130.12.

50. Wang Hsien-ch'ien, *Hsün Tzŭ Chi Chieh* 15.5*a*.

51. *Chuang Tzŭ* [commentary] 10.43*b*–44*a*.

52. Gale, *Discourses on Salt and Iron*, p. 123.

53. *Ibid.*, pp. 116–17.

54. Mei Yi-pao, *The Ethical and Political Works of Motse*, p. 229.

55. *Chuang Tzŭ* 10.28*a*.

56. Mencius 7(1)26.2.

57. Mei Yi-pao, *The Ethical and Political Works of Motse*, p. 189.

CHAPTER V

Mencius and the Emphasis on Human Nature

1. Takigawa Kametaro, *Shih Chi Hui Chu K'ao Chêng* 67.29, 121.3–4.

2. *Mencius* 4(2)31.

3. Chavannes, *Les Mémoires historiques de Se-ma Ts'ien* V.157–58.

4. Huan K'uan, *Yen T'ieh Lun* 2.13*b*.

5. Takigawa Kametaro, *Shih Chi Hui Chu K'ao Chêng* 74.12.

6. Chavannes, *Les Mémoires historiques de Se-ma Ts'ien* V.157–58.

7. *Mencius* 3(2)9.9.

8. *Ibid.* 7(1)26.

9. *Ibid.* 7(2)26.1.

10. *Ibid.* 3(2)10.
11. *Ibid.* 3(1)4.1–6.
12. Richards, *Mencius on the Mind*, p. 28.
13. Hu Shih, *Chung Kuo Chê Hsüeh Shih Ta Kang*, Chüan Shang 13.
14. See Creel, *Confucius, the Man and the Myth*, p. 194.
15. *Mencius* 4(2)22.2.
16. Takigawa Kametaro, *Shih Chi Hui Chu K'ao Chêng* 74.3.
17. *Mencius* 7(2)30.
18. *Ibid.* 6(2)13.
19. *Ibid.* 2(2)14.
20. *Ibid.* 3(2)4.
21. Richards, *Mencius on the Mind*, p. 55.
22. *Mencius* 2(2)13.1–2.
23. *Ibid.* 2(2)8.
24. *Ibid.* 7(1)9.
25. *Ibid.* 7(1)21.
26. *Ibid.* 6(1)16.1.
27. *Ibid.* 7(1)36.
28. *Ibid.* 3(2)2.3.
29. *Ibid.* 4(2)31.3.
30. *Ibid.* 2(2)11.3.
31. *Ibid.* 5(2)7.4.
32. *Ibid.* 7(1)8.
33. *Ibid.* 5(2)6.
34. *Ibid.* 6(2)5.
35. *Ibid.* 2(2)2.
36. *Ibid.* 5(1)5.
37. *Ibid.* 1(2)9.
38. *Ibid.* 4(1)6.
39. *Ibid.* 1(2)7.
40. *Shih San Ching Chu Su, Mêng Tzŭ Chu Su T'i Tz'ŭ Chieh* 2b.
41. *Mencius* 7(1)36.
42. *Ibid.* 7(2)34.
43. *Ibid.* 5(2)2.
44. *Ibid.* 1(1)4.
45. *Ibid.* 5(2)9.
46. *Ibid.* 1(2)8.
47. *Ibid.* 1(1)5.
48. *Ibid.* 7(2)4.
49. *Ibid.* 2(2)1.
50. *Ibid.* 3(1)3.
51. *Ibid.* 7(1)22.2.
52. *Ibid.* 1(1)3.3.

53. *Ibid.* 1(1)7.20.
54. *Ibid.* 1(1)7.24, 3(1)3.10.
55. *Ibid.* 2(2)4.
56. *Ibid.* 5(1)5.
57. *Ibid.* 5(1)6.
58. *Analects* 2.10.
59. *Mencius* 4(1)15.
60. *Ibid.* 4(1)1.
61. *Ibid.* 4(1)2.2.
62. *Ibid.* 6(2)10.
63. *Ibid.* 5(1)4.1.
64. *Ibid.* 7(2)3.1.
65. *Ibid.* 1(1)1.
66. *Ibid.* 4(2)32.
67. *Ibid.* 6(1)6.
68. *Ibid.* 2(1)6.
69. *Ibid.* 6(1)7.
70. Richards, *Mencius on the Mind*, p. 75.
71. *Mencius* 2(1)2.10.
72. *Ibid.* 2(1)2.9–16.
73. *Ibid.* 7(2)35.
74. *Ibid.* 1(2)1–5.
75. *Analects* 6.25, 12.15.
76. *Mencius* 1(1)7.20.
77. *Ibid.* 4(2)19.1.
78. *Ibid.* 4(2)12.
79. *Ibid.* 2(1)2.15.
80. Mei Yi-pao, *The Ethical and Political Works of Motse*, p. 165.
81. *Mencius* 6(1)7.
82. *Ibid.* 3(2)6.
83. *Ibid.* 1(1)7.20–21.
84. *Ibid.* 7(1)27.
85. *Ibid.* 7(1)4.1.
86. *Ibid.* 7(1)1.1.
87. See Creel, *Confucius, the Man and the Myth*, p. 194.

CHAPTER VI

The Mystical Skepticism of the Taoists

1. Lin T'ung-chi, "The Taoist in Every Chinese," p. 215.
2. Legge, *The Yi King*, p. 96.
3. *Mencius* 7(1)26.1.
4. *Huai Nan Tzŭ* 13.7a.
5. *Lieh Tzŭ* 7.1b–2a.

6. Howe, *Holmes-Pollock Letters*, II.22.
7. Legge, *The Writings of Kwang-zze*, I.390.
8. *Ibid.*, I.180.
9. *Ibid.*, I.345.
10. *Ibid.*, II.48.
11. *Lao Tzŭ*, chap. 33.
12. Legge, *The Writings of Kwang-zze*, I.243.
13. *Ibid.*, I.248.
14. Maspero, *Le Taoïsme*, pp. 227–42.
15. See Creel, *Confucius, the Man and the Myth*, pp. 122–23.
16. *Lao Tzŭ*, chap. 4.
17. Plato *Laws* 679.
18. *Lao Tzŭ*, chap. 16.
19. Legge, *The Writings of Kwang-zze*, II.11.
20. *Lao Tzŭ*, chap. 2
21. Legge, *The Writings of Kwang-zze*, I.374–78.
22. *Ibid.*, I.191–92.
23. *Ibid.*, I.196.
24. *Ibid.*, I.195.
25. *Lao Tzŭ*, chap. 24.
26. *Ibid.*, chap. 9.
27. Legge, *The Writings of Kwang-zze*, II.16.
28. *Lao Tzŭ*, chap. 33.
29. *Ibid.*, chap. 44.
30. *Ibid.*, chap. 46.
31. Legge, *The Writings of Kwang-zze*, II.60–61.
32. *Ibid.*, I.199.
33. *Lao Tzŭ*, chap. 23.
34. *Ibid.*, chap. 1.
35. *Ibid.*, chap. 56.
36. *Ibid.*, chap. 81.
37. *Ibid.*, chap. 20.
38. *Ibid.*, chap. 19.
39. *Ibid.*, chap. 47.
40. Legge, *The Writings of Kwang-zze*, I.185–86.
41. *Lao Tzŭ*, chap. 31.
42. *Ibid.*, chap. 46.
43. *Ibid.*, chap. 75.
44. *Ibid.*, chap. 57.
45. *Ibid.*, chap. 74.
46. Legge, *The Writings of Kwang-zze*, I.300–303.
47. *Ibid.*, I.390.
48. *Ibid.*, I.265–66.
49. *Ibid.*, II.60–61.
50. *Lao Tzŭ*, chap. 70.

51. *Ibid.*, chap. 56.
52. *Ibid.*, chap. 3.
53. Legge, *The Writings of Kwang-zze*, I.240.
54. *Ibid.*, I.332.
55. *Lao Tzŭ*, chap. 5.
56. Wang Hsien-ch'ien, *Ch'ien Han Shu Pu Chu* 30.38a.

CHAPTER VII

The Authoritarianism of Hsün Tzŭ

1. Plato *Cratylus* 389; *Republic* x.596; *Phaedo* 100.
2. Duyvendak, "Hsün-tzŭ on the Rectification of Names," pp. 228–30.
3. *Ibid.*, p. 234.
4. Lorraine Creel, *The Concept of Social Order in Early Confucianism*, pp. 135–36; Wang Hsien-ch'ien, *Hsün Tzŭ Chi Chieh* 1.2a.
5. Dubs, *The Works of Hsüntze*, pp. 301–4.
6. *Ibid.*, p. 310.
7. *Ibid.*, p. 58.
8. *Ibid.*, pp. 60–61.
9. *Ibid.*, p. 61.
10. *Ibid.*, p. 305.
11. *Ibid.*, pp. 113–14.
12. *Ibid.*, pp. 313–14.
13. *Ibid.*, pp. 113–14.
14. *Ibid.*, p. 36.
15. *Ibid.*, pp. 50–51.
16. *Ibid.*, p. 37.
17. *Ibid.*, pp. 96–97.
18. *Ibid.*, pp. 49–50.
19. *Ibid.*, p. 276.
20. *Ibid.*, p. 36.
21. *Ibid.*, p. 40.
22. *Ibid.*, p. 65.
23. *Ibid.*, p. 99.
24. *Ibid.*, pp. 100–101.
25. Duyvendak, "Hsün-tzŭ on the Rectification of Names," pp. 252–53; Wang Hsien-ch'ien, *Hsün Tzŭ Chi Chieh* 16.14b–15b.
26. Dubs, *The Works of Hsüntze*, pp. 44–45.
27. *Ibid.*, pp. 275–76.
28. Wang Hsien-ch'ien, *Hsün Tzŭ Chi Chieh* 11.18b.
29. Dubs, *The Works of Hsüntze*, pp. 179–81.
30. *Ibid.*, pp. 244–46.
31. *Ibid.*, pp. 173–76.
32. *Ibid.*, pp. 44–45.

33. *Ibid.*, p. 240.
34. *Ibid.*, pp. 213–46.
35. *Ibid.*, p. 124.
36. *Ibid.*, p. 121.
37. *Ibid.*, p. 109.
38. Wang Hsien-ch'ien, *Hsün Tzŭ Chi Chieh* 19.12*b*.
39. Dubs, *The Works of Hsüntze*, p. 125.
40. *Ibid.*, pp. 157–58.
41. *Ibid.*, pp. 167–69.
42. Wang Hsien-ch'ien, *Hsün Tzŭ Chi Chieh* 7.8*b*–9*b*, 8.9*a*–11*a*; Lorraine Creel, *The Concept of Social Order in Early Confucianism*, p. 128.
43. Wang Hsien-ch'ien, *Hsün Tzŭ Chi Chieh* 9.4*b*–5*a*.
44. *Ibid.* 9.2*b*.
45. Dubs, *The Works of Hsüntze*, pp. 190–91.
46. Duyvendak, "Hsün-tzŭ on the Rectification of Names," p. 240.
47. Wang Hsien-ch'ien, *Hsün Tzŭ Chi Chieh* 11.9*b*.
48. *Analects* 15.28.
49. Dubs, *The Works of Hsüntze*, p. 52.
50. Dubs, "The Failure of the Chinese To Produce Philosophical Systems," p. 108.

CHAPTER VIII

THE TOTALITARIANISM OF THE LEGALISTS

1. Chavannes, *Les Mémoires historiques de Se-ma Ts'ien*, II.62.
2. Wang Hsien-ch'ien, *Hsün Tzŭ Chi Chieh* 11.9*b*.
3. Wang Hsien-shên, *Han Fei Tzŭ Chi Chieh* 17.7*a*.
4. *Ibid.* 18.10*a*, 20.7*b*.
5. *Ibid.* 9.9*b*–10*a*, 11.
6. Creel, *Confucius, the Man and the Myth*, pp. 220–21.
7. *Lao Tzŭ*, chap. 3.
8. Fung Yu-lan, *A Short History of Chinese Philosophy*, p. 157.
9. Duyvendak, *The Book of Lord Shang*, pp. 14–16; Takigawa Kametaro, *Shih Chi Hui Chu K'ao Chêng* 68.7–9.
10. Duyvendak, *The Book of Lord Shang*, pp. 39–40.
11. *Ibid.*, pp. 131–59.
12. Takigawa Kametaro, *Shih Chi Hui Chu K'ao Chêng* 63.14–28.
13. Wang Hsien-shên, *Han Fei Tzŭ Chi Chieh* 19.1*b*–2*b*.
14. *Ibid.* 19.3*a*.
15. *Ibid.* 20.1.
16. *Ibid.* 19.1.
17. *Ibid.* 19.17*a*, 20.3.
18. *Ibid.* 19.8*b*.

19. *Ibid.* 18.1, 19.7*a*–9*a*.
20. *Ibid.* 19.9*a*.
21. *Ibid.* 19.1*a*–12*a*.
22. *Ibid.* 18.12*b*–13*a*.
23. *Ibid.* 18.2.
24. *Ibid.* 16.10*b*–11*a*.
25. Escarra, *Le Droit chinois*, p. 79.
26. Wang Hsien-ch'ien, *Hsün Tzŭ Chi Chieh* 5.3*a*, 8.1*a*.
27. Wang Hsien-shên, *Han Fei Tzŭ Chi Chieh* 19.5*b*.
28. *Ibid.* 9.10*b*.
29. *Ibid.* 18.4*b*.
30. *Ibid.* 18.5*b*–6*a*, 10*b*–11*a*, 19.13*b*–14*a*.
31. *Ibid.* 19.16*a*.
32. *Ibid.* 14.5*a*–6*a*, 18.2.
33. *Ibid.* 12.5*b*, 14.3*b*–4*a*, 18.12*b*.
34. *Ibid.* 18.7*b*, 19.7*b*–8*a*.
35. *Ibid.* 19.3*b*.
36. Duyvendak, *The Book of Lord Shang*, p. 83.
37. Takigawa Kametaro, *Shih Chi Hui Chu K'ao Chêng* 87.5.
38. Chavannes, *Les Mémoires historiques de Se-ma Ts'ien*, II.135.

CHAPTER IX

The Eclectics of Han

1. Dubs, *The History of the Former Han Dynasty*, I.19, 32.
2. *Ibid.*, I.91.
3. *Ibid.*, I.136–38.
4. *Ibid.*, I.24.
5. *Ibid.*, I.16, 75, 99–102.
6. *Ibid.*, I.15.
7. Gale, *Discourses on Salt and Iron*, pp. 77, 103, 121.
8. Dubs, *The History of the Former Han Dynasty*, I.75–77, 99–102, 130–32.
9. Wang Hsien-ch'ien, *Ch'ien Han Shu Pu Chu* 49.8*a*–9*a*.
10. Chavannes, *Les Mémoires historiques de Se-ma Ts'ien*, III.557–59, 568–69.
11. Dubs, *The History of the Former Han Dynasty*, II.16, 106.
12. Creel, *Confucius, the Man and the Myth*, pp. 239–40.
13. Dubs, *The History of the Former Han Dynasty*, II.51, 58–60.
14. Wang Hsien-ch'ien, *Ch'ien Han Shu Pu Chu* 56, 53.4*b*–5*a*.
15. *Ibid.* 58.1–4*a*.
16. Takigawa Kametaro, *Shih Chi Hui Chu K'ao Chêng* 112.4.
17. *Huai Nan Tzŭ* 1.2*b*–3*a*.
18. *Ibid.* 7.2*a*.
19. Legge, *The Lî Kî*, I.261–62, 288.

20. Escarra, *Le Droit chinois*, pp. 11–12, 256–57.
21. Legge, *The Lî Kî*, II.278–81.
22. *Ibid.*, I.364–67.
23. *Ibid.*, I.75; II.324.
24. *Ibid.*, I.237.
25. Tung Chung-shu, *Ch'un Ch'iu Fan Lu* 11.2b–3a.
26. See Creel, *Confucius, the Man and the Myth*, pp. 103–4.
27. Hu Shih, "The Establishment of Confucianism as a State Religion during the Han Dynasty," pp. 34–35.
28. Tung Chung-shu, *Ch'un Ch'iu Fan Lu* 10.4b.
29. *Ibid.* 10.5b.
30. *Ibid.* 10.1b.
31. Takigawa Kametaro, *Shih Chi Hui Chu K'ao Chêng* 130.9.
32. Hu Shih, "The Establishment of Confucianism as a State Religion during the Han Dynasty," p. 40.
33. Balázs, "La Crise sociale et la philosophie politique à la fin des Han," p. 92.
34. Wang Ch'ung, *Lun Hêng* 3.23a–27; 18.16a–22; 19.1a–11b; 20.1a–11a; 30.4a–8a.
35. *Ibid.* 9.
36. *Ibid.* 4.5b–7b.
37. *Ibid.* 3.19b–20b; 4.15a–16a; 18.1a–8a; 20.11a–19b.
38. *Ibid.* 22.12a.
39. Fung Yu-lan, *Chung Kuo Chê Hsüeh Shih* 588.
40. Huang Hui, *Lun Hêng Chiao Shih* 1236–37.

CHAPTER X

BUDDHISM AND NEO-CONFUCIANISM

1. Eliot, *Hinduism and Buddhism*, I.64.
2. *Ibid.*, I.99.
3. *Ibid.*, I.45.
4. *Ibid.*, I.98.
5. Soothill, *The Lotus of the Wonderful Law*, pp. 85–94.
6. Eliot, *Hinduism and Buddhism*, III.250.
7. Williamson, *Wang An Shih*, II.56, 251, 363–64.
8. *Ibid.*, II.201.
9. Shryock, *The Origin and Development of the State Cult of Confucius*, p. 139.
10. Balázs, "La Crise sociale et la philosophie politique à la fin des Han," p. 91.
11. Hodous, *Buddhism and Buddhists in China*, pp. 29, 31.
12. *Ibid.*, p. 52; Eliot, *Hinduism and Buddhism*, II.28–31.
13. Quoted by permission from an as yet unpublished manuscript.
14. Hodous, *Buddhism and Buddhists in China*, p. 18.

15. Reichelt, *Truth and Tradition in Chinese Buddhism*, p. 238.
16. Eliot, *Hinduism and Buddhism*, I.216–17, 251.
17. Hamilton, "Hsüan Chuang and the Wei Shih Philosophy," pp. 292, 307.
18. Hu Shih, "Development of Zen Buddhism in China," pp. 499–500.
19. *Ibid.*, p. 502.
20. Reichelt, *Truth and Tradition in Chinese Buddhism*, p. 308.
21. Fung Yu-lan, *Chung Kuo Chê Hsüeh Shih* 820–22.
22. Chu Hsi, *Chu Tzŭ Yü Lei* 1.3*a*.
23. *Ibid.* 12.8*a*.
24. Plato *Phaedo* 65.
25. Legge, *The Great Learning*, pp. 357–58.
26. Chu Hsi, *Ssŭ Shu Chi Chu, Ta Hsüeh* 5*a*.
27. Fung Yu-lan, *Chung Kuo Chê Hsüeh Shih* 920–23; translated by Derk Bodde in Fung Yu-lan, "The Philosophy of Chu Hsi," pp. 41–45.
28. *Analects* 2.15.
29. *Ibid.* 15.30, 2.18, 7.27. On the translation of the latter two passages see Creel, *Confucius, the Man and the Myth*, p. 135, lines 27–32, and p. 135, last line, to p. 136, line 2; see also p. 311, n. 24.
30. *Mencius* 2(1)6.
31. Han Yü, *Chu Wên Kung Chiao Han Ch'ang-li Hsien Shêng Chi* 11.3*b*.
32. Fung Yu-lan, *Chung Kuo Chê Hsüeh Shih* 809–10.
33. Huang Siu-chi, *Lu Hsiang-shan*, pp. 12–16.
34. *Ibid.*, p. 36; Lu Hsiang-shan, *Hsiang-shan Hsien Shêng Ch'üan Chi* 36.5*b*.
35. Huang Siu-chi, *Lu Hsiang-shan*, p. 60; Lu Hsiang-shan, *Hsiang-shan Hsien Shêng Ch'üan Chi* 35.3*b*.
36. Huang Siu-chi, *Lu Hsiang-shan*, p. 72.
37. Wang Yang-ming, *Wang Wên-ch'êng Kung Ch'üan Shu* 7.28*b*–30*b*.
38. *Ibid.* 3.50*b*–51*a*; Henke, *The Philosophy of Wang Yang-ming*, pp. 177–78.
39. Wang Yang-ming, *Wang Wên-ch'êng Kung Ch'üan Shu* 32.14*a*; Henke, *The Philosophy of Wang Yang-ming*, p. 13.
40. Legge, *The Great Learning*, p. 366.
41. Wang Yang-ming, *Wang Wên-ch'êng Kung Ch'üan Shu* 1.5*b*–6*b*; Henke, *The Philosophy of Wang Yang-ming*, pp. 53–54.

CHAPTER XI

THE REACTION AGAINST NEO-CONFUCIANISM

1. See Creel, *Confucius, the Man and the Myth*, p. 250.
2. See Goodrich, *The Literary Inquisition of Ch'ien-lung.*
3. Hu Shih, "Confucianism," p. 200.
4. See Creel, *Confucius, the Man and the Myth*, pp. 254–78.
5. *Analects* 9.1 and 5.12.
6. *Ibid.* 15.2.3.
7. *Ibid.* 6.25, 13.20.
8. *Ibid.* 4.9.
9. Ku Yen-wu, *T'ing-lin Hsien Shêng I Shu Hui Chi, Wên Chi* 3.1*a*–2*b*. This passage is translated, somewhat differently from the version I have given, in Freeman, "The Ch'ing Dynasty Criticism of Sung Politico-Philosophy," pp. 89–90.
10. Hummel, *Eminent Chinese of the Ch'ing Period*, pp. 351–52; Chiang Wei-ch'iao, *Chin San Pai Nien Chung Kuo Chê Hsüeh Shih* 23.
11. Huang Tsung-hsi, *Ming I Tai Fang Lu* (*Ssŭ Pu Pei Yao* ed.) 1*b*–2*b*.
12. These quotations from *Analects* 4.24, 1.14, 2.13, and 14.29 by Lu Shih-i (1611–72) are quoted in Chiang Wei-ch'iao, *Chin San Pai Nien Chung Kuo Chê Hsüeh Shih* 12.
13. *Yen Li Ts'ung Shu, Ts'un Hsing* 1.1. A part of this passage is translated, somewhat differently, in Freeman, "The Ch'ing Dynasty Criticism of Sung Politico-Philosophy," pp. 107–8.
14. *Yen Li Ts'ung Shu, Ts'un Hsüeh* 3.2*a*.
15. *Ibid.* 3.6*b*–7*a*.
16. *Yen Li Ts'ung Shu, Yen Hsi-chai Hsien Shêng Yen Hsing Lu* 2.8*b*.
17. *Ibid.* 2.27*b*.
18. *Yen Li Ts'ung Shu, Ts'un Hsüeh* 2.13*a*.
19. *Ibid.; Yen Li Ts'ung Shu, Yen Hsi-chai Hsien Shêng Yen Hsing Lu* 2.22*b*.
20. *Yen Li Ts'ung Shu, Ts'un Chih* 1–4.
21. *Ibid.* 1*a*, 7*b*–9*b*.
22. Tuan Yü-ts'ai, *Tai Tung-yüan Hsien Shêng Nien P'u* 1*b*–2*a*. Most of this passage is translated in Freeman, "The Philosophy of Tai Tung-yüan," pp. 55–56.
23. Tai Chên, *Mêng Tzŭ Tzŭ I Su Chêng* 1.1.
24. Tai Chên, *Yüan Shan* 2.
25. Tai Chên is here quoting from *Mencius* 2(1)6.3.
26. Tai Chên, *Mêng Tzŭ Tzŭ I Su Chêng* 2.7*b*–11*a*. This pas-

sage is translated, somewhat differently, in Freeman, "The Philosophy of Tai Tung-yüan," pp. 59–60.

27. *Encyclopaedia of the Social Sciences*, XII.588–89.

28. Hu Shih, *Tai Tung-yüan Ti Chê Hsüeh* 35.

29. Tai Chên, *Mêng Tzǔ Tzǔ I Su Chêng* 1.4. Translated somewhat differently in Freeman, "The Philosophy of Tai Tung-yüan," p. 64.

30. Tai Chên, *Mêng Tzǔ Tzǔ I Su Chêng* 1.12. Translated somewhat differently in Freeman, "The Philosophy of Tai Tung-yüan," pp. 63–64.

31. Tai Chên, *Yüan Shan* 20–21. Translated in Freeman, "The Philosophy of Tai Tung-yüan," p. 62.

32. Tai Chên, *Mêng Tzǔ Tzǔ I Su Chêng* 1.10.

33. *Ibid.* 1.1*b*–2*a*.

34. Tai Chên, *Tai Tung-yüan Chi* 9.12*b*.

35. Gardner, *Chinese Traditional Historiography*, p. 18.

36. Fang Chao-ying in Hummel, *Eminent Chinese of the Ch'ing Period*, p. 698.

CHAPTER XII

THE INFLUENCE OF THE WEST

1. *Hsüeh Hêng*, No. 18 (Shanghai, 1923), *Wên Yüan* 6–7.

2. Sun Yat-sen, *San Min Chu I, The Three Principles of the People*, p. 171.

3. Sun Yat-sen, *Chung-shan Ts'ung Shu* 4, *Hsüan Yen* 2.

4. *Ibid.* 4.

5. Hu Shih, "Confucianism," p. 200.

6. Chan Wing-tsit, "Trends in Contemporary Philosophy," in MacNair, *China*, p. 320.

7. Sun Yat-sen, *San Min Chu I, The Three Principles of the People*, p. 98.

8. Mao Tsê-tung, *Lun Jên Min Min Chu Chuan Chêng* 17.

9. Van der Sprenkel, *New China: Three Views*, pp. 109–10; Schwartz, *Chinese Communism and the Rise of Mao*, pp. 48, 75, 129, 199; American Consulate General, Hongkong, "Survey of China Mainland Press," No. 44 (January 9, 1951), pp. 11–13.

10. Schwartz, *Chinese Communism and the Rise of Mao*, pp. 198–99.

11. North, "The Chinese Communist Elite," p. 67.

12. See, for instance, Huan K'uan, *Discourses on Salt and Iron*, pp. 56, 88.

13. Sun Yat-sen, *San Min Chu I, The Three Principles of the People*, pp. 386–87, 437–44, 478; Chiang Kai-shek, *China's Destiny*,

pp. 152, 165, 228–29; Mao Tsê-tung, *China's New Democracy*, pp. 29–30.

14. Sun Yat-sen, *San Min Chu I, The Three Principles of the People*, pp. 17, 87–88.

15. North, "The Chinese Communist Elite," p. 68.

16. Sun Yat-sen, *San Min Chu I, The Three Principles of the People*, p. 277.

17. Schwartz, *Chinese Communism and the Rise of Mao*, p. 22.

18. Liu Shao-ch'i, *How To Be a Good Communist*, pp. 82–83.

19. Mao Tsê-tung, *On Practice*, p. 22.

20. Liu Shao-ch'i, *How To Be a Good Communist*, p. 101.

21. Mao Tsê-tung, *On Practice*, p. 23.

22. Taylor, "The Hegemony of the Chinese Communists, 1945–1950," p. 13.

23. Schwartz, *Chinese Communism and the Rise of Mao*, p. 12.

24. Payne, *Mao Tsê-tung*, pp. 30–31, 62.

25. Mao Tsê-tung, *China's New Democracy*, p. 48.

26. *Ibid.*, p. 61.

27. *Ibid.*, pp. 61–62.

28. American Consulate General, Hongkong, "Survey of China Mainland Press," No. 18 (November 28, 1950), p. 10; No. 39 (December 9, 1950), p. 34.

29. Liu Shao-ch'i, *How To Be a Good Communist*, p. 83.

30. *Ibid.*, p. 15.

31. *Mencius* 6(2)2.

32. Liu Shao-ch'i, *How To Be a Good Communist*, p. 16.

33. *Ibid.*, pp. 26–27.

34. Kuo Mo-jo, *Shih P'i P'an Shu* 63–92.

Index

Agricultural school, 70–71
Ai ("love"), 56
Alexander the Great, 9
Amitabha, 198
Analects, 33, 35, 49, 139, 204, 205
Ancestor worship, 11–12, 15
Antiquity, use of precedents from, 136, 223–24; by Confucius, 51; by Mencius, 85–87; by Mo Tzŭ, 51–52
Aristocrats, impoverished, 23–24
Art, Buddhist, 198–99

Balázs, Étienne, 181, 182
Barbarians, 20, 167, 235
Bodhisattvas, 193, 197, 199
Britain, 235, 236, 241
Buddha, 190–91, 202
Buddhism, 186–206, 217, 241; Indian, 186–91; introduction to China, 186, 191; proscription of, 195; relation to Neo-Confucianism, 205–6
Burning of the books, 157

Cannibalism, 53
Capitalism in China, 246
Ceremonial, Records on; see Records on Ceremonial
Chan, Wing-tsit, 242
Changes, Book of, 95, 172–73, 205–6, 207, 210
Chi K'ang Tzŭ, 42–44
Ch'i (state), 75–76, 115–16
Ch'i ("substance"), 207, 228
Chiang Kai-shek, 246, 249
Ch'ien Lung emperor, 227, 232
Ch'in, 116, 132–33, 137, 142–45, 155–58, 160; First Emperor of, 156–58, 161, 174
Chinese influence on European thought, 220
Ching-t'ien system, 82, 226

Ch'ing scholarship, 229, 232–34, 243
Chou, Duke of, 10–11, 13–14, 17–18
Chou dynasty, 10–24
Chu Hsi, 115, 195, 206–9, 211–12
Chuang Tzŭ, 99
Chuang Tzŭ, 64–65, 66, 97, 99–101, 103–9, 191, 201
Chün tzŭ, 27
Chung Yung; see Doctrine of the Mean
Classics, 30, 126–27, 136, 138–39, 151, 157, 159, 171–72, 192, 202, 206, 243; expurgation of, 218; see also under names of individual books
Commentaries: Chu Hsi's, 206, 213, 219; Han, 171–72, 233–34
Common people; see People; Plebeians
Communists, 2–4, 45, 244–57, 258
Confucianism, 159–60, 163–82, 202–14, 217–19, 229–31, 241–42; and Communism, 254–57
Confucians, 34–35, 37, 46–48, 50–53, 60–61, 65, 68, 115, 125, 133–34, 136, 138–39, 143, 147, 148, 150–53, 157, 158, 161, 164, 169; see also Disciples, of Confucius
Confucius, 24, 25–45, 224; and Buddhism, 199, 203–4; and Communism, 254, 256–57; in Legalist books, 138–39; legends concerning, 178; sacrifices to, 217, 261; temples to, 195, 199
Conservation of resources, 82
Contemplative Taoisms, 109–10
Contentment, 259–60

Davidson, J. LeRoy, 198–99
Decree of Heaven, 15–18
Democracy: in China, 114, 163,

218–19, 240, 243–44; Western, 240–41, 249, 250
Democratic ideas of Confucius, 27–29, 37, 41, 45, 218–19, 241
Destiny; *see* Fate
Dewey, John, 242
Dialecticians, 63–65, 126
Diocletian, 7
Disciples: of Confucius, 27–29, 43–45, 46–47, 65; of Hsün Tzŭ, 116, 133, 160; of Mencius, 71–73; of Mo Tzŭ, 61–62, 65
Diversified farming, 82
Divination, 172–73
Doctrine of the Mean, 205
Dubs, Homer H., 115, 133, 163–64
Duyvendak, J. J. L., 144

Economics of Mencius, 82–83
Education, 28, 83, 206, 243; Communist, 253; ideas concerning, of Confucius, 28–34, 41, 43–45; of Hsün Tzŭ, 125–31; of Mencius, 83, 91–92
Emotional discipline, Confucian, 32, 90–92, 128–29, 229, 231
Emperor, supernatural status of, 178–79
Escarra, Jean, 153
Ethics, 150; Buddhist, 199; of Confucius, 31–33, 38–42, 45; of Lu Hsiang-shan, 212; of Mencius, 83
Examination system, 159, 165, 170–71, 202, 206, 218, 243

Fa ("law"), 151
Fa chia, 140
Family, 13, 18–19, 137, 142, 143, 146, 149, 239; under Communism, 253; *see also* Ancestor worship; Filial piety
Fang Chao-ying, 233–34
Fate, 52–53, 222
Fêng shui, 199
Feudalism, 19–24, 79–80, 136, 255
Filial piety, 18–19, 46, 199
First Emperor of Ch'in, 156–58, 161, 174
Five elements; *see* Five forces

Five forces, 173–77, 199, 205
Forged documents, 16, 85–86, 233
Forster, E. M., 5–6
Four Books, 205
Funerals; *see* Mourning
Fung Yu-lan, 140, 184, 206

Gardner, Charles S., 233
Gautama, 190–91, 202
Goldsmith, Oliver, 220
Government: of Chinese Empire, 238–39; relation of, with philosophy, 159
Government, ideals of: Confucius', 39–42; Hsün Tzŭ's, 131–32; Legalist, 136–38, 149–55; Mencius', 78–85; Mo Tzŭ's, 48–51, 58–60; Taoist, 107–9, 111–14
Great Learning, 205, 208
Guest-officials, 68–69

Hamilton, Clarence H., 200
Han dynasty, 159–85
Han Fei Tzŭ, 133, 140, 145–50, 153–55, 167–70
Han Fei Tzŭ, 146, 168
Han Kao Tsu, 160, 161–65
Han learning, school of, 220–34
Han Yü, 34–35
Hawthorne, Nathaniel, 7
Hayakawa, S. I., 89
Heaven (deity), 15–18, 35, 36, 58–61, 76, 130–31, 177, 179, 199, 222
Hells, Buddhist, 198
Hereditary aristocracy, 11–12, 26, 131, 142, 143, 147, 148
Hereditary office, 22–23, 49–51, 77, 83–84, 166; attitudes concerning, of Confucius, 37, 41–42; of Hsün Tzŭ, 127, 131–32; of Mencius, 78–79, 83–84
Hinayana, 191, 193–94
Hinduism, 187–89
Historical Records, 68, 142, 156
Hitler, Adolf, 59
Hodous, Lewis, 197, 199
Holmes, Oliver Wendell, 97
Hou Chi, 11
Hsia dynasty, 16–17

Index

Hsiang Yü, 161–62
Hsü Hsing, 70–71
Hsüan, King of Ch'i, 68–69
Hsün Tzŭ, 65, 115–34, 137, 139, 140, 145, 148–49, 153, 160, 210
Hsün Tzŭ, 116
Hu Shih, 47, 71–72, 178, 181, 200–201, 219, 229, 241, 242
Huai Nan Tzŭ, 174–75
Huang Tsung-hsi, 222–23
Human nature, ideas on: of Chu Hsi, 207–8; of Confucius, 39–40; of Han Fei Tzŭ, 149–50; of Hsün Tzŭ, 119–25; of Lu Hsiang-shan, 212; of Mencius, 87–92, 119; of Tung Chung-shu, 178–79
Human relationships in Chinese life, 239–40
Human sacrifice, 37
Huxley, T. H., 237

I Ching; see Changes, Book of
Identification with the superior, 58–60, 65, 139
India, 9, 186–91, 207
Infanticide, 149
Informers, 57, 139, 142, 143
Inscriptions, 10, 11, 15, 221
Intellectuals, as Communists, 3–4, 244–52
Inventions, 5–6
Investigation of things, 208, 214

Japanese invasion, 241, 244
Jesuits, 219–20, 238

Kao Tsu, Han; see Han Kao Tsu
Karma, 187–88
Kleptomania, 54
Korean war, 252
Ku Yen-wu, 220–22, 232
Kuan Chung, 141
Kuan Tzŭ, 141
Kuan Yin, 197
Kumarajiva, 194
Kung Shu Pan, 55
Kung-Sun Hung, 170–71

Kung-Sun Lung, 63
Kung-Sun Yang; see Shang Yang
Kuo Mo-jo, 257

Land, ownership of, 137, 144
Language, Hsün Tzŭ's theory of, 116–19
Lao Tzŭ, 97–98
Lao Tzŭ, 97–99, 101, 102–8, 110, 112, 191, 192, 201
Law: Chinese concepts of, 152–53; Legalist concept of, 151–53
Legalism, 132–33, 135–58, 159, 165–71, 174, 180
Leibniz, G. W. von, 220
Li ("principle"), 207–8, 211–12, 214–15, 228, 230–31, 254
Li ("propriety"), 29–32, 46, 127–31, 207–8, 260–62
Li Ao, 210
Li Chi; see Records on Ceremonial
Li Ssŭ, 133, 145–46, 155–58
Liang (state), 68, 69
Lieh Tzŭ, 95–97, 100, 109
Linguistics, 220
Literary inquisition, Manchu, 218, 232
Liu Shao-ch'i, 256–57
Love, universal, 56–57
Lu, Duke of, 20–21
Lu Hsiang-shan, 209–13, 215, 222
Lü Hou (Empress), 160
Lun Hêng, 183–85

Mahayana, 193–94, 197
Manchu dynasty, 217–19, 220–21
Mao Tsê-tung, 246, 251–55
Maspero, Henri, 101
Meditation, 38, 190, 191, 198, 200, 203, 209–10, 211, 214–15, 224
Mencius, 68–93, 204–5, 207–8, 210, 212; and Communism, 256–57
Mencius, 71–72, 93, 205, 210, 229
Mill, John Stuart, 237
Ming dynasty, 213–14, 218–19
Missionaries, Western, 240–41, 246–47
Mo Tzŭ, 47–67, 70, 139
Mo Tzŭ, 47–51, 55, 62–64

Moism and Moists, 62–65, 70, 148, 158, 161, 175, 180–81, 241
Mongol dynasty, 217, 219
Monopolies, government, 167
Mou Tzŭ, 192, 196–97
Mourning, 30–31, 46, 53, 131
Music, 58
Mysticism, Taoist, 101–10

Names, Hsün Tzŭ's theory of, 117–19
Nationalists, 244, 249–50
Neo-Confucianism, 204–14, 219, 221–34, 254
New Tide, 242–43
Nirvana, 188, 192, 202
North, Robert C., 245

Payne, Robert, 254
Peasants as Communists, 245
Pelliot, Paul, 192
People, duty of rulers to, 17–18, 48, 83, 132, 138, 163–64, 179, 223; *see also* Plebeians
Philosophy, relation of, with government, 159, 180–82
Phonetics, 221, 232
Plato, 102, 208
Plebeians, 12–13, 22, 119–20, 160–64; *see also* People
Poetry, Book of, 11, 12, 13, 16, 18, 22
Population of China, 57–58, 146
Propaganda, Chou dynasty, 15–18; Communist, 247–48, 253–54, 256
Psychology: of Hsün Tzŭ, 118; of Mencius, 89–92; of Tai Chên, 228–29, 231
Purposive Taoism, 110–14, 139

Quesnay, François, 220

Realists, 140
Reciprocity, 40
Records on Ceremonial, 116, 175–76, 205
Reichelt, Karl L., 201
Reichwein, Adolf, 45

Reincarnation, 187–88
Religion, 22; of Confucius, 35–38, 44; of Hsün Tzŭ, 130–31; of Mo Tzŭ, 59–61; *see also* Ancestor worship; Buddhism; Hinduism
Renaissance, Chinese, 242–43
Revolution: American, 240, 241; Chinese, 241; French, 220, 240, 241
Richards, I. A., 71, 75
Ritual; see *Li* ("propriety")
Rousseau, Jean-Jacques, 7, 102
Russia, relations of, with China, 4, 248–49, 250

Sage-kings, 49–51, 60, 77, 85, 87, 122–24, 126, 131, 146–47, 209, 223, 225, 257
Schwartz, Benjamin, 250
Scientific attitude, 37–38, 229–30
Shang, Book of Lord, 144, 155
Shang culture, 10, 15, 16
Shang Yang, 141–44, 154, 169
Shên Pu-hai, 141
Shên Tao, 141
Shih ("power and position"), 141, 151
Shih Ching; see *Poetry, Book of*
Shryock, John K., 195
Shu ("methods"), 141, 151, 170
Shun, Emperor, 49–50, 78, 83–84, 85, 87, 147, 257
Slaves, 154, 163, 165, 167, 179–80, 196
Smith, Adam, 237
Socialist ideas in Confucianism, 245–46
Socrates, 208
Son of Heaven, 37, 179
Spencer, Herbert, 237
Spoken language in literature, 242–43
Spring and Autumn Annals, 177–79
Steiner, H. Arthur, 258
Sun Yat-sen, 18, 240, 241, 243, 246, 248, 249
Sung dynasty, 204
Supreme Ultimate, 206, 207

Index

Ta Hsüeh; see *Great Learning*
Tai Chên (Tung-yüan), 226–34
T'ang dynasty, 202–3
T'ang the Successful, 16–17
Tao ("way"), 32–35, 48, 101
Tao, 101–2, 103, 107, 110–11, 112, 207, 208–9
Tao Tê Ching; see *Lao Tzŭ*
Taoism, 32–33, 94–114, 165, 172, 174, 180, 196–97, 241; relation of, to Buddhism, 191–93, 201–2; relation of, to Legalism, 139; relation of, to Neo-Confucianism, 205–6
Taylor, George E., 254
Tê ("virtue"), 102
Teachers: Confucian, 46–47; Hsün Tzŭ's emphasis on, 121–25; special position of, 77, 124–25
Textual criticism, 232–33
Theater, 256
Thoreau, H. D., 7
Ti (deity), 17
Translation: of Buddhist scriptures, 194; of Western philosophy, 237
Tung Chung-shu, 170, 171, 176–79, 181
Tzŭ-hsia, 68
Tzŭ-ssŭ, 68, 72, 77

University, imperial, 159, 171
Usurping officials, 20–24
Utilitarianism: of Mencius, 86–87; of Mo Tzŭ, 57–58

Vedas, 187–89
Voltaire, 220

Wang An-shih, 195
Wang Ch'ung, 183–85
Wang tao, 83
Wang Yang-ming, 213–16, 218, 222
War, opinions on: of Confucius, 26–27; of Legalists, 139, 142, 143, 155; of Mencius, 81–82; of Mo Tzŭ, 53–56
Weber, Max, 38–39
Wei Yang; see Shang Yang
Well-field system, 82, 226
Wên, Han Emperor, 165–66
Western influence, 217, 219–20, 235–57
World Wars, 237, 246, 249
Wu, Han Emperor, 159–60, 166–71, 174
Wu, Liang Emperor, 194
Wu wei, 106, 192

Yang Chu, 70, 95–97
Yao, Emperor, 49–50, 78, 83, 85, 87, 146–47, 163, 257
Yellow Turbans, 196, 202
Yen (state), 75–76
Yen Fu, 237, 258
Yen Yüan, 224–26
Yin and *yang*, 172–76, 205
Yin dynasty, 17 n.
Yü, Emperor, 49–50, 83–84, 146

Zen, 200–202, 206, 210, 213, 216